Joel Bakan

THE NEW
CORPORATION

Joel Bakan is a professor of law at the University
of British Columbia. A Rhodes scholar and former
law clerk to Chief Justice Brian Dickson of the
Supreme Court of Canada, he holds law degrees
from Oxford, Harvard, and Dalhousie Universities. An internationally renowned legal authority,
Bakan has written widely on law and its social and
economic impact. He is the cocreator and writer of
a documentary film and television miniseries titled
The Corporation, which is based on his book of the
same name. He also wrote and directed the documentary film *The New Corporation,* which is based
on this book.

ALSO BY JOEL BAKAN

*Just Words: Constitutional Rights
 and Social Wrongs*

*The Corporation:
 The Pathological Pursuit of Profit and Power*

*Childhood Under Siege:
 How Big Business Targets Your Children*

THE NEW
CORPORATION

How "Good" Corporations
Are Bad for Democracy

Joel Bakan

VINTAGE BOOKS

A Division of Penguin Random House LLC
New York

A VINTAGE BOOKS ORIGINAL, SEPTEMBER 2020

Copyright © 2020 by Joel Bakan

All rights reserved. Published in the United States
by Vintage Books, a division of Penguin Random
House LLC, New York.

Vintage and colophon are registered trademarks
of Penguin Random House LLC.

Library of Congress Cataloging-in-Publication Data
Names: Bakan, Joel, author.
Title: The new corporation : how "good" corporations are bad for
    democracy / Joel Bakan.
Description: New York : Vintage Books, 2020. | Includes bibliographical
    references and index.
Identifiers: LCCN 2020011651 (print) | LCCN 2020011652 (ebook) |
    ISBN 9781984899729 (trade paperback) | ISBN 9781984899736
    (ebook)
Subjects: LCSH: Corporations. | Corporations—Corrupt practices. |
    Corporate culture—21st century. | Democracy—Economic aspects. |
    Democracy and environmentalism.
Classification: LCC HD2731 .B235 2020 (print) | LCC HD2731 (ebook) |
    DDC 306.3/42—dc23
LC record available at https://lccn.loc.gov/2020011651

Vintage Books Trade Paperback ISBN: 978-1-9848-9972-9
eBook ISBN: 978-1-9848-9973-6

Book design by Christopher M. Zucker

www.vintagebooks.com

Printed in the United States of America
10   9   8   7   6   5   4   3   2   1

For
Rebecca
Myim and Sadie
and Paul
with all my love

CONTENTS

Introduction   3

1. The New Corporation   7

2. Still Crazy After All These Years   36

3. The Corporate Liberation Movement   59

4. California (Bad) Dreaming   91

5. Being Corporate   107

6. Democracy Unbound   145

Afterword   177

Acknowledgments   189

Notes   193

Index   225

THE NEW
CORPORATION

INTRODUCTION

ON APRIL 19, 2019, the Business Roundtable, led by JPMorgan Chase's Jamie Dimon and composed of more than two hundred of America's top CEOs, heralded the dawn of a new age of corporate capitalism. Henceforth, the CEOs proclaimed, the purpose of publicly traded corporations would be to serve the interests not only of shareholders but also of workers, communities, and the environment. The declaration capped a two-decade-long trend of corporations claiming to be different, to have changed into caring and conscientious actors—ready to lead the way in solving society's problems. I call it the "new" corporation movement. And for those within it who occupy the rarefied heights of elite corporate boardrooms, life has been good. For a twenty-year run, productivity was up. Profits were up. Stock prices broke records. Innovation seemed boundless. New ways to make money were discovered each day. And the rich kept getting richer. No doubt the coronavirus pandemic has tamped down the rise, and it may be awhile before corporations regain their full swagger. But they almost certainly will—especially as governments shower them with bailouts and infusions of cash.

Less certain are the fates of the vast majority of people in the United States and around the world whose lives became increasingly precarious as Wall Street soared and who, as a result, now suffer inordinately from the pandemic. Over the last two decades, workers' wages stagnated, inequality spiraled, public services—including health services—were shredded, good jobs and unions disappeared, and people worked harder for less pay and with less security (if they worked at all). Today, half of Americans cannot pay an unexpected four-hundred-dollar bill without selling something or going into debt, and millennials are the first generation in U.S. history to be worse off than their parents. Proper health care and housing are beyond the reach of many, and for the first time, mortality rates in the United States began rising in 2014. Opioids destroy lives and communities, and "deaths of despair," from suicide and drugs and alcohol, are at all-time highs. Growing social division fuels hate and xenophobia, corrodes democracy, and enables the rise of demagogues, while climate change ravages the planet with ever-deadlier wildfires, floods, droughts, and hurricanes, heightening the risk of future pandemics, among other things.

Despite their claims to be ready to help, the "new" corporations cannot solve these global ills. But more important than that—and this is my central argument—they are a large part of the reason things have gotten worse so dramatically and quickly over the last two decades. Indeed, the publicly traded corporation (hereinafter "the corporation") never really changed, at least not *fundamentally.* It is the same psychopathic institution I diagnosed twenty years ago (in a book and a film, both called *The Corporation*). But it is more charming now. And it uses that new charm to convince us that it's benevolent, that we can drop our guard and let it take control.

Casting themselves as good actors, corporations cajole governments to free them from regulations designed to protect public interests and citizens' well-being, claiming they can be trusted to regulate themselves. They take over public services—like schools, water systems, and social services provision—saying they will run them better and more efficiently than governments, and they push for tax cuts with promises of jobs and other societal benefits. The result? Governments retreat from governing, corporations take greater control, and we become a society that no longer *has* corporations but that *is* corporate—the reason, I claim, "good" corporations are bad for democracy.

Fortunately, there is a counterforce. Global resistance to corporate power and rule has surged over the last decade, an antidote to both the false hope of the "new" corporation and the growing sense of hopelessness pervasive in society. More and more, through rising protest and political action, people refuse to accept the hollowing out of democracy and the severe threat corporations pose to people and planet. It may be that the coronavirus pandemic is weakening corporations' hold on society, as it lays bare the injustices and inadequacies of the current system, and fosters newly robust senses of community and democracy. That's cause for hope, no matter the many reasons for despair.

1 THE NEW CORPORATION

IT'S A COLD JANUARY NIGHT in Davos, high up in the Swiss Alps. Snow falls hard as Bibop Gresta, chair of Hyperloop Transportation Technologies, runs quickly down the town's main street, dancing nimbly among icy patches, trying not to slip and fall. Tuxedo clad and straining to see through fogged-up designer glasses, the forty-something entrepreneur is late for a party being hosted by JPMorgan Chase CEO Jamie Dimon and former British prime minister Tony Blair. Rumor has it Al Gore will be at the party (he is), and Canadian prime minister Justin Trudeau will show up (he doesn't). The usual coterie of business titans, high-tech entrepreneurs, and government and nongovernmental organization (NGO) officials will be there, networking boozily through the night, aglow with their own good fortune, champagne flowing and music booming. Welcome to Davos, the usually sleepy alpine village that transforms into a party hub for the global elite each January when the World Economic Forum (WEF) comes to town.

Davos is "a great occasion to meet a lot of the big players," says Gresta, a former Italian pop star ("I had twenty big hits, all terrible—it was the nineties," he jokes) turned high-tech entrepreneur. Now head of the company developing Elon Musk's idea of a Hyperloop—a trackless train that travels through a tube at speeds of up to eight hundred miles an hour, levitated and propelled by vacuums, magnets, and solar power—he's in Davos looking for financial backers. Dimon has agreed to meet him at the party. "I promised to be there early, to be received by him and by Tony Blair," he says, but in Davos "you're always late, there's always something happening, and you're trying to make the best of the time that you have." His previous meeting, with celebrity rapper Akon, had run late, then he lost valuable time changing into his tux—"to be recognized as credible, you actually have to dress in a certain way," he told me—and now his stylishly pointy shoes, which have no grip on the icy sidewalk, are slowing him down.

Also on her way to Dimon's party is Sandra Navidi, a New York consultant and author. As a Davos regular, Navidi doesn't even attempt stylish footwear on the ice-covered streets. Instead, she's wearing distinctly unfashionable snow boots (with pumps tucked away in an oversize purse), ready to navigate among the several parties she'll attend over the course of the evening. Well-known and liked in Davos, despite her gentle jabs at some of its elite attendees in her book, *Superhubs: How the Financial Elite and Their Networks Rule Our World,* Navidi sees the annual gathering as an opportunity to connect with "people who have the power to change things, and to get a sense of how they think and how they feel." She's looking forward to the usual networking and schmoozing at the party and also to saying hello to her friend Jamie Dimon, who, she says, "has a preeminent position among the titans of the financial industry; he's sort of their unofficial ambassador in Washington." When Navidi sees Dimon at the party, they share a hug and double-cheeked kiss.

Gresta, who has arrived at the party slightly late, though intact, waits for the right moment and then approaches Dimon, who greets him warmly before chiding him about his formal attire. The two talk for several minutes, a quick meeting but, Gresta tells me afterward, a good one. Dimon seems open to working with him, says Gresta, who is excited at the prospect, in part because of Dimon's commitment to sustainability and societal improvement at JPMorgan Chase. For Gresta, sustainability and improving society are central concerns, the reason he was originally drawn to the Hyperloop, which, he says, is *sustainable*—fueled by renewable energy and potentially creating more energy than it consumes—and also *improves society* by allowing people to connect across long distances faster. For these reasons, Gresta believes, Hyperloop Transportation Technologies "represents a new generation of companies that will change everything."

I became interested in Gresta and Navidi and decided to follow them around Davos because each embodies, albeit in different ways, the much-heralded "spirit of Davos." Hardheaded businesspeople and entrepreneurs, they believe in capitalism, work within it, and see it as key to creating a better world. But they're also highly critical of its current trajectory—its blinkered greed, spiraling consumerism, and harmful impacts on society and the environment. "This is stupid," Gresta says of today's capitalist system. "The ecosystem is in decline thanks to us. We need to do something to reverse this. It's not a matter of 'if'; it's a matter of 'when,' or we will actually disappear." For Navidi, capitalism's current excesses seriously threaten democracy, as a small clique of the global superelite accumulate power that "actually exceeds that of democratic people." As a result, she says, people lose faith in the system, grow alienated from it, and turn to self-proclaimed outsiders, populist strongmen like Donald Trump, who then further entrench elite rule and corrupt democracy.

Gresta's and Navidi's mix of idealism about capitalism as it could be and criticism of capitalism as it is mirrors views of their Davos host, Klaus Schwab. Schwab, an economist by trade, founded, and has always been head of, the World Economic Forum and its annual Davos meeting. He's deployed both for four decades to try to nudge capitalism toward a more enlightened and conscientious form. Today's capitalism—"neoliberal," as he describes it—is dangerously broken, a "free market on the rampage, a brakeless train wreaking havoc." Fixing it is central to the WEF's mission. "The World Economic Forum was never in favor of neoliberal globalization," he told me. "We always argued for the need to make globalization much more equitable." And the way to do that, he says—and has been saying for almost a half century—is to inject into corporations, and the globalized capitalist system as a whole, a new and deeper sense of social responsibility.

"In 1970, I was asked to write a book on modern management," Schwab says. "I had to ask myself the question: What is a company? What is the purpose of a company? Is it just to make money?" His answer was "no," that while corporations must make money, they're equally obliged to respect, and indeed promote, the interests of society and all whom their actions affect. "Stakeholder capitalism" is what he called his idea, and he's happy, he says, that it's now "more accepted than it was in the past," that we've reached the point where "social and environmental values have to be part of corporate action and corporate decision-making." Still, there's much work to do, he says. "New thinking on how we combine or how we blend moneymaking and social responsibility" is needed, and that's the reason "we at the World Economic Forum engage companies in corporate global citizenship."

Schwab believes the corporation needs a heart, like the Tin Man in the *The Wizard of Oz*. And as a kind of Wizard of Davos, he has made it his life's mission to make sure it gets one. Under his watchful eye, Davos has evolved over the years into *the* global hub for ideas and initiatives aimed at making corporations good global citizens. Its agenda is loaded with meetings and sessions on, among other things, climate change, sustainability, inequality, poverty, racism, sexism, LGBTQ rights, and migration, each examined in terms of how corporations can become part of the solution and less of the problem.

The spirit and ethos of Davos have always been extensions of Schwab's ideas—indeed, the focus of Davos 2020 was, as the World Economic Forum described it, "renewing the concept of stakeholder capitalism to overcome income inequality, societal division and the climate crisis." Davos is all about cultivating a new kind of capitalism where corporations operate with greater commitment to solving the world's problems. It's no surprise, then, that when business leaders make vows about social purpose, it's often at Davos—as when CEOs from fourteen major companies, including Nike, Microsoft, and Coca-Cola, jointly declared a "new frontier in corporate global citizenship," where corporations are obliged to take the lead in "building better governance systems and public institutions for society as a whole"; or when Bill Gates unveiled his idea of "creative capitalism" ("a reworking of Schwab's idea of global corporate citizenship," as *Forbes* described it at the time); or when CEOs from the world's largest companies committed to new standards for disclosing their companies' performance on social and environmental issues.

Nor is it a surprise that most people who attend Davos share its—and Schwab's—convictions. Cosmopolitan, progressive, and believing corporations should embrace social purpose and do good in the world, Davos capitalists are not like their Koch brothers, anti-globalist, xenophobic, and Trumpist counterparts. The latter can surely be found here, but they're a minority who belie the overall ethos. Walking the town's mellow brick roads, you're more likely to find members of the enlightened economic elite, capitalism's doves and lambs, not its lions and tigers and bears.

Typical is Richard Edelman, whose Edelman Trust Barometer is the gospel of global public opinion prognosticators. When I met him in Davos's main plaza, he excitedly told me about how corporations are changing for the better, now embracing social and environmental values as *core* values, "in the supply chain, in the hiring practices, throughout the corporation," compared with fifteen years ago when such values were relegated to the periphery, as mere "philanthropic exercises."

Valerie Keller, another Davos regular and the executive director of global markets at Ernst & Young, agrees with Edelman. She's seen "a sea change" over the last fifteen years as corporations commit more and more deeply to social purpose. Inspired by the trend and wanting to take it further, she launched Ernst & Young's Beacon Institute (along with Sir Richard Branson, Arianna Huffington, former Unilever chief Paul Polman, and 120 other global executives) "to say we stand for a world that works for everyone, and we stand for business, and big business to be the space where that change can happen." Which captures the ethos of most corporate executives today. Based upon Keller's polling of business leaders at Davos, 80 percent of them reject "Milton Friedman's premise that business's sole obligation is to return shareholder value." Instead, they believe "that in today's transformative age, business has a wider accountability and opportunity in society." That is a significant change, she says: "If we had taken that same poll five years ago, it would have been different."

I also bumped into the world's top business guru, Harvard Business School's Michael Porter, while sitting at an espresso bar in the Davos Congress Centre. In the early 2000s, Porter coined the term "shared value" to describe how corporations can (and should) make money by doing social good. Corporations are finally getting that message, he told me. "Over the last fifteen years," he said, "the corporation has really reshaped and redefined itself, and particularly the way it relates to society and its sense of what role it can and should play in society. It's quite remarkable how big a shift that's been." By assuming leadership roles in solving social and environmental problems, major corporations have been boosting profits and growth while also becoming, he says, "the most powerful force for addressing the pressing issues we face."

Everything about Davos—not least the presence and views of business thought leaders like Edelman, Keller, and Porter—suggests that Schwab's nearly half-century campaign to inject social purpose into the corporation is working. The same is true beyond Davos, in the wider world of big business. Corporations have changed their tune, it's undeniable. Eschewing narrow self-interest and proclaiming broader social purpose, they appear significantly different today from when I first diagnosed them as psychopaths nearly two decades ago. Indeed, business leaders regularly tell me that while I may have been right back then, things have changed. "Your calling corporations psychopaths had an impact," John Coyne, a top executive at Unilever, recently told me, "but I hope we are now on the road to recovery. There's a genuinely different dialogue that's taking place about corporations and the role that they play in society." And it's true, there is. On every global issue—the environment, climate change, world poverty, and now the coronavirus pandemic—

corporations position themselves as part of the solution, no longer the problem. And many now believe them, a real shift from a decade ago.

The early 2000s was a time of great anxiety about the corporation. People were worried about what corporations were doing to society and the environment and how globalization was fueling their growing power and influence. They were searching for ways to understand and change what was happening—a search my earlier book and film, *The Corporation,* were part of. But it was another film, released around the same time, that truly anticipated what was to come.

Monsters, Inc., an animated children's tale, tells the story of a sad and dreary authoritarian city-state called Monstropolis. Home to a varied assortment of monsters, the city is ruled by its energy company, Monsters, Inc., which in turn is run by a dictatorial CEO, Mr. Waternoose. Monstropolis is not part of the human world, but each night the energy company's monster employees, including protagonists Sulley and Mike, travel to the human world through portals that exit into children's bedroom closets. From there they frighten sleeping children, not out of an animus toward children but for purely economic reasons. Children's screams are what fuel the energy company, and terrifying children is how those screams are elicited and harvested.

The apparently terrifying Sulley and Mike turn out to have hearts of gold, however. And through a series of plot twists and turns, their latent goodness bursts to the surface. Realizing they love children, and that Monsters, Inc., can be fueled even more effectively by children's laughter, they set out to change the company. After several action-packed sequences, they overthrow the evil CEO, Mr. Waternoose, take over the company, and remake the business to be fueled by children's laughter rather than their screams. Now, with the monsters making children laugh by joking and having fun with them, Monsters, Inc., gets the fuel it needs. The company thrives. The city thrives. The children and everyone else live happily ever after. With the warm and literally fuzzy Sulley and Mike now in charge, Monsters, Inc., is benevolent, no longer evil.

Fast-forward to 2017, Super Bowl LI. Tom Brady and his New England Patriots rally from a record twenty-five-point deficit to beat the Atlanta Falcons in overtime, one of the greatest sports comebacks ever. But what also had people cheering that day were the television ads. Major companies—Budweiser, Coca-Cola, and Google among them—had paid top dollar to take subtle and not-so-subtle swipes at America's own Mr. Waternoose, Donald Trump. The ads promoted diversity, immigration, and globalism while the recently inaugurated president was aggressively pursuing the opposite. Though unprecedented for their explicit political overtones, the ads reflected, and were part of, a broader corporate pushback against Trump's presidency, which included Nordstrom refusing to carry a Trump brand; Amazon joining the state of Washington to sue Trump for his executive bans on travel from majority Muslim countries; and Coca-Cola, General Electric, Unilever, and ExxonMobil joining forces, along with numerous other companies, to condemn Trump for pulling the United States out of the Paris climate accord. "It is surprising," remarked the Schulich School of Business professor Dirk Matten at the time. "Business is about business, about caring about shareholders. And suddenly we see them deeply involved in the political arena."

But it wasn't that surprising. Even before Trump became president, major companies and their CEOs were emulating Sulley and Mike, acting like good guys, trying to do the right thing. "CEO activism" is how, in 2015, Professor Michael Toffel of Harvard Business School described the phenomenon of CEOs "taking stands on political and social issues unrelated to their companies' bottom lines." This was "something new," Toffel said. "Until recently, it was rare for corporate leaders to plunge aggressively into thorny social and political discussions. But the world has changed." Three years later, writing in 2018, Toffel said he "never imagined how significant this phenomenon would become." Police shootings, discrimination against LGBTQ people, women's rights, the environment, race issues, and regressive immigration bans and policies had prompted corporate leaders to speak out and take action. Recently, for example, more than 80 companies and CEOs issued statements of solidarity with Black Lives Matter and racial justice in the wake of the murder of George Floyd.

"CEO activism," though new, was part of a larger and longer-term shift that had begun in the early 2000s—the "new" corporation movement. Beaten down by anti-globalization protests at that time, discredited by the skulduggery of Enron and World-Com, targeted by a growing chorus of critics (including me), and increasingly distrusted by a worried public, business leaders began proclaiming it was time to remake the corporation and redefine its mission and mandate. Their calls for change grew only louder in 2008 when Wall Street's spectacular collapse revealed more corporate rot and prompted new rounds of protest and criticism, not least Occupy Wall Street. And change began to happen.

But it was a different kind of change from what Occupy protesters were demanding in the streets. The latter wanted curbs on corporations' power, taxes on their wealth, measures to narrow the gap between the 99 and the 1 percent, and restrictions on their political influence. Business leaders, in contrast, like Sulley and Mike—who could have started a revolution to wrest power from Monsters, Inc., and give it to "the people" ("the monsters") but instead chose to leave power where it was and make its exercise more benevolent—called for corporations to become more conscientious and socially concerned but refrained from challenging their growing power, influence, and impunity.

The results were nonetheless significant. "Around 2005," the political scientist Peter Dauvergne observes, "many of the world's biggest branded companies, from Walmart to Coca-Cola to Procter & Gamble, were suddenly making very sweeping promises of full sustainability, promises such as 100 percent carbon neutrality, zero waste to landfills, 100 percent recycling." Walmart, for example, pledged in 2005 "to be supplied 100 percent by renewable energy; to create zero waste; and to sell products that sustain people and the environment." Other major corporations made similar promises. Dauvergne says he initially thought "this was just more greenwashing," then on closer inspection realized something deeper was happening—"a proactive, real, and significant shift in how the biggest companies were dealing with sustainability."

It's true that in 2005 most large corporations were already practicing corporate social responsibility (CSR), and had been for years, many with well-publicized plans, glossy annual reports, inspiring websites, and officers and vice presidents dedicated to the cause. And it's also true that a handful of small, socially minded companies, including Ben & Jerry's, Tom's of Maine, Patagonia, Nature's Gate, and Interface, had gone beyond CSR to entrench social and environmental values at the core of their business models.

But what was new and different in 2005 was that the world's largest publicly traded corporations began doing the same, proclaiming that they, too, would embed social and environmental values deeply and across all operations. The problem with traditional approaches to CSR, these companies' leaders said, was that within their terms, social and environmental values were too confined and peripheral, reduced to "reputation-conscious public relations," as one pundit described it, rather than "embedded and integrated into the core operations of companies." Former British Petroleum head Lord John Browne, a "great proponent of CSR twenty years ago," told me that he and other business leaders realized CSR is actually "dangerous" because it dilutes companies' and leaders' commitments to social and environmental values. "Thinking about CSR as some department that is added on after you have got the business strategy right is wrong," he said. "You have to include all components of CSR in the business that you do." The problem with CSR, he explained, was that it had become "a codified activity about checking boxes and fulfilling certain criteria," effectively "relieving leaders of actively being involved" when they should be "thinking about purpose the whole time."

Lord Browne's idea that *purpose* should be the lodestar of corporate leaders is fundamental to the "new" corporation movement. "Profit cannot be your purpose," the leadership expert Daniel Skarlicki told me. "Profit is the result, but purpose is the process for getting there." And the way you find purpose, Skarlicki said, is to "go deep inside yourself," to "understand what you truly care about, access your heart, get out of your head, reflect on what matters to you as a human being." Ernst & Young's Valerie Keller agrees. Corporate leaders have to "get it both here, and here," she says, pointing to her head and her heart. That's what defines the kind of "courageous leader" needed to ensure companies commit "to solving global challenges, putting humans at the core of what business is all about," and shifting "the paradigm and the possibility of what it means to be a business on the planet."

When asked who among corporate leaders best exemplifies this ideal, most people—including Keller and also Edelman and Lord Browne—point to former Unilever chief Paul Polman. Unilever's John Coyne agrees. "We have a CEO," he proudly told me (while Polman was still in that position), "who believes that the cult of shareholder value has seen its day." A champion of "inclusive capitalism"—"the movement to make capitalism more equitable, sustainable, and inclusive," according to the Coalition for Inclusive Capitalism—Polman boldly proselytized new corporation ideals. "I don't think our fiduciary duty is to put shareholders first," he stated. "I say the opposite. What we firmly believe is that if we focus our company on improving the lives of the world's citizens and come up with genuine sustainable solutions, we are more in sync with consumers and society and ultimately this will result in good shareholder returns." Polman's Sustainable Living Plan, his signature achievement at Unilever, has since 2010, the company claims, reduced emissions by one million tons, achieved zero waste to landfill from factories, made substantial gains on sustainable sourcing for agricultural products, and improved the health and lives of close to half a billion people.

Polman and Unilever are not alone, however. Over the last two decades, all major companies have publicly eschewed narrow self-interest, embraced social purpose, and remade themselves (to greater and lesser degrees) to appear as conscientious and socially minded institutions—a kind of Ben & Jerry's–fication of big business. This "is not social responsibility," Michael Porter insists. "It is not on the margins of what companies do but at the center; it reconnects company success with social progress." Embracing social and environmental values is no longer "a CSR strategy," Coyne told me in a similar spirit. It's now part of "the corporate strategy for the company."

Visit the website of any major corporation and you'll wonder whether you've accidentally clicked on that of an NGO or activist group. These days, all corporate communications lead with social and environmental commitments and achievements. Walmart, for example, boasts that it has diverted 75 percent of its global waste from landfills, reduced greenhouse gas emissions by 35 million metric tons, protected nearly one million acres of wildlife habitat, cut fleet emissions by 650,000 metric tons, and supplied 26 percent of its energy from renewable sources (its ultimate goal being 100 percent). McDonald's uses 100 percent recycled fiber–based packaging, has significantly upped its sourcing of sustainable beef, fish, coffee, and palm oil, and increased energy efficiency by 20 percent. Apple powers its facilities worldwide with 96 percent renewable energy (compared with 20 percent in 2010), the average energy used by its products has decreased by 70 percent since 2008, two-thirds of its office waste is diverted from landfills, and 62 percent of the paper used in product packaging and offices comes from recycled fiber and 38 percent from sustainably sourced fiber. Recently, the company vowed it would become carbon-negative, not just carbon-neutral, by 2030.

The list goes on. All major companies boast of significant achievements across social and environmental issues. Whether it's sustainability, human rights, climate change, health, or biodiversity, they are at the forefront, they say. The recent coronavirus pandemic is a case in point. Walgreens, Target, and CVS executives were at President Trump's side when he announced a response plan, and since then, the president's Rose Garden pandemic briefings quickly became a forum for corporate CEOs to boast of their contributions. "Fantastic. Those are great companies. Thank you very much," said Trump after one such briefing that included executives of Honeywell, Procter & Gamble, and FedEx. In the meantime, Walmart, Amazon, McDonald's, and numerous other companies showcase sick-leave programs for employees, GM and

Ford repurpose production lines to make ventilators, *Forbes* gushes about the "50 ways companies are giving back during the coronavirus pandemic," and major corporations' ad campaigns tell us how much they care—that Walmart is "Here for you"; "we're never lost if we can find each other" on Facebook; and, as Uber reminds us, we should "stay home for everyone who can't."

It's no surprise really, all these good works. As Justin Bakule, former head of the Shared Value Initiative, told me (before the pandemic broke), corporations have changed, quickly and significantly, over the last two decades. Each year, Bakule helps *Fortune* magazine compile a list of companies that are "changing the world" (Jamie Dimon's JPMorgan Chase is on the 2019 list, along with Apple, Walmart, IBM, and Ernst & Young, among others). The list, he says, is "helping change the narrative, saying about companies like Walmart, McDonald's, and others, to the common reader, to the businessperson, 'Take another look. Let's see. Let's reevaluate. Let's not hang on to what we thought these companies were doing ten years ago or the moment where they had their worst day.'" Bakule believes we are reaching a tipping point toward a new kind of corporation.

In a now famous letter to world business leaders, BlackRock's Larry Fink echoes Bakule. "We're in a new age of doing business," he wrote in 2018. "You need to give back. You need to be part of the solution. Society is demanding that companies serve a social purpose." Sue Reid, vice president of climate and energy at Ceres, a nonprofit organization that cajoles corporations to embrace social purpose, notes "a palpable shift, an increasing momentum, that creates an awful lot of optimism" around corporate promotion of social and environmental values. The activist Tzeporah Berman, who in the 1990s chained herself to trees in British Columbia's old-growth forests to stop logging companies from cutting them down, says she sees "a new evolution of healthy corporations run by people who are trying to make the world a better place, a real change in the way that corporations are approaching environmental issues and social justice issues." There's certainly more work to be done, these and other advocates say. But the "new" corporation is becoming firmly rooted in global society. When, I asked Bakule, would we reach the tipping point and truly enter the new corporation era? "Within the next ten years," he told me.

Back at Davos, waiting in line for the much-anticipated speech by President Donald Trump, I notice a woman wearing a T-shirt emblazoned with the slogan "Not My President." It's the closest thing I've seen to a protest since arriving here. The woman's name, I learn when I walk over to talk to her, is Anya Schiffrin, a professor at Columbia University's School of International and Public Affairs. I tell Professor Schiffrin that I think she's very brave for wearing the T-shirt, especially since protests are banned in Davos during the WEF meeting (though permitted in Zurich, a hundred miles away). "We have to do something," she says as the man standing next to her nods enthusiastically. That man is fellow Columbia professor and Nobel Prize–winning economist Joseph Stiglitz. He's Professor Schiffrin's husband and also no fan of Donald Trump.

The previous night, I had watched Stiglitz fume against President Trump's economic policies. We were in a dark, low-ceilinged room in the basement of a shabby restaurant on the outskirts of town, attending a reception hosted by the Institute for New Economic Thinking. Crowded with somber-looking economists, the reception felt like a secret meeting of dissident intellectuals (which it kind of was). Stiglitz's speech was followed by equally passionate and worried words from fellow Nobel laureate Michael Spence and then Robert Johnson, president of the institute. Like the other economists in the room, Johnson dismissed the shibboleths most Davos denizens take for granted. When I asked him later about one of those in particular—the "new" corporation—he said it was a diversion, mainly about corporations "pretending what's good for them is good for us." His skepticism made me wonder why he was here. So I asked him. "Davos collects a body of very influential people," he told me. "If you can have influence here, you can have great impact. I think it's worth a try, but I don't come here expecting great success."

From the attention Professor Schiffrin was getting in the Trump speech line, it seemed at least her "Not My President" protest was having success. Which isn't all that surprising. Few among the Davos crowd openly admit to liking Trump. His economic nationalism and xenophobia—not to mention his crude and unsavory character and antics—clash with their enlightened cosmopolitanism. More their style is Prime Minister Trudeau, who had spoken earlier in the week, reciting his usual progressive, feminist, and globalist notions, along with the very Davos idea that (he quoted directly from Larry Fink's letter) corporations need to give back, to be part of the solution, and to serve a social purpose.

Yet Trump, the first sitting American president to address Davos, was the biggest draw of the week, his audience numbers far surpassing those of Trudeau and every other world leader who gave a speech—including Germany's Angela Merkel, the United Kingdom's Theresa May, France's Emmanuel Macron, and India's Narendra Modi.

The queue to get into the auditorium, unusually long and cranky (members of the world superelite don't like waiting in line), began moving slowly after several delays, and we entered the auditorium serenaded by the regal strains of a brass band from the local canton's militia. Once everyone was seated, President Trump, accompanied by Klaus Schwab, strode onto the stage. Seemingly oblivious to the presence of Trump and

Schwab, the band played on, and the two men stood awkwardly for a cringingly long time. When the music finally stopped, Schwab stepped to the podium to introduce Trump, who proceeded to rehash (though in more muted tones) his usual, and very un-Davos-like, celebration of greed-driven "America first" capitalism—altogether unsurprising.

What *was* surprising for many was Schwab's introduction. The expectation was that Schwab, the personification of conscientious capitalism, would try to create some distance, albeit diplomatically, between himself and Trump. Instead, he fawned over Trump. "I'm aware that your strong leadership is open to misconceptions and biased interpretations," he said, seeming discombobulated when his words were met with hisses and boos. "So, it is so essential," he continued, his voice becoming louder and a bit shrill, "for us in the room to listen directly to you." And then he said this: "On behalf of the business leaders here in this room, let me particularly congratulate you for the historic tax reform package passed last month, greatly reducing the tax burden of U.S. companies."

Now, to put things in context, Trump's tax bill, which he first promised as a candidate and then pushed through Congress in December 2017, arguably reflects precisely the free- market-on-the-rampage, brakeless-train-wreaking-havoc capitalism that Schwab condemns and works to change. As Stiglitz remarked after Trump's speech—I caught him hurrying along the concourse outside the auditorium, looking angry and energized—the tax bill would gut public funding for, among other things, education, health care, and regulatory enforcement, thereby "distorting the economy" and "undermining prosperity and productivity." Trump's 2020 budget plans bear out Stiglitz's concerns, with projected cuts of trillions of dollars from health care, social services, and education over a ten-year period and deep cuts to environmental protection and other regulatory areas. So why, I asked Stiglitz, would Schwab, who seems to know better, say what he said about Trump's tax reforms? He paused for a moment, shook his head, and said, "I was shocked by Klaus's endorsement of the tax bill."

But Stiglitz shouldn't have been shocked. To begin with, Schwab didn't really *endorse* the tax bill. Rather, he congratulated the president, not on his own account but "on behalf of the business leaders here in this room," for "greatly reducing the tax burden of U.S. companies." He presumed those business leaders would be happy with Trump's tax bill, and about that, he was right. As Sandra Navidi told me later, "I have not heard a single businessperson on the record or off say he or she is not happy with the tax reform—even if they're anti-Trump."

The tax bill provides a huge windfall to corporations and their shareholders. Jamie Dimon's JPMorgan Chase saved $5 billion in 2019, for example, part of the $32 billion combined savings of top U.S. banks that resulted directly from Trump's cuts. And even Dimon, no Trump supporter—indeed, the embodiment of a new corporation leader, who quit a presidential advisory panel in protest of Trump's refusal to condemn white supremacists in the wake of the Charlottesville violence; and who has boasted he's smarter than Trump and could beat him in an election—said of the tax bill that "if you want America to be competitive, you need a competitive tax system."

In that statement, Dimon reflects the views of the business leaders in the room of Trump's speech, the ones on whose behalf Schwab thanked the president. As a headline and subsequent bullet point on CNBC's website summed it up: "Often critical of Trump's rhetoric, CEOs in Davos have to admit they like what they see. Bristling over some of his social rhetoric, CEOs have embraced tax reform and economic policies under Trump." Indeed, as President Trump's administration prepared to implement his 2017 tax plan, big corporations—including notable "new" corporations like Coca-Cola, General Electric, and IBM—lobbied intensively, and successfully, for even more cuts, securing new exemptions that reduced to almost nothing their tax liabilities for offshore profits, saving them tens of billions of dollars and allowing some of them, like Google, to abandon elaborate offshore tax-avoidance schemes.

It is therefore not surprising, let alone "shocking," that Schwab would thank Trump for his tax cuts on behalf of business leaders. Nor is it surprising that those business leaders would support Trump's tax bill—even though most of them, like Dimon, are striving to make their companies conscientious and social purpose oriented. It's naïve to expect, or hope, they would oppose tax cuts that gut government's capacity to protect social and environmental values, even the very same values they purport to champion. After all, leaders of the "new" corporation movement—companies like JPMorgan Chase, Apple, Walmart, and General Electric—make a great effort to avoid taxes, whether by squirreling money away in offshore tax havens, concocting complicated subsidiary regimes, or lobbying governments to cut taxes (either on their own or through organizations like the U.S. Chamber of Commerce, which pushed for Trump's tax package and now extols it for "unleashing a new era of growth for the American economy"). Why would these companies suddenly *not* want lower taxes?

And despite their claims to care, they're happy to offload onto others the costs of their profitable tax-reduction strategies. Recently, such costs were horribly on display as death, suffering, and economic hardship followed governments' bungled responses to the coronavirus pandemic. Corporate-driven tax cuts, including Trump's, were part of the reason government action was so woefully inadequate. Those tax cuts led to spending cuts—to health care, hospitals, and emergency preparedness—which in turn led to, among other things, shortages of testing kits, medical supplies, hospital beds, and health-care workers. At the same time, large segments of the population, especially in the United States, went without health care when they became ill because they were uninsured and couldn't afford it. And many were forced to go to work sick because neither employers nor government provided paid leave.

In short, the pandemic painfully reveals how the same tax cuts and avoidance that helped corporations reap record profits over the last few decades also starved governments of the means to protect citizens in the face of a global crisis. It's true that some of those corporations voluntarily provided help—Amazon CEO Jeff Bezos, for example, donated $100 million to food banks (an amount equaling roughly eleven days' worth of his personal earnings)—but it represented a thin sliver of what they saved through tax cuts and avoidance. "If Bezos really wanted to be socially responsible," former secretary of labor Robert Reich told me, "instead of contributing to food banks, he would lobby for higher taxes on himself and all of the other billionaires in America so that we have enough money to provide what everybody in this country really needs." As for those other billionaires, one study reports America's superrich boosted their collective fortune by $248 billion during three of the pandemic's worst weeks. Over that same time, tens of millions of ordinary citizens suffered palpably, many dying, because revenue-starved public systems were inadequate to the task of protecting citizens' health and well-being.

That, along with so much that came before it, starkly reveals the paradox inherent in Schwab's introduction of Trump—that "new" corporations say they care about social and environmental values, yet they don't want to pay taxes to protect and promote those values. The paradox is easily solved, however, if we assume that the ways corporations have changed, though real and significant, are not *fundamental*. Making money for themselves and their shareholders remains their top priority, as it always has been. So while they might care about social and environmental values, they care only *to the point* such caring might cut into profits. Then they stop caring. Paying taxes is a drag on profits, so corporations avoid, evade, and oppose doing so and also cheer, thank, lobby, and help elect politicians, like Donald Trump, who reduce their tax burdens. And as the next chapter shows, the same is true for everything else—while corporations may pursue social and environmental good, they do so only in ways and amounts likely to help them do well, and they continue to do bad when that is the best way for them to do well.

Like any good party, which depends on tacit agreement among participants to keep unseemly truths (jealousies, resentments, and betrayals) tucked beneath a veneer of celebration and conviviality, Davos is vulnerable to the party spoiler—the guy or gal who dredges those unseemly truths to the surface. Donald Trump was the Davos party spoiler. Because he showed up, Schwab had to introduce him. And in introducing him, Schwab had to choose between being honest (disclosing business leaders' affection for the tax bill) and being duplicitous (distancing himself from Trump). To his credit, he chose the former, and the Davos party was spoiled, the curtain pulled back on the Wizard of Davos. Now the unseemly truth was in plain view—the corporation's mandate is to make money for itself and its shareholders, and it will pursue that mandate relentlessly, and damn the consequences.

Despite shiny talk of conscientious commitments, corporations embrace social and environmental values to help them make *more* money—not to make less of it. Klaus Schwab acknowledges this. He doesn't say corporations should become good actors because it's the right thing to do, even if it costs them money. He says they should "blend moneymaking and social responsibility" because that's in their "long-term interests"—in other words, their self-interest. Valerie Keller similarly suggests corporations "harness the power of purpose" because that will "drive performance and profitability." John Coyne says sustainability is essential to "grow our business" and thereby deliver returns to "shareholders and other stakeholders." Paul Polman believes corporations will "perform better for . . . shareholders" if they "create long-term value that sustains human endeavor without harming the stakeholders and broader environment." Bill Gates cajoles corporations to "benefit from doing work that makes more people better off." Michael Porter says his "shared value" "reinforce[s] corporate strategy" and allows corporations to "[reap] the greatest business benefits."

No one says corporations should do good for the sake of doing good. What it's really about, as Bakule describes it, is "aligning self-interest—corporations' business interests—with society's interests—doing well by doing good."

And that's the key concept here, "doing well by doing good"—making money *through* social and environmental values rather than in spite of them. There are many ways corporations do this. They may profit from products that are good for the environment—like Walmart's sale of Earth Friendly Products; Honeywell's "technologies that address some of the world's toughest challenges in . . . clean energy generation"; Tesla's electric vehicles (and those of most other major automakers). Or they may tap new markets with social and environmental initiatives—like Unilever training rural Pakistani women to be beauticians (creating a new market and sales force for its beauty products); JPMorgan Chase investing in a renewal program in Detroit (creating new clients for its services and new opportunities for its clients); Coca-Cola mounting youth empowerment programs in Brazil's impoverished favelas (creating loyal customers for its products).

Doing good can also build positive reputations that help corporations attract customers, employees, and investors, and thereby "do well." As Daniel Skarlicki says, "If you want to future-proof your business, you have to consider that your customers, employees, and investors are millennials, and millennials are demanding values, they care about social and environmental issues." Positive reputations also help companies gain the blessings of communities where they operate, creating so-called social license to operate, which is especially important for extractive businesses.

Moreover, corporations save money by doing good, in numerous ways. Marriott reduces laundry costs by asking customers to reuse towels to "help save the planet"; Honeywell built a LEED (Leadership in Energy & Environmental Design) gold-certified production plant in Kansas City that uses half the energy of the plant it replaced; Levi Strauss & Company plans to "harvest raw materials from people's closets," as former vice president Michael Kobori described it to me, a sustainability measure that would help the company save money when sourcing fabric for its jeans.

In all these ways (and others too), corporations do well by doing good. Sustainability and social responsibility programs yield tangible economic benefits as well as reputation boosts and marketing angles that enhance corporations' competitive advantage. Shareholder value is maximized, and corporate interests are served. But still, there's the other side of the "doing well by doing good" equation— the "doing good" side. It needs to be asked: How much social and environmental good can corporations actually do in their pursuit of doing well? That is the key question of the next chapter, but for now it bears noting that "doing well" always sets the limit for what, and how much, good a corporation can do. That's a profound limit. And it's one that's dictated by law.

Corporations are created by law. Through law, groups of share-holders are granted single identities, corporate personhood, which in turn shields them from legal liability for debts and wrongs the businesses they invest in are responsible for. Share-holders are further protected by the "best interests of the cor-poration" rule, which demands directors and managers always prioritize their interests. That rule results in the corporation having a fundamentally self-interested institutional nature, which significantly constrains what leaders can do when trying to nurture their companies toward goodness. In short, the law *demands* corporations do well, while it *permits* them to do good (but only when that helps them do well).

It would be different, of course, if corporate law were differ-ent. And some corporate law scholars say it's changing. Their arguments are rooted in a famous 1930s exchange in the pages of the *Harvard Law Review* between Merrick Dodd and Adolf Berle. Dodd argued the corporation is "an economic institution which has a social service as well as a profit-making function." Berle countered that "all powers granted to a corporation or to the management of a corporation [are] at all times exercisable only for the ratable benefit of the shareholders as their interest appears." Berle won the debate, at least in terms of how corpo-rate law developed over the course of the twentieth century.

More recently, corporate law scholars say the law is shift-ing toward Dodd's position. Professor Lynn Stout, for example, argues forcefully that U.S. corporate law does not—and should not—demand that shareholder value be prioritized over social and environmental values. Her view is supported by court deci-sions and legislation in various U.S. states that permit corporate decision-makers to consider nonshareholder interests in determining what is in the "best interests" of their companies. Beyond the United States, more evidence can be found in European corporate law, which tends to be less shareholder driven than its U.S. counterpart, and in Canada, for example, where the Supreme Court recently held that "in considering what is in the best interests of the corporation, directors may look to the interests of, *inter alia,* shareholders, employees, creditors, consumers, governments and the environment to inform their decisions."

These are important shifts, which include "benefit corporations," or B corps (discussed in chapter three). But they fall far short of dethroning shareholder value as the corporation's overarching obligation. Even Professor Stout acknowledges that creating wealth for shareholders remains the corporation's *fundamental* mandate. Shareholders will "tolerate at least *somewhat* diminished returns" in exchange for corporations upholding social and environmental values, she says. But that wording implies they still expect *mainly* undiminished returns—that companies won't pursue those values in ways that *significantly* encroach on their returns.

Indeed, no one seriously suggests corporations are *not* legally required to promote shareholder value. Rather, what they say is that corporations may, and sometimes must, consider nonshareholder interests in determining their own "best interests"; or that they can or should sacrifice short-term share price gains for longer-term shareholder value; or, as Stout suggests, that they can provide *somewhat* diminished returns in exchange for social and environmental good. None of that denies corporations are legally compelled to prioritize self-interest in the form of creating shareholder value, whether in the short or the long term. Reforms may promote better corporate ethics and behavior, but it "would be foolish," as one commentator says of the above-mentioned Canadian Supreme Court decision, "to assume directors do not have a primary mandate to ensure a corporation is profitable."

And it really cannot be otherwise in light of the corporation's role in capitalism. The modern corporation was invented in the mid-nineteenth century to help create the large pools of investment capital needed to finance new and growing industrial ventures, like railways, steamship lines, and factories. Everything about its legally created structure is geared to that end. Corporate law is fundamentally *about* capitalism. It's designed to incentivize investment and thereby produce the fuel, capital, that the system needs to operate. To that end, the legal "best interests of the corporation" principle guarantees investors their money will be used for *their* benefit. Without it, they wouldn't invest, and the whole system, not just the corporation but capitalism itself, would grind to a halt. Which is why maximizing shareholder value—by prioritizing profit, growth, and competitive advantage—will always be the corporation's overarching mandate, at least in capitalist systems.

Corporations can still pursue social and environmental goals, of course, but only ever in ways that serve their "best interests." New corporation leaders know this. They're not naïve, nor are they outlaws. "Doing well by doing good [is] the current corporate consensus," as the *Financial Times* reports. No business leader is ready to abandon "doing well"; nor, legally, are they permitted to. The "new" corporation movement suggests only that "doing well" be understood and practiced in broader and more nuanced ways. "Many people say it's all about shareholder value, and I agree with that," Lord Browne told me. "But shareholder value is not just about extrapolating today's revenue and today's profits. It's about all the costs and all the risks." Still, with "doing well" the corporation's primary goal, and that being legally required, the earlier question posed—How much social and environmental good can corporations really do?—truly needs an answer.

Before getting to that answer, one final point must be made: it's crucial while pursuing it to stay focused on the corporation *as an institution,* on how its legal structure compels the people who run companies to do what they do. Those people, as is true in all institutions—churches, universities, governments, unions, schools, and the military, to name a few—are varied and retain diverse viewpoints about how to do their jobs and about life in general. Some may genuinely want to steer their companies in directions that promote social and environmental values, while others less so, and still others (though increasingly few) not at all. Some may personally believe in the corporate values that frame their work, while others may not, embracing different, and even contradictory, values outside their corporate jobs. What all have in common, however, despite all these differences, is that when they go to work, they're bound by the institutional imperatives of the corporations they work for.

Moreover, while those institutional imperatives are essentially the same for all corporations, different understandings and ways of operationalizing them result in different cultures at different companies. Just as the people who work for corporations differ the one from the next, so too do corporations themselves. Some are robustly committed to social and environmental values, while others less so. But their common institutional makeup imposes limits on how different they can be.

In previous attempts to explain this, I've resorted to ice hockey as an analogy, and it's helpful to do so again here. Ice hockey is a violent game, combining high speed, hard surfaces, and intense physical contact. The game's rules and structure encourage levels of violent behavior that outside the game—at work or at the mall, for example—would result in criminal prosecution. Yet hockey players are not necessarily violent people. They become violent when they're on the ice because that's what the game demands of them. And even when they're on the ice, they're not equally violent. Some are pugnacious players, fighting, slashing, and checking hard, while others rely on superior skating and puck-handling skills. Moreover, what's true of players is true of teams—some teams, as a whole, play a more violent game, others less so. Yet despite all these differences, hockey is hockey. It has a set structure and rules that determine what teams can, cannot, and must do when they're on the ice.

The same is true for the corporation. Despite all the differences that exist among corporations, as well as among those who run them, corporations are still corporations. Like hockey teams, they all play by the same rules, and those rules profoundly shape and limit their decisions and actions. And just as we can intelligibly assess the game of hockey as a whole—claiming, for example, that it is by nature a violent game—so too can we intelligibly analyze the corporation as an institution.

2 STILL CRAZY AFTER ALL THESE YEARS

MY INTERVIEW WITH LORD JOHN BROWNE got off to a rocky start. Waiting beforehand with a film crew in the hallway of L1 Energy's London headquarters, where Browne is the executive chair, I noticed a man storming toward me, fuming with anger. "This is terrible, terrible. You must remove it all, now," Lord Browne shouted at me, waving his arms at equipment cases my crew had left strewn about the hallway. "This is an office, not a studio." He was right, of course. The cases shouldn't have been there. They were a blight and, even worse, a safety hazard. And as I well knew, Lord Browne does not like safety hazards. Safety was a near obsession for him during his twelve years at the helm of BP, where he initiated programs that significantly reduced worker deaths and injuries from slips, trips, and falls—exactly the kinds of accidents the errant cases might have caused.

I apologized to Lord Browne and, with my crew, quickly moved the offending cases into a nearby storage room. He seemed satisfied and sat down for the interview. I began by asking him about safety. In 2010, BP suffered one of the world's worst safety disasters, the *Deepwater Horizon* explosion. Lord Browne had left the company three years earlier, but I wanted to know what he, having been chief architect of its safety culture, felt about the horrific failure. He began by telling me about another disaster.

"In 2005, when I was CEO of BP, we had a terrible tragedy," he told me. "Fifteen people died in a refinery explosion in Texas City in Texas." A backfiring pickup truck ignited a vapor plume caused by a chemical-filled distillation tower boiling over, and a huge explosion followed. This happened despite "years of trying to improve safety at BP" and the fact that "injuries, accidents, and fatalities were all on a significant downward trend, and safety was a top priority." After the explosion, "we were at pains to say safety must never be compromised for financial performance. I believe we had done that before Texas City, but after Texas City we redoubled those efforts to make sure that safety took primacy." By the time he left the company in 2007, Browne said, BP had put the right measures in place. "I thought: 'This is great, this company has got it.'"

Three years later, the *Deepwater Horizon* explosion killed eleven workers and nearly destroyed the Gulf of Mexico ecosystem. Lord Browne found it "so depressing," not only because of the loss of life but also because another safety accident had occurred. There were some "terrible echoes of history," he said. "I was watching on television the oil coming out of the seabed, which you could see in real time, and I thought to myself that the reputation of the company I had spent a lot of time with was going out to the sea, just as the oil was."

Though Lord Browne takes no responsibility for the tragedy ("I wasn't there, and I didn't know what had happened," he told me), postmortems of the disaster tell a different story— that, as Abrahm Lustgarten, the author of *Run to Failure: BP and the Making of the Deepwater Horizon Disaster,* described it to me:

"John Browne's fingers are all over that accident—the failures of maintenance, the poor decisions that led to it, echo and track what he instituted in the company decades before, the culture that he built."

From the time Lord Browne took control of BP in 1995, and even before that, while heading BP's exploration and production group, he worked hard to transform the company from a small two-pipeline concern into a top-tier oil and gas producer. Cheered on by investors and the business press, who dubbed him the "Sun King" for his efforts, he built a business model that squeezed out obstacles to profit and growth and yielded much of each. Through it all, Lord Browne proclaimed the importance of protecting workers and promulgated legions of rules—like no coffee cups without lids, no talking on cellphones while driving or operating equipment, no going up and down staircases without holding handrails—that reduced worker deaths and injuries. These *personal* protective measures aligned well with the BP business model—they cost little, saved money by reducing injury-related work time losses, and bolstered the company's image. In the meantime, however, more costly and disruptive *process* safeguards—relating to upkeep of wells, drilling rigs, and pipelines—were being dangerously diminished.

Leading up to the Texas City disaster, for example, the plant's process safety budget was cut twice, by 25 percent (in 1998) and then by another 25 percent (in 2005, just before the explosion). And this despite the fact that "much of the refinery's infrastructure and process equipment were in disrepair" and there had been "numerous previous fatalities . . . and many hazardous material releases," as the U.S. Chemical Safety and Hazard Investigation Board (CSHIB) reported in its official postmortem of the disaster. "BP did not take effective steps to stem the growing risk of a catastrophic event," the board concluded, "leaving the Texas City refinery vulnerable to catastrophe." In the end, the "very low personal injury rate at Texas City gave BP a misleading indicator of process safety performance."

After the Texas City explosion, three more deaths occurred at the refinery. In 2009, the federal Occupational Safety and Health Administration (OSHA) cited BP for "failure to abate" hazards at Texas City and for 829 "willful" safety violations at its U.S. refineries (compared with 33 overall in the United States for all other oil and gas companies combined). The company had "yet to achieve an effective safety culture," the chair of the CSHIB stated in response to OSHA's findings against it. Moreover, within a year of the Texas City disaster, an oil rig in the Gulf of Mexico, the *Thunder Horse,* sank during a hurricane, a result of shoddy construction, and Alaska's North Slope suffered its largest oil spill ever owing to BP's failure to maintain an aging pipeline (for which the company was criminally charged and pleaded guilty).

The path from Texas City to the *Deepwater Horizon* is tragically clear. Throughout Browne's tenure and afterward, BP cut corners on process safety. Parallel to the company's industry-leading personal safety record was an industry-leading string of spills, explosions, and legal infractions. "They were producing a lot of standards, but many were not very good, and many were irrelevant," says Nancy Leveson, an MIT industrial safety expert who advised the National Commission on the BP *Deepwater Horizon* Oil Spill and Offshore Drilling. The company lacked clear rules, for example, on how to conduct a "negative-pressure test," which might have prevented the *Deepwater Horizon* explosion. Just before that explosion, Leveson told colleagues that BP "was an accident waiting to happen." In its final report, the national commission identified BP's focus on "individual worker occupational safety but not on process safety" as a root cause of the tragedy.

"John Browne came in and he grew BP almost overnight,

pushing the largest cost cut that I've heard of at any corporation in any kind of industry," as Lustgarten summarizes it. "You can't do that without cutting corners on maintenance of equipment, without pushing timetables, like what led to the *Deepwater Horizon* disaster. That's the culture that he built."

It's easy to charge Lord Browne with hypocrisy, to suggest he cynically championed personal safety to mask his company's dangerous neglect of process issues. But I don't think that's entirely accurate or fair. Lord Browne truly cared about his workers' well-being, at least that's what I took from my interview with him. But his commitments failed to extend beyond, or at least not far enough beyond, personal measures. He construed safety to cohere with a business model that was intolerant of the costly drags on profit and growth that more stringent process measures would have caused. Which makes his avowals at once genuine and blinkered, reflecting a more complicated process than hypocrisy—and one that's arguably more dangerous.

People who manage and run large publicly traded corporations, like Lord Browne, are not guided by their own lights. Whatever their personal values and ideas might be, when they go to work at their companies, they, like hockey players skating onto the ice, are bound by the rules of the game. No doubt there's wiggle room. There's an envelope to be pushed. But there's still an envelope. And it severely constrains what they can do. Their decisions *must* always advance their companies' financial self-interests and hence that of their shareholders. The corporate form is agnostic about *how* they do it. But it demands they do it.

Therefore, when corporations and their leaders pursue social and environmental values—such as safety, sustainability, social responsibility, human rights, responding to a pandemic, or whatever else—they inevitably stop short of measures that interfere with profits or contradict business models. Koch Industries' claim to practice sustainability, for example, is not in itself untrue, as the company does have programs to reduce waste, save energy, recycle resources, and prevent pollution. But coal mining, arguably a profoundly *un*sustainable practice, nonetheless continues. Honeywell showcases its new LEED gold-certified manufacturing plant in Kansas City as a model of sustainability. But what goes on inside that plant? The manufacture of nuclear weapons components—again not very sustainable. British American Tobacco boasts of biodiversity around its tobacco fields. But the company makes a product that kills people and makes them ill (the World Health Organization has called tobacco production an "inherent contradiction" with social responsibility). FedEx claims "we actively promote and support a culture of health and safety for the benefit of our employees," while fending off unions and compelling employees with COVID-like symptoms to work during the pandemic. Google vaunts its use of renewable energy while it sells AI solutions to fossil fuel companies to help them boost production. Amazon promises after George Floyd's murder to "stand in solidarity with the Black community . . . in the fight against systemic racism and injustice," while marketing products that promote surveillance, fear, and racial-profiling in communities and police forces.

The point is simple. Corporations pursue social and environmental values, as they do everything else, in ways that serve *their* ends. Though loudly proclaiming commitments to such values, they always limit their actions to measures that promote, or at least don't threaten, profitable practices and basic business models.

Walmart, for example, while claiming to be among the world's most sustainable companies, is guided by an "entire corporate philosophy," as Peter Dauvergne describes it, that "is about growth and expansion, promoting consumption of more low-priced, short-term, nondurable, wasteful products." Indeed, since its 2005 sustainability pledge, Walmart has added three thousand new big-box stores worldwide to the sixteen hundred it had at the time. And "as it grows," adds Stacy Mitchell, author of *Big-Box Swindle,* it "pushes out existing enterprises and local economic systems and replaces them with its own, often far more polluting, global supply chain and sprawling stores."

There are myriad other examples. Procter & Gamble "decreases the amount of materials used to create and package our [Pampers disposable] diapers by 50%," it boasts, while aggressively expanding global markets for a product widely believed to be unsustainable. Coca-Cola uses renewable and recyclable plant-based plastics to make its bottles, while promoting bottled water, a product that, as Consumers International describes it, "represents the very antithesis of what sustainability means." Unilever claims to sustainably source palm oil, a key ingredient in many of its products, while pushing market growth for those products in the Global South and thus increasing overall demand for palm oil.

Sustainability is effectively defanged when it is narrowly conceived to align with business models and interests. Corporations pursue it, but only where there's little cost, little risk, and little disruption to their business models, along with, ideally, substantial benefits to themselves and their shareholders. Those are the hallmarks of even the most seemingly ambitious corporate sustainability programs. In a UN-conducted survey, CEOs themselves report feeling constrained by institutional mandates to pursue only small-scale sustainability projects with limited impacts. They express doubt that "greater scale, speed, and impact" is possible without "radical, structural change to markets and systems."

No such doubt is found, however, in corporations' slick TV

ads, Internet videos, and sustainability and CSR reports, where they exhibit boundless desire and potential to "do good." Nor is it found in the sunny talk of "new" corporation advocates, like Michael Porter, who proclaim that corporations are "the most powerful force for addressing the pressing issues we face." The fact is, corporations behave and talk differently than they used to, in ways that create patinas of plausibility for vastly exaggerated claims. That's a dynamic at play not only for sustainability but also for other pressing issues, like climate change.

Big oil and gas companies currently claim they're no longer the problem but now part of the solution to climate change. "We believe climate change is real," Royal Dutch Shell CEO Ben van Beurden recently declared. "The world needs to go through an energy transition to prevent a very significant rise in global temperatures, and we need to be part of that solution in making it happen." To that end, Shell promises to reduce the carbon footprint of its energy products 20 percent by 2035 and 50 percent by 2050, positioning it, claims van Beurden, to "meet the goals of the Paris Agreement on Climate Change." Shell, along with the world's other major oil and gas companies, actively helped forge that agreement (with one Shell executive even boasting his company could "take some credit" for certain of the accord's provisions). "Governments were responding to business's push for a climate agreement" in Paris, rather than the other way around, Levi's former vice president Michael Kobori told me, and having played a lead role in its progeny, oil and gas companies vociferously, though unsuccessfully, defended the accord against President Trump's threat to pull the United States out of it.

Compared with notorious past strategies of denial and obstruction, fossil fuel companies' current efforts to "do good" around climate change seem, at first glance, a positive development. On second glance, however, the picture looks less rosy. It's true the Paris accord's process signaled "a new way of behaving" for big oil and gas companies, as Lord Browne described it to me, but it also provided those companies an opportunity to seize control of the agenda and ensure the resulting agreement would "not limit them too much, not be too aggressive at moving to a clean energy future," in the words of Robert Weissman, president of Ralph Nader's Public Citizen. There are no limits in the accord on continued exploration and drilling or on tar sands exploitation (which experts say could alone defeat Paris targets), pipeline construction, or hydraulic fracturing ("fracking"). The accord contains no legally binding emission targets, no timeline for emission reductions, no enforcement mechanisms, no concrete regulatory proposals, and no plans to end fossil fuel subsidies.

Thanks to big oil's "help" in crafting it, the Paris accord is toothless. And that is potentially catastrophic.

Scientists have already sounded the alarm. The world is currently on course for a 3-to-5-degree Celsius temperature rise, which they claim would be cataclysmic. It's still possible to hold that to between 1.5 and 2 degrees, they say, but that would require immediate and radical action. For a 1.5-degree cap, carbon emissions would have to be cut 45 percent from 2010 levels and hit zero by 2050, according to the Intergovernmental Panel on Climate Change (IPCC), the United Nations body for assessing climate science. For a 2-degree cap, the next decade requires a 20 percent cut and emissions reaching zero by 2075. The Paris accord's promise to hold rising temperatures to 2 degrees, and ideally 1.5 degrees, was its great achievement. But it's shamefully offset by an even greater failure—the lack of concrete and enforceable measures to hit its targets. Under the cover of good intentions and new ways of behaving, big oil and gas companies pushed for and got an agreement that leaves hydrocarbon-driven business models largely unfettered and relegates humanity's survival to the realm of hope rather than action.

Corporations' participation in the Paris accord, a form of "doing good" as they portray it, undoubtedly helped them do well. But it is highly questionable whether any good at all was done for society and the environment. *The Economist* notes "a single, jarring truth: Demand for oil is rising and the energy industry, in America and globally, is planning multi-trillion-dollar investments to satisfy it." Oil and gas companies are boosting production and creating new fossil fuel megaprojects. By 2025, for example, ExxonMobil expects to have pumped 25 percent more oil and gas than in 2017. In the meantime, as *The Economist* reports, "the consequence for the climate could be disastrous if the rest of the industry pursues even modest growth."

The net effects of corporations' new commitments to help solve the climate crisis are to bolster influence and promote self-interested plans for moving forward. "Corporations are having a dramatic impact on public discourse," Dauvergne observes, "as people increasingly turn to them for solutions, and increasingly accept corporate explanations of what progress actually is." Actively presenting themselves as solution providers, no longer problem creators, corporations push back against scientific consensus, claiming we have more time, and less need for action, than scientists call for. The story they tell is that renewable energy is a long way in the future, and in the meantime, "lighter" carbon fuels like natural gas (typically extracted through fracking) are the answer. Because it's "impossible to displace carbon fully for a long time," as Lord Browne rehearses the story's logic, "displacing the energy mix toward a lighter carbon content" is the best we can hope for now.

The underlying premise—that radical and immediate action on climate is neither possible nor necessary—serves to prolong society's dependence on fossil fuels and therefore protect the industry's core business model. It's a classic "new" corporation strategy. With climate change no longer plausibly deniable, corporations stop denying it, congratulate themselves for being good actors, and then set to work to ensure that *how* the issue is understood and addressed leaves their business models and interests intact. The result is to stave off urgent and far-reaching measures scientists are calling for, including speedy moves to renewables. The UN Intergovernmental Panel on Climate Change, for example, concludes that keeping global warming to either 1.5 or 2 degrees would demand "rapid and far-reaching," "unprecedented"—though, they say, possible—changes in land use, energy, industry, buildings, transportation, and cities. The self-interested "solutions" promised by fossil fuel corporations contradict that scientific consensus, their built-in delay tactics aimed at preserving core business models rather than promoting society's best interests.

"The real danger," as the youth environmental activist Greta Thunberg described it at a 2019 UN climate conference in Madrid, "is when politicians and CEOs are making it look like real action is happening, when in fact almost nothing is being done, apart from clever accounting and creative PR." The slick messaging coming from industry is seductive and lulls us into believing corporations have everything under control, that we're in good hands. Since 2005, fossil fuel companies, and their financiers, have upped both spending and efforts to pump out that message, claiming, in response to growing public concern and scientists' increasingly dire warnings, that they care about climate change and are doing everything they can to stop it.

In his 2020 letter to CEOs, for example, Larry Fink, head of BlackRock, the world's largest money manager (managing nearly $7 trillion in assets), promised action on climate change. There's compelling scientific evidence that "climate risk will impact both our physical world and the global system that finances economic growth," and he's concerned about it, he wrote, alongside the "millions of people [who] took to the streets to demand action on climate change." Vowing to "place sustainability at the center of our investment approach" and, among other things, dump bonds and stocks that generate more than 25 percent of revenue from coal production, he nonetheless made it clear these moves were aimed primarily at helping investors make money. "Our investment conviction is that sustainability- and climate-integrated portfolios can provide better risk-adjusted returns to investors," he wrote.

Dumping coal is, of course, a shrewd business move, as coal stocks have tanked, with that of one major producer in Black-Rock's portfolios, Peabody Energy, losing three-quarters of its value since 2018. But beyond coal, there's no sign BlackRock will divest itself of still-profitable fossil fuel assets. The company manages more than $100 billion in oil and gas investments, including in major companies aggressively expanding production, like ExxonMobil, Shell, Chevron, and BP. Unless and until BlackRock no longer "does well" by investing in such companies, it's nearly certain it won't "do good" by disinvesting.

"The message that corporations now acknowledge the climate crisis and are undertaking measures to address it is absolutely bogus, self-serving," Grand Chief Stewart Phillip, head of the Union of British Columbia Indian Chiefs, told me. He worries that the wildfires, melting glaciers, rising oceans, and drought resulting from climate change are coming faster and with more severe consequences than expected and notes their disproportionate impact on indigenous people. Yet with all the fine talk from the corporate world, "nothing has changed," he said. And he's right. The fossil fuel industry continues to boost production, drilling, and fracking, developing one new megaproject after another, as it boasts ever louder about how much it cares.

The inevitable result, as scientists have been predicting for some time, is a rapidly warming planet. And in addition to the devastating effects Chief Phillip worries about, there's another one too—a heightened risk of deadly pandemics. Most emerging infectious diseases—including the current coronavirus, as well as AIDS, Ebola, West Nile, SARS, MERS, and many more—are zoonotic, meaning they jump to humans from nonhuman animals. Climate change destroys animal habitats by causing wildfires, hurricanes, floods, thawing, and drying, bringing animals and humans into closer proximity. That, in turn, increases the chances of humans contracting zoonotic infections. It was a forest fire connected to a drought, for example, that caused fruit bats in Malaysia to relocate to trees on farms, where they infected pigs with the Nipah virus. The pigs then infected farmers, and more than a hundred people died.

The point is, "disease, it turns out, is largely an environmental issue," as *The New York Times* summarized it in 2012. And it's not only climate change but other environmental issues too. A Hendra virus outbreak in Australia, which killed humans and horses, was blamed in part on suburbanization that drew fruit bats into backyards and pastures. On the U.S. East Coast, deforestation destroyed habitats for wolves, foxes, and hawks, natural predators of white-footed mice. The latter, a repository for larval ticks, flourished as a result, fueling a dramatic rise in Lyme disease. Deforestation in the Amazon by 4 percent caused a 50 percent increase in the incidence of malaria because mosquitoes thrive in recently deforested areas.

Displacement of human beings as a result of climate change is a further factor likely to fuel pandemics as global warming accelerates. One effect of such warming is that equatorial regions will heat up, forcing populations to migrate north and south to cities with livable environments and economies that are still intact. Cramped shantytowns, refugee camps, and the like will crop up in those cities, creating sites for easy transmission of infectious disease. Already, as migrants are relegated to crowded refugee camps, with little access to sanitation, food, water, soap, and health care, a perfect storm for the rapid spread of infectious diseases is created, a tragedy for residents of those camps and a catalyst for the further spread of pathogens.

In short, the coronavirus pandemic needs to be seen as a warning of yet another devastating effect of climate change—its acceleration of infectious disease spread—revealing, once again, that "new" corporations' claims to care and have solutions are not only false but also dangerous.

Nutritional health is another area where corporations present themselves as part of the solution, no longer the problem. Food and beverage companies have been particularly active on this front. Coca-Cola, for example, pledges "to being part of workable solutions to the problems facing society related to obesity," committing to "partnering with . . . academia," and promoting "evidence-based science." Nestlé, the world's largest food and beverage company, recently rebranded itself as a "nutrition, health and wellness company," with a "long-term goal of creating shared value" and "enabl[ing] healthier and happier lives for individuals and families, with a strong focus on infants and children." Unilever's Sustainable Living Plan includes a promise to "improve health and well-being for more than a billion by 2020."

Through such commitments, corporations purport to "do good" in relation to health. But again, as with sustainability and climate, their conceptions of health, and what needs to be done to promote it, are narrowly tailored to advance their own interests. Take, for example, big food and beverage companies' promise to fight hunger and malnutrition by selling products to the world's poor. Often aligned with NGOs, including United Nations agencies, they target starving and malnourished people in the developing world for sales, creating new markets for products that health-conscious consumers in the developed world are turning away from. "At a time when some of the growth is more subdued in established economies," as Nestlé CEO Mark Schneider describes it, "strong emerging-market posture is going to be a winning position."

In one effort to tap those emerging markets, Nestlé created a direct-sales force of pushcart vendors in poor and remote regions of Brazil. The company says the program helps remedy hunger and malnutrition by making food available to underserved populations. But the bulk of sales from its pushcarts are of high-calorie, low-nutrient products like Kit Kat and Chandelle pudding. "They are going into the backwoods of Brazil and selling their candy," as Barry Popkin, W. R. Kenan Jr. Distinguished Professor of Nutrition at the UNC Gillings School of Global Public Health, describes Nestlé's program. And as it and other companies increasingly ply their goods to the world's poor (between 2011 and 2016, packaged food sales have grown 25 percent worldwide, compared with just 10 percent in the United States), impoverished people abandon traditional diets in favor of processed products—the leading cause, say experts, of an obesity epidemic that now exists alongside hunger and malnutrition in the Global South.

Making matters worse, corporations have begun targeting the poor with sugar-laden drinks that they say will help solve malnutrition, especially for children and women. These are among the array of "nutraceutical" products that now are a booming business across the Global South. In India, for example, nutraceuticals account for "the most successful sector of the food and pharmaceuticals market," according to one analyst, with sales doubling from $2 billion to $4 billion between 2010 and 2017 and projected to hit $10 billion by 2020 and $18 billion by 2025. Advocated as a "humanitarian technology capable of relieving suffering and ameliorating the loss of life in contexts of crisis," as one commentator describes the central pitch for nutraceuticals, they are widely regarded as a "clear case of 'doing well by doing good.'"

Again, there's little doubt corporations "do well" by selling nutraceutical drinks. But what about the "doing good" part? Companies boast of significant health benefits. Coca-Cola, for example, claims its Vitingo, an orange-flavored drink fortified with vitamins and minerals, will help solve India's "high burden of micronutrient deficiency, especially among school-age children, women, and children below 5 years old." Nestlé markets the meal-replacement beverage Boost with promises it can maintain muscle and support bone health and is "suitable as a mini-meal." GlaxoSmithKline says its Horlicks drink, marketed aggressively among India's poor, "can build and strengthen the body, brain, muscles and bones," especially for women and children. When Unilever recently announced plans to acquire Horlicks, it noted that the product "is aligned with Unilever's stated strategy of increasing its presence in health-food categories and in high-growth emerging markets." There are many more products and similar claims.

But the supposed health benefits of the drinks are "just tall claims made by the makers," charges the nutrition advocate Arun Gupta. There's no independent science to verify the claims (though companies often say they are "scientifically proven") and no regulatory standards or oversight. Indeed, the products may actually do more harm than good, not least because of their high sugar content. Coca-Cola's Vitingo, for example, contains 4 teaspoons of sugar per serving, Horlicks has close to 3 teaspoons, and Boost has 5.5 teaspoons. One serving of each drink equals roughly the entire maximum sugar intake *per day* recommended by the World Health Organization for children (3 to 6 teaspoons).

And again, as with climate change, corporations' self-interested conception of an issue, hunger and malnutrition in this case, serves to frame public and policy debates in ways that help industry, not necessarily others. The idea behind companies' seemingly benevolent nutraceutical push is that solutions to poverty-caused malnutrition are found in "the corporate laboratory and marketing agency," as one commentator describes it. And as governments and NGOs embrace that idea, which increasingly they do, the effect is to obscure how social conditions and economic structures make it difficult, and often impossible, for people to have a balanced diet. In that way, the notion that consuming nutraceuticals can help solve hunger and malnutrition diverts focus from roots and causes and forestalls the kinds of real change that are necessary.

In relation to all the issues examined—hunger and malnutrition, climate change, sustainability, and industrial safety—corporations say they are out in front, taking the lead, no longer the problem but now part of the solution. What we see, however, is that in each case their efforts to "do good" are driven primarily by the imperative to "do well." No doubt those efforts can yield benefits to society, but inevitably they are severely limited. Moreover, as I've shown, the kinds of "good" corporations do in pursuit of "doing well" are sometimes positively harmful—as where sugary drinks are marketed as promoting health. Or, more broadly, where corporations proliferate their self-interested conceptions of values like sustainability, climate change mitigation, and health through lobbying, marketing, and public relations and capture and narrow how those values are understood in public opinion and addressed by governments.

All of which is why I agree with Warren Buffett's skeptical assessment of corporations that "do good." "It's very hard to evaluate what they're doing . . . it's very, very hard," he says. "The government has to play the part of modifying a market system." Which is true, as the next chapter shows. But for now, it's important to note that even when governments do play that part, by passing laws and regulations that *demand* corporations "do good," it's still often not enough. And that's in large part because the logic of "doing well by doing good" leaves open, and implicitly condones, the possibility that corporations might "do bad," including breaking the law, when that, rather than "doing good," is the best way to "do well."

It's International Anti-Corruption Day, December 9, 2014, and people are in the streets worldwide, protesting against the growing corruption in both corporations and government. They've "had enough of corruption and they want to do their part to stop it," says Transparency International's former managing director Cobus de Swardt, explaining why his group helped organize the day. For Volkswagen, this is the perfect day to release an Internet video celebrating the company's anticorruption crusade. The video is animated and begins with a narrator solemnly declaring that "the reputation of our brand is our most valuable asset." Villains and monsters appear on the screen, and the narrator continues: "That's why it has to be protected from threats no matter where they come from; from threats no matter what form they take." A posse of superheroes then swoops in to vanquish the villains and monsters. "Superheroes always know what to do, and so do we," the narrator says as the word "COMPLIANCE" appears on the screen. "All we ask you to do is follow the rules."

At the time the video was released, Volkswagen was thought of as a paragon of corporate virtue. The company, ranked among the "10 companies with the best CSR reputations" by *Forbes* magazine, had just won an award at the World Forum for Ethics in Business. "It's fair to say," noted a report in *Triple Pundit* in 2014, that "no other automobile and transportation manufacturer has gone as far as VW in adopting and instilling social and environmental, as well as economic, sustainability at the core of its organizational values and priorities." For its own part, the company claimed in 2014 that "environmental considerations are factored into every decision we make" and promised it would become "the world's most environmentally compatible automaker" by 2018.

Things didn't quite work out that way. Despite its apparent good intentions and all the praise showered upon it, Volkswagen was, in 2014, enmeshed in a scandal of breathtaking scope and cynicism. For the previous six years, it had secretly installed "defeat devices" in diesel-fueled vehicles that switched off emission controls once regulatory testing was complete. An "intentional effort . . . to evade law and lie to regulators . . . [that] went to the top of the organization," as one U.S. attorney described it, the scheme doctored vehicles to emit up to forty times more pollutants than legal limits allowed, dumping tens of thousands of extra tons of air pollution into the atmosphere, directly causing, according to some studies, illness and thousands of deaths. In 2017, VW pleaded guilty to charges of conspiracy to commit fraud, obstruction of justice, and falsifying statements. The presiding judge chastised the company for "very, very, very serious crimes" and sentenced it to a $2.8 billion fine, a slice of the $25 billion in fines and settlements it would end up paying worldwide. "Who has been hurt by this corporate greed?" the judge asked. "From what I can see, it's not the managers at VW, the ones who get paid huge salaries and large bonuses, as always it's the little guy."

With its emissions cheating, Volkswagen sought to "do well by doing bad." The company saved billions by not retrofitting engines to meet regulatory standards, while it gained a competitive advantage by falsely marketing vehicles as low emitters. VW is not alone, however, as a company whose actions blatantly, and criminally, belie its words. There are scores of others that "do bad"—cheat and break the law—when that, rather than "doing good," is the best way to "do well."

Johnson & Johnson, for example—a "distinguished company," according to the American Academy of Pediatrics, and one that claims its *"first* responsibility is to doctors, nurses and patients, to mothers and fathers . . . who use our products and services"— recently pleaded guilty to crimes that endangered women, children, and the elderly. The company was caught committing a slew of offenses: hiding from consumers and regulators the fact that its infant and children's Tylenol and Motrin were adulterated with harmful nickel/chromium particles; fraudulently marketing drugs for off-label use by elderly patients to treat dementia (a practice it continued even after deaths among such patients prompted a warning from the Food and Drug Administration); promulgating false, misleading, and dangerous marketing campaigns of opioids that, in the words of one judge, "caused exponentially increasing rates of addiction [and] overdose deaths"; and deliberately suppressing the fact that its talc-based products, including its baby powder and Shower to Shower powder, were suspected of containing asbestos and heightening risks of ovarian cancer.

With respect to the latter, when demand for its baby powder plummeted around 2006, partly in response to emerging asbestos-related concerns, Johnson & Johnson marketers began targeting African American women, 60 percent of whom used the powder, compared with 30 percent of the general population. Company documents show a deliberate and aggressive campaign that included distributing free samples in churches and beauty salons in African American neighborhoods, running print and digital campaigns, and broadcasting radio ads aimed at "curvy Southern women 18–49 skewing African American." When contacted by Reuters to explain its practices, the company's response was that it targeted numerous demographics. "We're proud pioneers of the practice of multicultural marketing," it said. Johnson & Johnson stopped selling talc-based powder in North America in May 2020.

Returning to BP, the *Deepwater Horizon* explosion resulted in $24 billion in fines, just shy of Volkswagen's $25 billion. Together the two firms sit atop corporate crime's "Most Wanted" list. But they have lots of company, with many major corporations having received multibillion-dollar fines. Among them are *drug companies* Pfizer, GlaxoSmithKline, Eli Lilly, and Purdue Pharmaceuticals; *energy companies* Wisconsin Power and Light, First Energy, Anadarko Petroleum, Duke Energy, and American Electric Power; *banks* JPMorgan Chase, Goldman Sachs, Citigroup, Deutsche Bank, Credit Suisse, HSBC Holdings, and Wells Fargo; and *big-tech companies,* for whom tax evasion and antitrust are the favored legal infractions, with Google, Apple, Amazon, and Microsoft all getting themselves into trouble with the law.

The sad truth is that over the last two decades, corporations have been on a crime spree, even while claiming they have become conscientious and caring. The top corporate fine in the early 2000s was Hoffmann-La Roche's $500 million (roughly

$1 billion in today's dollars), which pales in comparison with VW's current record of $25 billion. Corporations are breaking the law "on a grander scale than anything we've seen," says Robert Weissman. And there's "zero reason to think even these very large fines are deterring corporate crime and wrongdoing because the ones who get caught typically don't pay as much as what they made from their wrongdoing."

Corporations have no internal constraints to stop them from flouting the law. Their legal makeup compels them to pursue profit and growth but say nothing about whether they have to abide by the law in doing so. As a result, decisions to break the law depend, as do all others, on whether the benefits outweigh the costs. Companies weigh the probability of getting caught, the likely dollar value of fines and settlements if they do get caught, potential reputational and customer loyalty losses, and the risk of governments clamping down with more stringent laws. Corporations consider all these factors and often anticipate likely fines for knowingly breaking the law, even setting aside funds to pay them. It's all part of a cost-benefit calculus that incentivizes corporate lawbreaking and helps explain why most corporations commit offenses, some routinely. It may not be good behavior, but it helps them do well.

Corporations break the law. They're programmed to act out of self-interest. They lack the capacity to care genuinely about anything but themselves, routinely exploit and cause harm to others, and mimic concern when that serves their self-interest. On these bases, I have argued in the past that the corporation, as an institution, is imbued with the flawed character of a human psychopath. The "new" corporation movement professes to answer that criticism. But as you can see, despite all the posturing, the corporation's character remains fundamentally the same. In 2011, the American Psychiatric Association added a new criterion to the diagnosis of psychopaths: "use of seduction, charm, glibness, or ingratiation to achieve one's ends." That's helpful for understanding this "new" corporation. It's still a psychopath—just a more charming one now. And more dangerous because of that.

3 THE CORPORATE
LIBERATION MOVEMENT

IN 1720, the British South Sea Company collapsed after revelations that its wildly inflated stock price was based on fraudulent and fabricated claims. The resulting South Sea Bubble, the world's first corporate scandal, crashed Great Britain's economy, not least because the British government had been the company's main investor. Ensuing social unrest spread quickly from London to the countryside, where in acts of "fairly direct class hatred," as one historian describes it, peasants began poaching deer on aristocrats' lands. In October 1721, sixteen men, their faces painted black, invaded the Bishop of Winchester's estate, stole three deer, and killed two. Dubbed the Waltham Blacks (they were from the village of Waltham Chase), the group conducted further raids, creating a furor among aristocrats and demands for reprisal.

In 1723, Parliament responded with the Black Act, a law that punished by death anyone suspected of poaching, even when there was no proof of wrongdoing. For the historian E. P.

Thompson, that law stands as a hideous example of the law's capacity for brutal injustice. But there's another way to look at the story, he says. "If I judge the Black Act to be atrocious," he writes, "this is according to some ideal notion of the standards to which the law, as a regulator of human conflicts of interest, must always seek to transcend the inequalities of class power which, instrumentally, it is harnessed to serve." It's that "ideal notion" of law, Thompson says, that we need always to remember and aspire toward. Though "the law's operation has, again and again, fallen short of its own rhetoric of equity, the notion of the rule of law is itself an unqualified good."

History is replete with laws, like the Black Act, that unjustly magnify the power of the powerful and cause pain, horror, and dispossession for others. Racial apartheid and segregation, colonialism, slavery, genocide, repression of all kinds, patriarchy, human rights, and labor abuses—all have been articulated, justified, and executed through law. Yet history also reveals that law sometimes fulfills Thompson's "ideal notion"—that it stands up to injustice and protects those vulnerable to being harmed and exploited. It's this Janus face of law that best explains its relationship to corporations. Law creates corporations to pursue profit and growth regardless of the harms and exploitation they cause to others, making them dangerous and sometimes unjust institutions. Yet law also regulates corporations, protecting people, communities, and the environment from the predatory behavior it licenses. And therein lies its "ideal notion."

Since the early twentieth century, regulation has been the main way governments protect people and public interests from corporate harms. In the early 1930s, President Franklin D. Roosevelt promulgated his New Deal, a massive regulatory intervention designed to rein in corporate power and shield people from the ravages of the Great Depression. Roosevelt's intention was clear. "We were not to be content with merely hoping for these [constitutional] ideals," he proclaimed, but "were to use the instrumentalities and powers of Government actively to fight for them . . . against the misuse of private economic power." Law was, in Roosevelt's plan, tasked with promoting justice by curbing economic power, an "ideal notion" that inspired not only the New Deal but a plethora of regulatory regimes across the industrialized world over the decades that followed. By the 1970s, robust regulations—protecting, among other things, consumers, workers, the environment, health, safety, and human and civil rights—were commonplace.

The purposes of regulation have always included promoting citizens' freedom and giving effect to their democratic rights, as well as protecting public interests. Individuals are not free when corporations have impunity to act in ways that inflict harm upon them—when, for example, they get injured working for a company or are defrauded by a bank, poisoned by pollution, discriminated against for a job, or become ill with a pandemic virus due to inadequate workplace safeguards. "Corporations' freedom detracts from our freedom, and it's a zero-sum game," as the *Guardian* columnist George Monbiot describes it—the reason legal curbs on corporate freedoms are needed to protect citizens' freedom. Those curbs are also important for helping ensure citizens' democratic rights are effective. As the main device governments use to control corporations, regulation is the channel through which we, the citizens who elect those governments, shape the rules that govern corporate conduct. When regulations are rolled back, so too are democratic controls on corporations and thereby the scope of citizens' democratic rights.

Beyond freedom and democracy, another rationale for regulation is that corporations are themselves products of regulation. The corporation was not created by the market's invisible hand or by any other supernatural entity. It did not evolve out of the universe's baryonic matter or the principles of physics. It's a creation of the state, of laws that conjure it into existence, deem it to be a "person," define and protect its rights and privileges, shield its owners from legal liability, and provide it with a mandate to prioritize its owners' best interests. Corporations—indeed, corporate capitalism—could not exist without these legal entitlements. From that follows a key rationale for regulation: that it's needed as a legal hedge against dangers created by the law itself, in the form of the corporation (recall law's Janus face).

Despite all these good reasons for regulation, a worldwide unraveling of regulatory systems is currently under way, and it has been since the early 1980s. Now it's being fueled by the "new" corporation movement.

Frustrated with regulatory limits on their pursuit of profit, corporations rebelled in the early 1980s. In an all-out attack on regulation, they lobbied, sponsored public relations campaigns, and created free market–friendly think tanks. They backed politicians such as British prime minister Margaret Thatcher and U.S. president Ronald Reagan (who blamed the previous Jimmy Carter administration for its "continuing devotion to job-killing regulation"). And soon governments—everywhere and of all political stripes—were purging regulations and curbing the creation of new ones, a trend that continues today. Most recently, the Trump administration vowed "deconstruction of the administrative state," as then Trump adviser Stephen Bannon described it, by, among other things, appointing a parade of anti-regulation regulators to the cabinet ("for a reason, and that is the deconstruction," Bannon said of the appointments) and by promulgating an executive order requiring departments to eliminate at least two laws for every new one created.

The scope of Trump's attack on the regulatory system is

unprecedented, with myriad regulations being slashed and blocked. He and his administration have scuttled long-standing public lands protections, opening national parks, monuments, and pristine wilderness areas to mining and fossil fuel drilling. They've rolled back rules relating to emissions from coal-fired power plants, offshore drilling (put in place after the *Deepwater Horizon* disaster), automobile tailpipe emissions (allowing cars on the road to emit an extra billion tons of carbon dioxide over their lifetimes), and numerous other environmental harms. They're weakening "infection control" requirements in nursing homes designed to contain the spread of viruses, like coronavirus. They're deregulating banks and financial institutions, leaving consumers and investors vulnerable—it's "probably the most anti-investor and [anti–]consumer protection administration in decades, if not ever," according to Dennis Kelleher, president and CEO of Better Markets, an advocacy group for stricter financial regulations. And the Trump administration has reduced worker safety protections and child labor laws, weakened union rights and wage protections, and diminished employment standards and worker health benefits. Just a few examples from a long and rapidly growing deregulation list.

Still, the Trump administration's attack on regulation is only the latest—albeit perhaps the greatest—victory in corporations' decades-long fight against legal controls. By the time Trump was elected president, the idea that government oversight is essential to democratic governance had already lost its privileged place in the political imagination, globally and across political lines. It had largely been replaced by the contrasting view that regulation stifles economic progress and that corporations should be free of it. "For four decades," as the commentator Jeff Wise describes it, "politics and industry have been increasingly captivated by the idea that government regulation of business is generally a bad thing. Regulation has gone out of fashion."

Key to understanding regulation's demise is the rise of the "new" corporation. With it, a new, apparently publicly minded, and therefore politically powerful rationale emerged to justify freeing corporations from legal bonds. Its logic is simple—because corporations now truly care about social and environmental values, they should be *trusted* to respect those values on their own, rather than *compelled* by law to do so. In short, they should be left to *self*-regulate rather than *be* regulated. The idea quickly gained momentum and was widely embraced by economists, business leaders, and policy makers, who called for, as soon-to-be British prime minister Gordon Brown expressed it in 2005, the "old model of regulation" to be replaced with a "better approach [that] trust[s] in the responsible company."

This new anti-regulation rationale differed from earlier ones, which had focused mainly on the virtues of free markets. Henceforth the emphasis would be on public interests and the responsibility of corporations to protect them. Deregulation was thus given a new progressive shine. Corporate leaders could embrace social and environmental values while insisting that self-regulation regimes, not legal measures, were the best way to protect them. They could defend lobbying for rollbacks of laws designed to protect the very values they solemnly professed by claiming those laws were now redundant and unnecessary. All of which has helped companies push harder, and more successfully, than ever to free themselves from regulation.

Even in the midst of a deadly pandemic, the U.S. Chamber of Commerce (which includes all "new" corporations as members) lobbied hard to avoid deployment of a law, the Defense Production Act (DPA), to require manufacturers to produce life-saving and desperately needed medical supplies. The lobby was largely successful, with Trump going so far as to claim use of the DPA would be akin to Venezuelan-style nationalization. "We're a country not based on nationalizing our business," he said. "Call a person over in Venezuela, ask them how did nationalization of their businesses work out? Not too well."

Though the Trump administration eventually compelled GM to make ventilators, it stopped far short of sweepingly deploying the DPA, drawing scathing criticism from the author and former military court judge James E. Baker. With the DPA, said Baker, "the federal government has all the authority it needs to close the supply gap, allocate resources among states, and prepare for the production and distribution of the vaccine to come." Yet, he said, "so far, the administration appears to have responded like a parent doling out candy to a child: one piece at a time." And that has remained true throughout the crisis, thanks to pressure from the U.S. Chamber of Commerce and other corporate lobbyists.

In the meantime, the American Petroleum Institute (API), which lobbies on behalf of oil and gas companies—the very ones now purporting to provide leadership and solutions in relation to climate change—wrote to President Trump requesting he waive regulatory compliance obligations relating to, among other things, the EPA's "routine testing and reporting requirements." In a separate letter to the EPA, the group asked for more specific regulatory relief, in relation to pollution monitoring, detection and repair of leaky equipment, and greenhouse gas reporting. The Union of Concerned Scientists quickly tweeted in response: "We can't use one crisis like #coronavirus to make another crisis like climate change worse." But the Trump administration went even further than what the API asked for, suspending enforcement of all environmental laws for any violation "that results from the COVID-19 pandemic."

Banks also attempted to leverage the coronavirus crisis, lobbying for long-sought-after rollbacks of measures designed to ensure they have sufficient cash on hand to buffer economic crises. The lobby, conducted by the Bank Policy Institute, whose members include the likes of JPMorgan Chase, Citigroup, and Bank of America, was widely condemned by experts as opportunistic and likely to make a bad situation worse if successful. Earlier deregulation had fueled easy access to credit, allowing corporations to debt-finance operations and spend record profits buying back their own shares. Just before the pandemic, debt in the U.S. corporate sector was at 75 percent of gross domestic product, higher than the previous record set in 2008. Then when the pandemic hit, with no cash on hand to help them weather the storm, they—the very same companies that paid little or no taxes for years—went hat in hand to the government demanding taxpayers bail them out.

"This is how the coronavirus will destroy the economy," Ruchir Sharma, chief global strategist at Morgan Stanley Investment Management, said at the time. "This once-in-a-century pandemic is hitting a world economy saddled with record levels of debt."

But, in the end, this is what deregulation is really about: citizens paying the price for corporate profiteering. "New" corporations may profess to care about society and the environment, but they will always push governments to free them from legal constraints, leaving citizens to suffer the consequences of their profit-driven irresponsibility.

In 2017, for example, Jamie Dimon and his Business Roundtable (whose members include CEOs from leading "new" corporations like Coca-Cola, Salesforce, Johnson & Johnson, and Procter & Gamble) asked the Trump administration to make cuts to a list of "top regulations of concern," ones "unduly burdensome" to big business. Among those were ozone and coal-fired plant emission standards, clean water rules, worker overtime and fair pay requirements, and net neutrality rules. In other words, those same "new" corporation leaders who, like Dimon, often criticize President Trump's stances on social issues cheer him for his deregulation agenda and work to leverage it to their advantage, all the while claiming to be champions of the very social and environmental values their efforts deprive of legal protection. In short, purporting to be "good" has turned out to be highly effective for corporations seeking to avoid legal prohibitions on being bad.

And it's not just about Trump, as already noted. The new anti-regulation rationale is helping fuel the creation of self-regulation regimes around the world, effectively turning global governance on its head. In most cases, these new regimes don't operate alongside legal regulations or bolster their enforcement. They replace them, relegating once-central legal rules to the margins and leaving policy decisions traditionally made by governments in the hands of corporate decision-makers. That is the net effect of the current proliferation of voluntary standards and codes of conduct worldwide—propagation of self-regulation and corporate liberation from mandatory legal rules.

The advantages for corporations are obvious. They're freed to create their own rules and decide when and how to follow them rather than being bound by government's mandatory edicts. Less obvious is whether and how self-regulation serves the interests of everyone else.

When President Trump delivered his speech in Davos, he boasted of his administration's achievements in dismantling regulation. "We have undertaken the most extensive regulatory reduction ever conceived," he proclaimed. "I pledged to eliminate two unnecessary regulations for every one new regulation. We have succeeded beyond our highest expectations. Instead of two for one, we have cut twenty-two burdensome regulations for every one new rule." Whether those numbers are real or "made up," as Joseph Stiglitz suggested after the speech (and it should be noted that Trump recently revised the ratio to thirteen to one), "the issue in regulation or deregulation is not the number, that's really absurd," Stiglitz continued. "Do you want to have another financial crisis?" he asked. "Well, if you do, let's get rid of the financial regulations. Americans care about the environment. They don't want to eat poisoned food. The regulations we have are designed to protect things like the environment, banking, and safety."

Things like flying without fearing your plane will crash.

When government departments were asked to respond to Trump's two-for-one executive order, the Federal Aviation Administration (FAA) made a list of three hundred regulations to be cut, whittled that down to ninety, and, as reported in the minutes of a September 2018 meeting, set about "working through the list as needed for the 2-for-1 offsets." These would be enshrined within the FAA Reauthorization Act of 2018, which limits the agency's authority over safety to the point, according to *Forbes* magazine, where it must "put the interests of business ahead of aviation safety." The FAA itself has warned the new law might "not be in the best interest of safety," because of its requirement that regulators delegate responsibility to manufacturers for certifying nearly all steps in the making of new planes. As one labor group described it, the act would make the FAA a "rubber stamp" and allow it to scrutinize safety only after a crash had occurred and "people are killed." But the new law is really just a culmination of industry's decades-long lobbying efforts to remove government safety oversight of its operations and leave companies free to regulate themselves.

Prior to the new law, FAA oversight had already been largely eviscerated owing to persistent industry lobbying since the

1990s. The law was not yet in effect when, for example, two Boeing 737 Max jets crashed in 2018, the first from Indonesia's Lion Air, the second, several months later, from Ethiopian Airlines. At the time of this writing, lawsuits and investigations are still under way, but what's emerged already is that both crashes, which killed all onboard, are linked to deregulation. The cause of each appears to be faults with the 737 Max's Maneuvering Characteristics Augmentation System (MCAS), a novel combination of sensors and software designed to correct pitch in ways that make the plane feel and fly like a regular 737. In the wake of the crashes, an FAA-commissioned investigation by technical experts from its own ranks, as well as NASA and international civil aviation authorities (known as "the Joint Authorities"), concluded there was insufficient oversight by the FAA of MCAS certification and that "FAA involvement in the certification of MCAS would likely have resulted in design changes that would have improved safety."

Problems around MCAS certification were symptomatic of broader regulatory deficiencies rooted in a culture where self-regulation had almost completely replaced true regulatory oversight. Nearly every aspect of the 737 Max's certification was in the hands of Boeing, not the FAA, the Joint Authorities reported, among which were "safety critical areas, including system safety documents related to MCAS." Staffing at the FAA was woefully inadequate, with a paucity of experienced engineers to assess compliance with regulations and conduct on-site inspections and audits. This has to be remedied, the Joint Authorities concluded, by ensuring "there is a sufficient number of experienced specialists to adequately perform certification and oversight duties" and that "responsibility for finding compliance [is] not constrained by a lack of experienced engineers."

Making matters worse, the Joint Authorities found, Boeing employees responsible for these oversight roles were impeded from communicating concerns and adverse findings to the FAA. The employees worried about "fear of reprisal" from the company and were subject to "undue pressure . . . which may be attributed to conflicting priorities and an environment that does not support FAA requirements." The resulting "burdens and barriers" could "prevent 'free' communication" between employees and the FAA, the Joint Authorities observed, which might stand in the way of the FAA receiving the "adequate level of information" it needed to perform its duties properly. The Joint Authorities recommended changes be made to ensure Boeing staff "have open lines of communication to FAA certification engineers without fear of punitive action or process violation." Recent revelations of cover-ups, incompetence, and Boeing employees mocking the FAA add to concerns about the regulatory culture revealed by the Joint Authorities' report.

The 737 Max crashes are stark and tragic reminders of what happens when governments retreat from regulating and leave corporations to regulate themselves. They're part of a long litany of corporate calamities connected to deregulation. Yet corporations keep insisting regulation is unnecessary, and governments keep agreeing.

Trump's deregulation-by-numbers approach is patently absurd, as Stiglitz suggests. It's arbitrary in automatically presuming half (at least) of existing regulations are disposable, and it implicitly ignores the rigorous, "very fact-intensive" (as Stiglitz describes it) process of creating regulations. In the U.S. system (and it's not dissimilar elsewhere), for example, proposed regulations must first pass cost-benefit tests, then be vetted by lawmakers and stakeholders, and finally be defended by regulators. If any of these steps are ignored, aggrieved parties can take regulators to court. If Congress doesn't like a regulation, it can overrule it. Trump's two-for-one rule effectively presumes the regulatory system is defined by thoughtless processes making superfluous rules. "He doesn't understand our regulatory process," says Stiglitz. "It's not a good thing when the president of the United States doesn't understand how our democracy works. That's an embarrassment."

But Trump can't be fully blamed (or take credit) for the two-for-one rule. He borrowed the idea from the United Kingdom, where in 2010 the government created a "one-in, one-out rule," later replacing that with a "one-in, two-out rule" and then a "one-in, three-out rule." Those rules, like the president's two-for-one rule, had immediate impacts. When, for example, an all-party parliamentary committee called for regulations requiring apartment buildings to have fire-resistant cladding and sprinklers, the government said no. The committee's honorary administrative secretary, Ronnie King, a former fire chief, speculated it was because "if you bring in a new regulation, you have got to give three up to get it." King's speculations were subsequently confirmed when, in response to further calls for fire-safety rules, then housing minister Brandon Lewis claimed, "We should intervene only if it is entirely necessary, and only as a last resort."

Three years later, on June 14, 2017, a fire broke out in Grenfell Tower, a twenty-four-story apartment block in London. The blaze spread quickly, engulfing the entire building and killing seventy-one people. The building's exterior had been fitted with cheap flammable cladding, and there were no sprinklers, both factors behind the tragedy and each a result of inadequate regulation. "The whole system of regulation, covering what is written down and the way in which it is enacted in practice, is not fit for purpose, leaving room for those who want to take shortcuts to do so," concluded an official investigatory report. After the blaze, in an open letter to the prime minister from leading health and safety professionals and organizations, the signatories demanded an end to "arbitrary rules . . . such as a requirement to abolish two health and safety regulations (and more recently, three) for any new one adopted." The consequence of that rule, they said, was that "even when it was recommended and accepted that mandatory fitting of sprinklers would make homes or schools safer, this was rejected in favour of nonregulatory action."

Inadequate regulation, often a result of industry's promise to self-regulate, is at the root of many recent disasters. Collapsed mines, pipeline spills, food and water contamination scares, consumer fraud, cancer clusters, fires, crashes, explosions—time and again corporations, in the pursuit of profit, endanger people and the natural environment. The *Deepwater Horizon* rig exploded, for example, after British Petroleum had pushed for deregulation and self-regulation enabling it to cut corners on process safety. The 2008 financial collapse was a direct result of government deregulation under pressure from Wall Street. A horrific train crash in Lac-Mégantic, Quebec, which killed forty-seven people and wiped out an entire town, happened after a government safety council warned of likely disaster because "rail companies are allowed to regulate themselves."

Each story, and there are, unfortunately, many more, reveals the tragic inadequacy of corporate self-regulation. No doubt corporations *can* self-regulate, but *how* they do so—what interests they protect, to what extent, and by what means—always is tailored to serve, or at least not undermine, *their* interests. The result is that while corporations may protect public interests to some extent, they do so only in ways that align with the profit motive. Self-regulation "stands in relation to regulation as self-importance stands in relation to importance, and self-righteousness to righteousness," as the economist Willem Buiter describes it. It is inherently conflicted and profoundly limited in protecting citizens and public interests.

The weight of scholarly opinion confirms Buiter's skepticism. "Voluntary approaches deliver little or no improvement in firms' performance beyond business-as-usual," concludes a broad survey of self-regulation regimes, published in the book *Decision Making in Environmental Law* and echoing findings from similar surveys. Examinations of particular self-regulation regimes reach similar conclusions. One study, for example, finds the Children's Food and Beverage Advertising Initiative, a self-regulation regime designed to combat obesity by curbing marketing of unhealthy foods to children, to be "more a smokescreen than a solution." Another finds that the chemical industry's Responsible Care self-regulation regime serves as a cover for companies to continue "lobbying efforts to weaken legislation," while having no "intention to comply with their commitments." And one more reveals the Trump administration's rollback of climate regulations, lobbied for by industry with promises of self-regulation, could have the effect of increasing U.S. carbon emissions by more than two hundred million tons a year by 2025. Implicit in these smokescreen self-regulation proposals is the replacement of mandatory legal rules with much less effective (and sometimes not effective at all) voluntary standards.

The truth is that self-regulation cannot escape the conflict of interest that intrinsically plagues it. Corporations can no more be trusted to protect public interests than foxes to guard chicken coops. It's not in their nature. Despite that truth, regulation has gone out of fashion, governments are in retreat, and corporations are ever freer to do as they please. They've been liberated from legal controls under the cover of self-regulation.

Why are we letting this happen?

Stacy Mitchell is an activist. As codirector of the New Hampshire–based Institute for Local Self-Reliance, she recently wrote a blog about Amazon's monopolistic power and how it threatens communities and democracy. When readers wrote in, outraged by what she had revealed, they told her they would immediately cancel their Prime accounts and boycott the company. That didn't make her happy. The fact that people's first response was to take action as *consumers,* she told me, reflects a disturbing mindset. "We have so internalized our identities as consumers that we've lost the ability to exercise our citizen muscle," she says. Her readers' responses to the Amazon piece would have been "music to corporations' ears," because "by keeping us in that consumer mindset, they render us powerless."

Companies would much rather face the ire of disgruntled consumers, who "can't have any real effect," than contend with "the real power we have as citizens to change laws and regulations to control how they are allowed to behave." It's not that consumer choices don't matter, says Mitchell. They do. Buying green products, boycotting bad actors, supporting small businesses—all are good things to do, but none have more than a minuscule impact on the problems they aim to solve. They make barely a dent on issues like climate change, human rights abuses, deforestation, ocean pollution, and other major social and environmental ills. Instead, what's needed are wide-ranging legal and policy solutions. Yet as we fall under the sway of corporations' deceitful message that they are "good" actors and we can buy our way to a better world, Mitchell says, we neglect our power as citizens to demand the laws and policies we need.

One example she cites is the local-food movement. Though it has many positive impacts—like a resurgence of farmers markets, local food being carried by major grocery chains, and a proliferation of farm-to-table restaurants—it's had little impact on the overall food system, where Walmart continues to capture a quarter of Americans' grocery spending and food packers and dairy companies ramp up consolidation. To challenge those kinds of developments, Mitchell says, we need to confront, in legal and policy domains, the fact that, for example, 80 percent of farm subsidies are directed to large-scale farms producing commodity crops for the processed-food industry; and that large grocery chains like Walmart are underscrutinized by antitrust regulators as they push out local and smaller-scale grocers. Overall, the local-food movement, by emphasizing that change can come through responsible consumer choices, unwittingly pulls focus from the need for citizens' political action.

Narratives about consumer choice and responsibility also help shield corporations from blame for fueling harmful consumerism. Our sense, for example, that it's all right to buy more and more plastics, electronics, and fabrics, all shipped in cardboard boxes, because the materials will be recycled, is, according to the *New York Times* reporters Tala Schlossberg and Nayeema Raza, "the greatest trick corporations ever played." The evidence is overwhelming that recycling doesn't work—much of what goes into recycling bins ends up in landfills or is burned, causing pollution and greenhouse gas emissions. Even if it did work as it should, however, recycling could never fully offset rising production and use of plastics, cardboards, and fabrics. By advocating for recycling, corporations deceitfully imply they can continue to boost production without worry and that consumers, not they, are responsible for the consequences. "It's a lie," Matt Wilkins writes in *Scientific American,* "that wasteful consumers cause the problem and that changing our individual habits can fix it."

And it's the same for climate change, where corporations deflect blame by insisting we are *all* responsible for the problem. Petro-Canada, for example, has stickers on its gas pumps: "Play your part on helping reduce climate change by using our products responsibly." ExxonMobil says in an ad that "using energy responsibly has never been more important." The American Petroleum Institute provides advice on "steps you can take to make your home more energy efficient." Such advice on how we, as individuals, can reduce carbon fuel use is not itself problematic and indeed can be helpful. The problem, however, is that, like recycling, it's part of a larger narrative that "plays perfectly into the hands of industry," as the climate advocate Anjali Appadurai describes it. "We feel guilt and shame, like we're never doing enough, and because our natural instinct is to shine blame back on ourselves, we get distracted from the real systemic roots of the problem—the fact just one hundred companies have created more than two-thirds of global emissions."

It's no surprise corporations actively promote the idea that consumer and lifestyle choices are key to solving environmental problems. Not only does it foist responsibility onto the individual, but it also implies that with sufficient consumer support, corporations can provide solutions. Broader anti-regulation campaigns are thus lent synergistic support. As the political scientist Peter Dauvergne describes the link, with "governments shifting responsibility to corporations, and those corporations becoming largely self-regulating, they're increasingly asking consumers to be advocates, to be responsible, which in turn supports the idea that they, corporations, not governments, should assume responsibility." The inevitable result, he says, echoing Mitchell, is "to sap the energy of political citizenship, and shift people away from pushing their governments to demand corporations shift and change in fundamental ways."

One particularly effective and deceptive way corporations encourage the idea of consumer power is through certification regimes. By labeling products as having met certain standards in their production—organic, fair trade, sustainable, ocean- or forest-friendly, low-energy, biodegradable, recyclable, and so on—certification purports to provide a basis for consumers to choose products that support social and environmental values (and avoid ones that don't). Typical are fair-trade certifications, used for products like fruits, vegetables, coffee, and chocolate, which certify that standards relating to health, well-being, sustainability, and equity have been met in corporate supply chains and production. With slogans like "Transformation through trade," "Shopping fair trade means taking a stand for a system that treats everyone with respect," and "Improve lives with every purchase," they reinforce the idea that consumers can create a better world through what they do and don't buy.

That message is problematic for inflating the impact of responsible consumption, as already noted. But there's a further issue as well—even on their own terms, certification regimes fall short. And that's because they encounter the same conflicts of interest that plague all self-regulation—standards and procedures are determined and enforced by the corporations they govern, which means they must ultimately align with profitability. As concerns fair trade, for example, big food companies "watered down standards to certify things overnight," according to the fair-trade activist Dana Geffner, thus permitting certification of products in which up to 80 percent of ingredients don't meet fair-trade standards. Certification ends up being little more than "fairwashing," says Geffner, "helping multinational corporations lead marketing efforts with small gestures of goodwill that help hide the bad will, and to try to stop people from seeing them as problematic overall."

Defenders of certification regimes highlight the involvement of NGOs, suggesting that this ensures adequate accountability and oversight. Increasingly, corporations are turning to NGOs to help them run and monitor these and other self-regulation regimes, putatively easing concerns about diminishing government oversight. When a respected NGO like the World Wildlife Fund (WWF), the Nature Conservancy, Save the Children, or the United Nations becomes involved in a self-regulation regime, fears of corporate impunity are allayed as the publicly minded organization presumptively takes government's place as overseer. It's a nice story. But it doesn't work.

NGOs tend to be pliant allies rather than independent watchdogs when they partner with corporations, not least because they often rely on their corporate partners for funds. Whether it's the WWF partnering with the LEGO Group to reduce energy used in manufacturing, the Environmental Defense Fund partnering with FedEx to reduce emissions from delivery trucks, or Save the Children partnering with GlaxoSmithKline to bring down the number of children dying from treatable and preventable diseases, activist NGOs, "by becoming a part of the corporate structure," Dauvergne observes, "start shifting what they've been demanding." No longer do they vigorously push, criticize, and challenge corporations—instead they become "cooperators and supporters, muting their criticism, and becoming passive parts of the system."

Which means NGO oversight can often be worse than nothing. "Being satisfied with relatively small and often inconsequential victories, and celebrating that as sustainability, NGOs end up actually promoting unsustainable growth," says Dauvergne. Because of the limits imposed by their partnership roles with corporations, and the way those roles mute criticism, the impact of NGOs ends up being little more than "tinkering with the system to make it go more smoothly, but not in a different direction." At the same time, he adds, NGO involvement cultivates the belief that we're making progress, thereby forestalling the kind of resistance to corporate rule we really need—namely, "large numbers of people pushing from the margins for a different system."

Before leaving certification regimes, it's important to consider one more kind, where the thing to be certified is not a product but rather the corporation itself. Beginning around 2007, many states and some jurisdictions outside the United States introduced legislation to create a new kind of corporation, the "benefit corporation" (often called the "B corp"). Its key feature is to legally obligate corporate decision-makers to consider the social and environmental impacts of their decisions. To become a B corp, a business must first be assessed and then certified as meeting certain standards. In most regimes, that job is delegated to nongovernmental organizations. B Lab, a nonprofit company created by three American entrepreneurs, does the lion's share of this work in the United States and increasingly in other countries too. It requires applicants for certification to complete online assessments of their business's impacts on workers, customers, community, and the environment and also to include in their governing documents requirements that corporate decision-makers "balance profit and purpose." For its assessment and certification services, B Lab charges applicants an annual fee, which the nonprofit uses—along with donations from numerous foundations and for-profit corporations—to run its operations.

There are lots of upbeat claims, though little hard evidence, that B corp certifications (whether by B Lab or anyone else) improve corporations' performance on social and environmental issues. The paucity of evidence is not surprising. That a company has filled out an online survey and included some general avowals in its corporate articles is no assurance it will behave any differently than it otherwise would have. There's no monitoring of B corps, no enforcement, no inspections, no penalties—in short, nothing that comes close to actual oversight. Like fairtrade certifications, B corp certifications promise considerably more than they can deliver.

It's questionable whether for corporations that are not publicly traded, and thus have no fiduciary duties to shareholders, certification adds anything at all, since they already can "balance profit and purpose" as they wish. For major publicly traded corporations, on the other hand, it's important to note that none have become B corps, despite B Lab's attempts to entice them with less stringent requirements. No doubt they fear even the hint of possibility that shareholder value could be encroached upon. And that keeps them away.

For these reasons, B corp certifications are unlikely to have any significant positive impact on how corporations behave, whether those corporations are publicly traded or not.

They may, however, have negative impacts. B corp advocates see corporations as potentially a "force for good," in B Lab's words, able to help solve "the world's biggest environmental and social challenges . . . like wealth inequality, climate change and social unrest." That, in turn, supports the "new" corporation ideas that corporations should take the lead on social and environmental issues and that they can regulate themselves. In regard to the latter, for example, the benefit corporation advocate Dennis Tobin says their purpose is to "enable for-profit companies to pursue profit and do it in a way that's acceptable," which in his view is preferable to "a paternalistic regulatory approach." In other words, benefit corporations provide an *alternative* to regulation and thereby potential fuel for deregulation. Which is why, says Carol Liao, a University of British Columbia law professor, benefit corporations end up being "a distraction from meaningful regulatory reform . . . that . . . erode true legal reform."

Still, activists and progressives, along with socially minded businesspeople, flock to B corps believing they are the solution we need. Senator Elizabeth Warren proposes a B corp–like regime that requires large corporations (annual revenue of more than $1 billion) to consider the interests of customers, employees, and communities in their decisions. That may address such corporations' reluctance to become B corps, but it doesn't solve the larger issue—that the change is unlikely to make much difference in how they behave.

There's a basic fallacy in the belief that tweaks to publicly traded corporations' mandates will significantly impact their behavior: It ignores the mutual dependence between those companies and the broader capitalist system. Recall that corporations, at least publicly traded ones, exist for the primary purpose of incentivizing investment in industrial enterprise. They do that, in part, by legally guaranteeing investors that *their* interests will always be prioritized. That guarantee is essential. Without it, investors wouldn't invest, and capitalism would collapse. Which means that even when corporations are required by their mandates to consider social and environmental interests, they'll only do so in ways that align with their *fundamental* missions to make money for investors. Regardless of tweaks to their legal structures and institutional natures, they *cannot* abandon that mission.

B corps work alongside and in synergy with voluntary codes of conduct, corporate-NGO partnerships, and consumer choice and responsibility narratives to create what appear to be regimes of effective oversight—and ones that are *non*governmental. The result is to create faith in self-regulation and thereby a sense that government oversight is no longer needed, thus paving the way for deregulation. That faith is fostered as well by another kind of self-regulation regime: offsets.

The pope typically doesn't get involved in debates about regulation and deregulation, but he recently waded into one. Worried that we "have come to see ourselves as [the earth's] lords and masters, entitled to plunder her at will," His Holiness sees "offsets," a mode of self-regulation designed to address environmental ills, as likely to entrench that mindset further. Offsets allow corporations to cause environmental harm in one place if they create an equal environmental benefit somewhere else. A polluter in Canada, for example, can offset its carbon emissions by funding protection of a carbon-absorbing forest in Malaysia. The same amount of carbon emitted by the Canadian polluter is, in theory, absorbed by the trees in Malaysia, bringing net emissions to zero and allowing the polluter to claim it is "carbon neutral" while still spewing greenhouse gases into the atmosphere.

Offsets are now industry's climate strategy of choice and also favored by many governments and NGOs. Critics like Pope Francis see them as voodoo environmentalism. For him, carbon offsets are "a ploy which permits maintaining the excessive consumption of some countries and sectors," while forestalling the "radical change which present circumstances require." Seeming "to provide a quick and easy solution under the guise of a certain commitment to the environment," offsets are more likely, he says, to "lead to a new form of speculation which would not help reduce the emission of polluting gases worldwide." Not only are offsets unlikely to work, says the pope, but by allowing corporations to pay for the right to do wrong, they license bad behavior and thus perpetuate rather than curb it.

Pope Francis's point can be illustrated by applying offset thinking to other kinds of wrongs, like cheating on a spouse. A parody website called CheatNeutral.com highlights the absurdity of carbon offsets by doing just that, setting up a scheme where cheaters can offset their infidelity by paying a fee to fund "monogamy-boosting offset projects" (such as couples therapy). "When you cheat on your partner," the site explains, "you add to the heartbreak, pain and jealousy in the atmosphere. CheatNeutral offsets your cheating by funding someone else to be faithful and *not* cheat. This neutralizes the pain and unhappy emotion and leaves you with a clear conscience." In other words, the wrong of a cheater's infidelity is made right when that cheater supports someone else's fidelity, flying in the face of our (not to mention Pope Francis's) conviction that cheating is wrong and that it should be *stopped,* not offset.

That's what regulations do. They *stop* (or at least limit) bad behavior. That's their purpose and effect. They protect citizens and ensure their freedom by mitigating threats to health, safety, security, and the environment. Like other kinds of self-regulation, offsets restrict governments to ancillary roles, perhaps as facilitators but never as sovereign overseers. They presume self-regulating corporations will voluntarily do the right thing if properly incentivized and that that can take the place of legal limits.

The source of offsets' appeal for companies is that they allow business as usual to continue, relatively unfettered. A recent promotional video from UN Climate Change plays on that appeal, portraying a man trying to reduce his carbon footprint by giving up his car, not flying on airplanes or eating steak, and even attempting to stop breathing. "That's slightly impractical," the narrator states wryly. "So, here's the real solution." The viewer is then directed to a website to purchase carbon offsets. Though the video was taken down after allegations that it mocked people's attempts to become more responsible around climate, it demonstrates the mindset underlying offsets—don't change your behavior, just pay to offset your harm.

With scientists now declaring that radical measures are necessary to avoid potentially cataclysmic consequences from climate change, this licensing of business as usual could be disastrous. The most we can expect from offsets, if they work properly, is to neutralize carbon emissions, while not reducing them overall. But even worse, they don't work properly—not even close to it. One study, for example, found only 2 percent of offset projects certified by the UN's Clean Development Mechanism (CDM) had a "high likelihood" of reducing carbon emissions, while 85 percent had a "low likelihood." In other words, the CDM is issuing permits to emit carbon on the assumption that emissions are offset, but the projects supposedly offsetting those emissions are not in fact doing so. Which means the CDM is actually *boosting* emissions rather than curtailing them—indeed, by an estimated 750 million extra tons a year.

Moreover, while their benefits remain uncertain, the harm caused by offset projects is real. When, for example, a Dutch energy company offset emissions from a new coal-fired power plant by financing forest preservation in Uganda, six thousand forest dwellers were evicted by the Ugandan government, some victimized by rape, arson, and shootings. In Panama, the Barro Blanco hydropower dam was registered by the CDM to issue offset credits despite opposition from the Ngäbe people, who were never consulted, never consented, and had their communities and religious and cultural sites flooded as a result of the dam (the project has now been de-registered). In Honduras, a "climate friendly" palm oil plantation was registered by the CDM, despite the fact that twenty-three Honduran peasant farmers with legitimate claims to the land had been assassinated in the lead-up to registration. In Durban, South Africa, a "green" waste dump in a poor black area was registered by the CDM as a methane-capture site, even though the site was a cancer cluster as well as a source of heavy metals leaching into surrounding water and soil. These are among many cases where local and typically disenfranchised communities pay steep prices for projects that allegedly offset environmental harm in other places.

Harm also occurs to local communities at industrial sites that rely upon offsets. When companies are permitted to carry on with polluting activity because they've paid for offset credits, emissions may be neutralized on paper, and perhaps in the atmosphere (though, as noted, that's a real question), but they are no less real for the local communities and ecosystems where they happen. The Dutch coal-fired power plant, for example, offset its emissions by funding forests in Uganda, giving it license to emit pollutants that, though having been offset, had ill effects on people's health and the natural environment in communities near the plant. And this doesn't even take account of the fact that the company sourced its coal from West Virginia, where mining operations were wreaking environmental havoc by blasting away mountaintops.

Offset regimes are increasingly being used in areas other than carbon reduction. One of these is water conservation, where the results are just as uncertain and the harms just as real.

In 2007, Coca-Cola faced a public relations crisis. College students across the United States had launched a boycott to support farmers in India who alleged their water and livelihoods were being stolen by the company's operations. Then CEO E. Neville Isdell acknowledged the farmers' concerns and announced a new program to address them. Henceforth, Coca-Cola would "replace every drop of water we use in our beverages and their production to achieve balance in communities and in nature with the water we use," and, he said, it would become "water neutral" by 2020. In 2015, the company proclaimed it had achieved water neutrality a full five years ahead of schedule, taking out a full-page ad in *The New York Times* to boast that "for every drop we use, we give one back" (a claim it continues to make in its marketing campaigns).

The claim is based on an offset regime. Coca-Cola doesn't literally give back each drop of water it uses but rather purports to replenish it through programs that, among other things, provide safe water and improved sanitation to communities, protect watersheds and aquifers, and make water available for productive use. Such replenishment programs are initiated, the company says, "where there is demonstrated need and we have the resources and partnership opportunities to make a lasting impact." Importantly, the replenishment is "not always to the aquifer from which the water was originally sourced" (though best estimates are that it is about half the time).

Coca-Cola's offset program is plagued by problems analogous to those of its carbon offset counterparts. Chief among these is harm caused to the areas where it extracts water. As the philosopher Michael Sandel explains, "If a company extracts enormous amounts of water from certain communities, but replenishes the aquifer someplace else, does that really set the slate clean? What about the communities whose aquifers have been drained and depleted?" There is indeed something near Orwellian in the claim of "water neutrality" when, inevitably, extraction depletes the water that locals depend upon for survival.

And the point isn't lost on those people. India's water-stressed communities are well aware that offsets don't help them when Coca-Cola depletes their local resources. Which is why they continue to oppose the company's operations. In 2014, for example, a heavily protested plant in Mehdiganj was ordered closed by local officials (who also blocked a planned expansion) because it extracted excessive amounts of groundwater and dumped unlawful amounts of pollutants. Then, in 2015, after much protest from local residents fearful of water shortages and industrial pollution, authorities canceled a planned land allocation for a Coca-Cola bottling plant in Tamil Nadu.

In addition to harming local communities, Coca-Cola's water neutrality program is ineffective and misleading. As with carbon offset regimes, it falls significantly short of what it promises. To begin with, only 1 percent of the water Coca-Cola uses to produce a bottle of Coke is slated for replenishment. That's because water used in agricultural production of ingredients (28 liters of water to grow beets for the sugar used in half a liter of Coke) and in manufacturing processes (7 liters) is not replenished. Only the 0.4 liter of water that actually makes it into the bottle of Coke is replenished. Therefore, despite the company posturing that every drop it uses to make its beverages is replenished, 99 percent of the water used to make it is not. And that's when the system works perfectly.

Moreover, many projects counted toward replenishment don't actually replenish. When, for example, the company increases the amount of safe drinking water available in one area to offset water use in another, that may be laudable, but it is not *replenishment,* as the net effect is to *increase* water use. Other times, replenishment projects just don't work, like a trench-digging program in Mexico, credited with replenishing thirteen billion liters of water by stopping erosion, that ended when scientists revealed it was actually increasing erosion. (No surprise, the company left the thirteen billion liters on the books as having been replenished.) Problems like these result, in part, from the absence of independent oversight. Though Coca-Cola partners with NGOs to help it run and monitor its water neutrality program—the World Wildlife Fund and the Nature Conservancy chief among them—these organizations receive millions of dollars from the company, which means they cannot provide truly independent oversight.

What makes it all the more galling is that Coca-Cola has known from the start that "water neutrality" is a deceptive idea. "In a strict sense, the term 'water neutral' is troublesome and even may be misleading," it acknowledged in an early concept paper. "Individuals, communities and businesses will always have a residual water footprint. In that sense, they can never become water neutral." So why would the company use the concept? Marketing. "Alternative names to 'water neutral' that have been suggested include water offset, water stewardship, and water use reduction and reuse," the concept paper stated. "However, none of these other terms seem to have the same gravity or resonance (inspiration) with the media, officials or NGOs as the term neutrality. For pragmatic reasons it may therefore be attractive to use the term 'water neutral,' but there is a definite need to be clear about precisely what it entails if reduction of water use to zero is not possible." The company has clearly ignored its own warning.

Coca-Cola's water neutrality program has the same fundamental flaw Pope Francis identifies for carbon offsets—by licensing business as usual, it perpetuates rather than challenges a mastery and plundering vision of our relationship to planet Earth. Its claim to neutralize depletion with offsets helps the company justify extracting more and more water, especially as it expands operations throughout the Global South. And with growing numbers of communities becoming water stressed, the overall effect is to legitimate a dangerously unsustainable business model. "It's such a nineteenth-century economic model," says the historian Bartow Elmore. "Perpetual growth—the endless pursuit of selling more products next year than you did last year: a fifth grader could tell you that's not sustainable. Coke is symptomatic of the economy that is ecologically unsound."

In the end, offsets are yet another way industry staves off government regulation with promises of effective self-regulation. And like all the others examined—certification, voluntary codes of conduct, corporate-NGO partnerships, and consumer responsibility—offsets are profoundly misleading and fail to do what they promise.

This chapter began with a simple idea. While law bolsters and enables the power of the powerful, it also, in its "ideal notion," extends protection to those who are vulnerable to that power. Regulatory laws manifest that ideal. Designed to protect people and the environment by curbing corporations' predilection to cause harm, they offer a hedge against corporations' rapacious pursuit of profit, itself programmed by law. Precisely because of that, corporations fight regulation and have from the very start. They began to win in the 1980s and then, in the early 2000s, bolstered their cause with a new and powerful rationale. Now socially responsible and publicly minded, they said, they no longer needed to be regulated but could regulate themselves. That argument has been highly effective in supporting corporations' campaigns to liberate themselves from government oversight.

The fight for corporate liberation has yielded results on other fronts as well. In 2010, the United States Supreme Court decided in *Citizens United v. Federal Election Commission* that corporations should be free to finance election campaigns of political candidates, because as "persons," they enjoy free speech rights. As a result, corporations are able to deploy their vast wealth (which is, literally, the consolidation of thousands, even millions, of shareholders' dollars) to help elect anti-regulation politicians and thus bolster their power to push for deregulation. In this way, judicial deregulation of political spending promotes government deregulation in all other spheres.

However, *Citizens United* only accelerates a broader diminishment of law's role in policing corporations, now being fueled by the putatively progressive story of the "new" corporation. There's little room in that narrative for a vision of government as robust sovereign and democratic controller of corporations. Instead, governments are understood to be, at best, on an equal plane with corporations, to be partners and collaborators that may help facilitate self-regulation but not take regulatory control. Klaus Schwab describes this understanding, which he passionately advocates, as one of "strong collaboration between government and business, a permanent platform for public-private cooperation to create the necessary self-regulation principles, rules, and protocols."

While Schwab also insists that "democracy is probably the most precious good that we have," his advocacy of self-regulation and partnership helps promote a larger narrative that favors private ordering over public oversight and thereby limits democracy. Public oversight is, after all, *about* democracy—about democratically accountable authorities curbing self-interested private actors from causing harm to public interests. Regulation is what allows us, as citizens, to have a say in the balance struck between corporate profit seeking and social and environmental concerns. Take it away and citizens lose whatever political purchase they might have on corporate behavior. Which is why, as Robert Weissman observes, "the model of self-regulation and collaboration is antidemocratic, not just sort of different from democracy but against democracy." By liberating corporations from regulation, we liberate them from *us*. That's a profound—and profoundly undemocratic—shift.

4 CALIFORNIA (BAD) DREAMING

BACK AT DAVOS, while I'm standing with Bibop Gresta on a mountaintop overlooking the town, admiring the fifty-million-year-old Swiss Alps stretching out before us, Gresta describes for me his vision of "a new generation of companies that can solve all the problems of humanity" (his Hyperloop, he says, being among the first). Intrigued, I ask him where, with corporations poised to solve all the world's problems, democratic governments fit in. His answer: Nowhere. Democracy is just a "meme," he says. It's time to leave it behind and "start from scratch, take out all the government concepts—government will be gone very soon." Businesses, relying upon "the best minds and best practice" and aiming to solve world problems, will take care of society, and if other forms of governance are still necessary, "technologies will substitute for government completely" and avoid "all the crazy, dyslexic anomalies attached to being human."

Like Gresta, many in Silicon Valley believe the era of democratic government is—or at least should be—over. Their creed is captured by words from John Perry Barlow's famous 1996 manifesto, "A Declaration of the Independence of Cyberspace": "Governments of the Industrial World, . . . on behalf of the future, I ask you of the past to leave us alone. You are not welcome among us. You have no sovereignty where we gather." In a similar spirit, the Silicon Valley blogger Mencius Moldbug (real name Curtis Yarvin, a computer scientist) says democracy should be replaced with rule by engineers and all government authority transferred to the tech industry. The Stanford University professor and venture capitalist Balaji Srinivasan proposes creating an "opt-in society, ultimately outside the U.S., run by technology," while Patri Friedman (Milton Friedman's grandson) has actually designed such a society, Seasteading, to be built on a floating platform in the ocean. Democratic government is an "obsolete political system," says Friedman, a belief seconded by Seasteading backer Peter Thiel, who believes governments should be replaced by "benevolent" monopolies like Google, Facebook, and Amazon.

Such extreme libertarianism is not shared by all denizens of Silicon Valley, however. A recent survey of Valley elite found that most disagree with the statement "I would like to live in a society where government does nothing except provide national defense and police protection, so that people could be left alone to earn whatever they could" and that most tend to be pro-abortion, pro–gun control, pro–LGBTQ rights, and against the death penalty. In other words, they are liberals, not libertarians. Still, there is one thing agreed upon by the Valley's liberals and libertarians alike: government regulation is bad. That united front is no surprise. Though companies in all industries demand freedom to pursue profit without constraint, for big-tech companies such freedom is essential to their business models.

———

On May 15, 1911, the Supreme Court ordered that the Standard Oil Company be broken up. From the time John D. Rockefeller founded it in 1870, the company had bought up competitors, taken control of everything (refining, marketing, and distribution), and institutionalized preferential treatment from the railroads and pipelines it owned. By the early twentieth century, it controlled 90 percent of oil production in the United States and was, the Supreme Court ruled in *Standard Oil Co. of New Jersey v. United States,* in clear violation of the 1890 Sherman Antitrust Act's ban on monopolies. According to the court, Standard Oil had "combin[ed] in one corporation the stocks of many other corporations aggregating a vast capital," which indicated "an intent and purpose to dominate the industry connected with, and gain perpetual control of . . . its products in the channels of interstate commerce." The remedy: "dissolution of the offending combination." The case was decided at a time of strong and widespread resolve to break up monopolies, based on a belief that the megacorporations spawned by industrialization could destroy competition and undermine democracy.

After a seven-decade-long run, that resolve began to crumble in the early 1980s when Ronald Reagan swept to power promising deregulation. Antitrust laws, which aim to avoid monopolies and promote competition among corporations, were targeted, and though existing laws remained on the books, including the Sherman Antitrust Act, they were substantially weakened by interpretations (inspired by scholars from the Chicago School of economics like Robert Bork) that presumed corporate bigness maximized efficiency and was therefore a good thing. On that basis, courts and regulators allowed corporations to grow and to expand into new areas, with few limits, a trend that continues today and paves the way for massive consolidation and concentration in all industries.

Nowhere, however, has that consolidation and concentration happened as fast and deep as in the tech industry. There, synergies between lax regulation and business models based on monopoly drive meteoric growth. Depending, as they do, on becoming platforms that *everyone* uses, and that *everyone* must therefore join (so-called network effects), companies like Facebook, Google, and Amazon succeed by creating monopolies, whether over search engines (Google), retail (Amazon), or social networking (Facebook). They monetize users (through fees, commissions, advertising, and data mining), connect with them at lightning speed over the Internet, and have relatively low capital costs. All of which incentivizes, and indeed requires, quick expansion within their sectors—and beyond. Amazon, for example, has now expanded into pharmaceuticals, finance, groceries, cloud computing, shipping and logistics, movies, television, and voice-activated hubs; and Google, Apple, and Facebook have made similar moves into news, entertainment, education, smart device hubs, and health.

The result is a handful of companies whose size and scope threaten not only competitive markets but democracy itself. Silicon Valley has become "the new Rome of our time," as Anand Giridharadas, the author of *Winners Take All: The Elite Charade of Changing the World,* describes it, with big-tech companies imperiously pursuing control of everything. If we don't do something about it, says Giridharadas, "we're going to live in a world in which they are governing us privately through the profit motive. But *governing* us." Already, big-tech companies leverage their considerable power to control government agendas. Barely present in Washington, D.C., a decade ago, they now are among the capital's top lobbyists, with total spending from Amazon, Apple, Facebook, and Google doubling between 2016 and 2018 (from $27.4 million to $55 million).

However, political influence is only one tactic tech companies deploy against regulation. Another, stealthier and increasingly powerful, is to use technology itself to avoid regulation. By creating *direct* relationships with consumers and workers, corporations are able to operate beyond regulators' reach and thereby subvert governments' democratic authority to control them.

The Internet of Things (IOT) lies at the frontier of this new technological deregulation. Creating Internet connectivity and sensors across life's infrastructure—appliances, smartphones, wearables, vehicles, utility systems, clothing, door locks, and so on—it vastly expands data-mining domains, while also creating direct channels for corporations to control people's behavior. Eventually able to "capture and utilize every bit of data which you share or use in everyday life," as the Analytics Vidhya website exclaims, the IOT—and this is its supposed allure—will ultimately "make machines smart enough to reduce human labor to almost nil." The problem, however, is that it may equally reduce the effectiveness of democratic regulation to almost nil. Its direct monitoring and control of consumers effectively "strip[s] away governance and the rule of law," says Shoshana Zuboff, Charles Edward Wilson Professor of Business Administration at the Harvard Business School (retired), and thereby "annihilate[s] the freedom achieved by the rule of law."

That is because the IOT effectively allows companies to bypass legal constraints by *directly* controlling behavior. A bank, for example, can use the IOT to shut off and lock an Internet-connected vehicle, locate it, and repossess it if its owner fails to make a payment. An insurance company can cancel a policy if vehicle sensors indicate the owner has been driving unsafely. In these ways, the IOT helps banks and insurance companies in their businesses. For consumers, however, the effect is to subvert legal protections. Typically, a bank wanting to seize a car, or an insurance company wishing to cancel a policy, has to go through legal processes—prove facts; prove that contract terms comply with consumer protection law; prove that a consumer is in breach of a contract; prove that the remedy sought (like repossessing a car or canceling an insurance contract) is appropriate. With the IOT, in contrast, they can do what they want directly, by way of, as Zuboff describes it, "a privately administered compliance regime of rewards and punishments . . . aimed at modifying and commoditizing behavior for profit."

Health providers might lock people out of their fridges if they eat too much ice cream. Banks might lock them out of their homes if they miss a mortgage payment. An employer might discipline an employee who has left her house when she's supposedly home sick. When corporations know everything *that* we do, and hold the on-off switches to every piece of our lives' infrastructures, they're able to control *what* we do, in ways that best serve *their* interests. Where it all leads, says Zuboff, is to a "new kind of sovereign power" where "human autonomy is irrelevant and the lived experience of psychological self-determination a cruel illusion"; where "human persons are reduced to a mere animal condition, bent to serve the new laws of capital imposed on all behavior through an implacable feed of ubiquitous fact-based real-time records."

As more and more of our thoughts, feelings, and behaviors are translated into data and mined by corporate-controlled machines, we lose not just our privacy but potentially our autonomy. And that is a scary prospect. It's still early days and hard to predict exactly how the vast and increasing amounts of data being collected about us will be used. But one thing is certain—for the corporations doing the collecting, creating profit will always be the overarching goal. That will drive the kinds of data-collecting technologies they develop and the ways in which they use the data they mine. And perhaps just as certain, profitability will lie in finding ever-new ways to control and modify behavior, at the expense of our freedom as citizens and consumers—and as workers too.

Laws designed to protect workers' well-being and humanity have been in place for more than a century in the United States, first prompted by the notorious 1911 Triangle Shirtwaist Factory fire, where 146 workers, mainly immigrant teenage girls, died. Exit doors had been locked to prevent employees from stealing and taking breaks, and fire escapes were inaccessible. Widespread outrage in the wake of the tragedy fueled labor activism and compelled lawmakers to ban dangerous sweatshop conditions and protect workers' safety. It was the beginning of a twentieth-century trend—notably consolidated by Franklin D. Roosevelt's Fair Labor Standards Act and National Labor Relations Act—to redefine the employment relationship in ways that protected workers. The basic infrastructure—minimum wages; maximum hours and days per week; child labor bans; health and safety protections; the right to form unions, strike, and bargain collectively—remains in place today, though it has been substantially weakened.

Corporations opposed worker protection laws from the start, routinely breaking them and lobbying to roll them back. Over the last century, they successfully tamped down these laws, not least by securing anti-union "right to work" legislation in many states. Today, they harass and threaten pro-union employees, sometimes fire them, and spend billions each year to avoid unions.

Google, for example, recently hired IRI Consultants, a firm that offers "union vulnerability assessments" and coaches corporations on tactics to avoid unions. Worker unrest had been growing at the company, first becoming apparent when, in the fall of 2018, employees organized a worldwide walkout to protest the way sexual harassment complaints against company executives were being handled. Since then, employees have complained about meetings being monitored, complaints stifled, and workers fired for taking a stand. Though no major union drive has happened, conditions are ripe for one. And Google is taking no chances. In hiring IRI Consultants, it followed a course advised by a recent Amazon training video—"recognize the early warning signs of potential organizing and escalate concerns promptly." Amazon recently followed its own advice, summarily firing employees who led protests and walkouts in response to the company's disregard for workers' health and safety during the coronavirus pandemic.

Anti-union tactics are pervasive across all industries, not just tech, which helps explain why union density rates in the private sector reached an all-time low of 6.3 percent in 2018, a decline from 16.8 percent in 1983 and 31 percent in 1967. "Every time a worker stands up to try to organize a union in any part of the country, he or she is met with threats, abuse, videos that threaten them, threaten their job," as the political commentator Jonathan Tasini described it to me. "There's lots of reasons why unions have declined, but the fundamental reason, the number one reason, is there's a multibillion-dollar industry whose one goal is to destroy unions in America."

But now, in addition to all of that, corporations are finding powerful new ways to control workers directly through data, a kind of technology-enabled deregulation of the workplace. The basic idea is to deploy devices to monitor employees' actions in real time and create feedback loops that control their behavior. It's eerily similar to a device called a Cowlar, a smart collar designed to fit around the neck of a cow and used by dairy farmers to monitor cows' milk output, temperature, activity, and location so as to maximize production.

Amazon warehouse workers don't wear smart collars, but the scanners they carry serve similar ends, tracking every movement and action, starting a countdown timer that moves them from task to task, rating productivity and sending admonishments for moving too slowly. The results are Kafkaesque as employees run to keep up with productivity targets, are disciplined for not meeting those targets, and are then disciplined again for *running,* which is against the rules. During twelve-hour shifts, workers might cover fifteen to twenty miles on their feet, routinely popping painkillers to persevere (dispensed in single-dose packages from workplace vending machines), as their scanners feed managers real-time performance metrics. They have no "expectation of being treated like human beings," says Emily Guendelsberger, a journalist who embedded as an Amazon employee and wrote a book about her experience—a point underlined by recent allegations that Amazon workers are at greater risk of contracting COVID-19 due to the frantic work pace, lack of restrooms (making proper handwashing impossible), and poor sanitation at warehouses. "Amazon has always treated its workers as though they weren't really human," observes Stacy Mitchell. "And now in the context of this pandemic, it is squeezing people even further, as the pace of work increases and even minimal kinds of safety measures are absent."

Yet Amazon and other companies continue work on developing technologies "to increase the workload and pace of work, with new methods of monitoring workers," as a report coauthored by the economist Beth Gutelius describes it. The report cites, as just one example, a video game that pits workers against each other to assemble customer orders faster. *Mission Racer,* projected on screens installed next to workstations, converts actual physical labor into video game racing cars, with the cars moving faster around a track as workers more quickly pick warehouse items and deposit them into boxes. Problems are further exacerbated, says Gutelius, by the increasing automation of Amazon (and other) workplaces through artificial intelligence and robotic software—Amazon uses more than two hundred thousand robotic vehicles, called "drivers," in its U.S. delivery fulfillment centers, a figure that is double the number from 2018 and more than ten times the number from 2014—which, according to Gutelius, adds more work, increases pressure on workers to speed up their tasks, and contributes to worker burnout.

The trend is clear. Technologies that monitor and control workers' behavior will soon be a part of all workplaces. One recent invention is an employee ID badge that hangs around an employee's neck on a lanyard and transmits data from embedded microphones, motion detectors, and other sensors. There's a biomeasuring wristwatch designed to monitor traders' emotions and indicate "in real time who is freaking out," according to the MIT professor who developed it. Banks are considering emotional monitoring of employees, and a Chinese company collects data about emotional states, stress, and fatigue from brainwave-scanning sensors in employees' headgear. The possibilities for employee surveillance and reward and punishment feedback loops are limitless and fast unfolding. "We are only scratching the surface right now," says Ben Waber, CEO of Humanyze, the company that produces the smart ID badges.

Silicon Valley celebrates innovation and disruption as key to creating a better world. But the main targets for disruption by workplace innovations are employees' rights to be protected from harmful and dehumanizing treatment. Those rights, a product of a century-long struggle by workers and their unions, are now being bypassed by technologies that enable employers to monitor and control employees' every move. It's like a high-tech mash-up of Orwell, Dickens, and *The Grapes of Wrath,* a world where twenty-first-century technology re-creates nineteenth-century workplace conditions.

Pushing in the same direction is another disrupting trend—the tech-driven eradication of the workplace.

On September 26, 2018, Fausto Luna, an Uber driver, died when he jumped in front of an A train at the 175th Street station in Washington Heights. He's one of eight New York City professional drivers who died by suicide in 2018, and while each driver's story is different, the common thread is overwhelming financial hardship. With the rise of Uber, professional driving changed from being a difficult way to make a living to a nearly impossible one, as the ride-hailing app skirted regulations designed to limit available cars and thus protect drivers' earnings. Prior to Uber, taxi drivers in big cities made $12 to $17 per hour. Now they average $9 to $11 per hour. For Uber drivers like Luna—many of whom are professional drivers doing extra time to supplement depressed incomes—there are stories of sleeping in cars to help make ends meet, using food stamps, and being stuck with crippling debt for vehicles they bought believing Uber's wildly inflated claims about likely income. In the meantime, since 2015 Uber has unilaterally raised its share of driver revenue from 20 percent to 25 percent, translating into an extra $3 billion for the company.

The overarching effect of Uber has been to transform a job protected by regulations and employment law—professional driving—into one that is precarious and unprotected. Through its app and algorithms, the company connects drivers to customers, claiming to be nothing more than a matchmaker, not an employer. Its "driver partners" are independent contractors, it claims, in business-to-business relationships with the company and therefore beyond the scope of employment protection. Though some municipal governments are starting to catch up with Uber—New York City, for example, imposed a minimum hourly wage for drivers—it's questionable whether this will become a trend. Moreover, with Uber heavily subsidized by investors who are now demanding profitability, the company will likely resist wage increases even more vociferously than it has—or swap them for rate hikes that diminish service for poorer customers and in poorer districts.

Having disrupted, and effectively decimated, urban taxi systems—which were regulated precisely to ensure a balance among the needs of owners, drivers, customers, and city transportation—the public is left with an unregulated alternative, largely free to do what it wants to become profitable.

Uber is not the only company developing apps that evade the employment relationship. Similar platforms are emerging across sectors (a few examples: Upwork, TaskRabbit, UpCounsel, Postmates, and CrowdMed) and within corporations too. Amazon Flex is an example of the latter. It promises "Great Earnings. Flexible Hours. Be Your Own Boss" for its nonemployee delivery drivers, who use an app to claim delivery shifts, drive their own vehicles to an Amazon warehouse, pick up packages, and then deliver them. The system is rife with abuse, overwork, and underpayment, all untouched by law because the workers are not technically employees.

We're quickly moving toward a future where work is no longer organized as employment but instead is broken down into segmented steps that workers are hired to do on a piece-meal basis, brokered by fee-collecting Internet platforms. "The digital economy will sharply erode the traditional employer-employee relationship," states a recent International Monetary Fund report, as we move toward "crowd-based capitalism in which most of the work-force shifts from a full-time job as a talent or labor provider to running a business of one, in effect a microentrepreneur." The proliferation of digital labor platforms across increasing numbers of sectors, both low skilled and professional, means that "nonemployment work arrangements will expand . . . possibly taking full-time jobs out of companies and converting them into sets of projects and tasks." As jobs are broken down into discrete gigs, effectively undoing employment relationships and the efficacy of unions, the report concludes, it will become much easier for companies to dispense with human workers altogether and automate their operations—which, of course, is precisely what Uber plans to do.

Technologies that control employees (like Amazon's scanners) or that negate employment altogether (like Uber's app) are powerful new weapons in corporations' persistent fight to roll back the legal protection of workers. They highlight the fact that despite dramatic technological change, some things remain the same—like how businesses try to squeeze as much labor for as little cost as they can from the people who do work for them. The intrinsically exploitative potential of that dynamic, tragically illustrated by the Triangle Shirtwaist Factory fire, is what prompted governments to promulgate protective laws a century ago. The need for protective laws is as pressing now as it was then. And that's especially true as corporations deploy technologies to undermine legal protections originally put in place to defend personal liberty and human dignity in the face of wanton profit seeking.

In my interview with Klaus Schwab, he told me that he thinks the digital revolution could turn out to be a "renaissance for humankind." There are, however, he said, some "very black clouds on the horizon." The examples discussed above hint at what some of those might be. Adding to that list are a host of other ills, such as the strategic cultivation of addiction by gaming and social media corporations; their targeting of ever-younger children with devices and platforms; and the corruption of public discourse and elections through disinformation, hate, and incendiary speech (fueled by social media business models based on profitably amassing users and attention without regard to content). But perhaps the most worrying dark cloud of all is the prospect of corporations leveraging for profit our increasingly pervasive belief that technology can "solve all the problems of humanity," as Bibop Gresta proclaimed on the Davos mountaintop, and thereby avoid, especially in how we govern ourselves, "all the crazy, dyslexic anomalies attached to being human."

Humanity's imperfections—political fighting, wars, poverty, intractable divides, the trials of love and friendship, bodies that deteriorate and die, endless social dysfunction—have, throughout history, driven us to seek transcendent worlds where perfection rules. That was religion's allure, and now we put our faith in machines to do the same. Unfettered by emotions, fallible bodies, limited minds, innate biases, and self-interest, they promise to achieve better outcomes, in all endeavors, than our imperfect human selves. Hence the frenzied development of machines to take over the work of judges, journalists, politicians, drivers, pilots, doctors, artists, poets, teachers, sexual partners, friends, and just about everyone else.

No doubt in some areas, especially those demanding mainly technical skills, machines can do better than humans. What's worrying, however, is the way they're being touted as superior in *all* domains, including where judgment, emotion, intuition, compassion, trust, and human connection are crucial. The "crazy, dyslexic anomalies attached to being human," as Gresta describes it, are part of who we are and what we, as human beings, need to work out and with. By surrendering all we do as humans to machines out of some sense that they are better, more perfect, beings than we are, we effectively give up on ourselves. We signal that "humans cannot be trusted," as Professor Sun-ha Hong, an expert in artificial intelligence, describes it; that "we need to get rid of human emotion, we need to get rid of human experience and discretion because they will get things wrong; that we need to rely instead on the more consistent, objective, and rational results of anonymous data and numbers."

As a result, we "delegitimize humanity itself," says Hong. We no longer value our human capacities, flawed as they are, to reason, feel, exercise judgment, and have wisdom. We stop aspiring to develop those capacities, since it appears they're no longer needed. Indeed, he says, "we reject human reason itself, believing we need to rely more on algorithmic rules, this technology of strangers." Among other things, that is disastrous for democracy, says Hong, because democracy depends on the capacity of citizens to trust one another and to believe we can persuade one another with well-reasoned arguments. The more we delegate governance and other intrinsically human endeavors to machines, the more we lose our capacity to determine our collective fate through reasoned and democratic deliberation. Thus, we abandon "the genuine heritage of the enlightenment."

Silicon Valley and its behemoth tech companies cry foul when faced with regulation, claiming it curtails innovation. And they're partly right—it does curtail innovation. Innovation is, after all, a mixed bag. Internal combustion engines, extractive machines, mass production and retailing, big-brand cigarettes and alcohol, television, pharmaceutical drugs, airplanes, nuclear weapons, fast food, large-scale agriculture—these were all innovations of the industrial age. They contributed, in different ways, to social good and prosperity. But they also caused untold harm—destruction of the natural environment, climate change, labor abuse, monopolies, illness, and death. Since the early twentieth century, regulation has been the mechanism for democratic societies to find the right balance between the good and the harm corporate-driven innovation causes.

What was true of the industrial age is no less true of these postindustrial times. Tech companies are different in many ways from their nineteenth- and twentieth-century counterparts. But producing innovations without downside dangers and risks is not one of them. As long as corporations remain institutionally compelled to prioritize financial self-interest above all else, regulation is necessary.

Contrary to the story told by tech entrepreneurs—that everything has changed, that tech will solve the world's problems, and that we don't need governments anymore—the twenty-first-century tech corporations share with their twentieth-century industrial counterparts the same economic logic. They leverage new technologies to consolidate power, destroy competition, and exploit workers and consumers. They cause harm to people and planet, and use their inordinate influence to push for laws and policies that favor them at the expense of others. There may be new challenges to regulating business effectively in the digital age, but what remains unchanged is the need to protect citizens and society from the worst of corporations' psychopathic tendencies.

5 BEING CORPORATE

WHEN MIKE MERRILL BECAME the world's first (and only, as far as
I know) publicly traded person, it was because, he told me, "I
love the culture of business, I love a boardroom, I love a conference call, I love a whiteboard." Having sold shares in himself,
he now vows to live his life according to how his more than
five hundred shareholders vote on questions he posts online. For
instance: Should he grow a beard? (A majority of shareholders
said "No.") Should he become a Republican? ("Yes.") Should he
join Spotify? ("Yes.") Should he get a vasectomy? ("No.") Should
he become a Dodgers fan? ("No.") Should he propose to his girlfriend? ("Yes.") The shareholders cast their votes in ways they
believe will boost Merrill's financial value and hence the value of
their shares. They "act in their own best interest," says Merrill,
who believes that that "is also in my best interest" and happily
surrenders to them his freedom to choose how to live his life.

Merrill feels, he says, that he's created a "community through
capitalism," though members of his actual community, close

friends and family, are less enamored. "Some feel like, 'Oh, I should have more say in your life because of our personal relationship.'" His response? "I tell them, 'You should buy shares because this is a really important thing about my life.'" His father owns shares; his mother does not. His girlfriend (at the time I first spoke with him), Marjarike, owns many shares. She first became a shareholder, she told me, "to see what was going on in there—who else is this guy going out on dates with?" Merrill had been dating numerous women, trying to find the right person—or at least the person his shareholders would approve. He wrote up reports after each date and submitted them for votes. Marjarike, a hedge fund analyst, figured out how to crash his market and then swooped in to buy a large bloc of shares. With that, she says, "I voted for myself, voted against other people," and secured shareholder approval to become Mike's girlfriend. "Plummeting his stock price was a very romantic gesture," she says.

When the relationship got serious, Merrill put the big question to his shareholders (the "proposal proposal," as he describes it): Should he marry Marjarike? The shareholders said "Yes." He proposed. Marjarike said "Yes." But the two never wed. Marjarike began to feel uncomfortable as their relationship progressed, with shareholders deciding even the most intimate aspects of the couple's lives. Merrill says he "wanted to keep pushing forward and exploring and experimenting," but Marjarike had doubts. When during our interview, for example, she asked Merrill whether he would put the name of their first child to a shareholder vote, his answer, "That would be amazing," was clearly not the right one. Marjarike stared at him, incredulous, visibly disturbed. Not long after that, they split up. Marjarike sold her shares in Merrill, who, when asked later how he felt about the breakup, said that what he found most moving through the ordeal was "how quickly the shareholders bought out her stake, because she was not offering the best price."

I was amused by Merrill's experiment when I first heard of it, but also disturbed, and I wasn't really sure why until I met the philosopher Wendy Brown. She described for me a fundamental shift she'd seen in society over the last twenty years. "Economization," she calls it—the "soaking into everything of economic values, a quiet and slow invasion into all the different cells of life." It's happening society-wide (as we'll get to in a moment), but it begins within our psyches, she says. There, we are remaking ourselves, at least figuratively, in the image of the corporation—exactly what Merrill does literally. "Corporations understand themselves as rising and falling according to their shareholder value, needing to attract investors," Brown told me. "And increasingly, human beings also understand themselves as little bits of capital, needing to attract investors and invest wisely in themselves."

When she said that, the penny dropped. I realized that what's so disturbing about Merrill's experiment is not that it's absurd. It's that it's not absurd enough—that it too closely resembles our current reality.

I asked Brown for some examples of economization, and she talked about love. "Remember how important falling in love was in college?" she asked. "It was a big part of things, very intense." Today it's different, she says, relating a story about a young woman, a student of hers. "I don't have time to invest in a substantive relationship, all that emotionality and so forth," the student told her. "I'm too busy building my résumé. When I knock off at night and I want to have sex, I call my buddy, have sex, and go to sleep." There's a larger story, Brown says, in the student's sense that she needs to *invest* in herself, to increase her market value, even if that means forgoing love. It reveals how economic imperatives increasingly trump everything else, how making "wise investments in ourselves, to attract investors and enhance our value," becomes the be-all and end-all—just as with Merrill.

Whether we're building résumés, going to the gym, counting steps, rating others and being rated by them, collecting "friends" and "likes," monetizing homes and cars, volunteering, meditating, learning, or whatever, boosting the value of the portfolios that are ourselves has become our main aim, says Brown. We think of ourselves, our social links, our moral and political lives, mainly in economic terms. Values we once thought beyond financial considerations are now routinely linked to them (as reflected in article titles like "Study Finds That Diverse Companies Produce 19% More Revenue"; "Sustainability Is 'Good for Humanity, but It's Better for Business'"; "Childhood Poverty Costs U.S. $1.03 Trillion in a Year, Study Finds"). "All kinds of things we might have considered or treasured for their own sake," says Brown, "have changed in their value, been turned into investments" as noneconomic ways of being and thinking, those "oriented toward democracy, or toward the soul," are pushed to the edge.

This trend, says Brown, threatens our freedom and democracy and ultimately the "Enlightenment dream," which, she fears, is "coming to a kind of end." After all, she asks, "what did the Enlightenment promise us? It promised us freedom on the basis of being able to think for ourselves and thus govern ourselves, the premise that if we were released from myth and tradition, and constraints by church and other forms of power, we could think and reason and discover, not only what was true in the world but also what was true for ourselves." Though economization doesn't coerce us at the point of a gun, or order our lives through the medieval myths and rigid hierarchies of pre-Enlightenment times, it subordinates us nonetheless, only now to economic imperatives. And that, says Brown, "all but extinguishes the real freedom to make ourselves according to our own lights."

How, then, are these processes linked to the "new" corporation? Closely. Corporations institutionalize the core economic values and imperatives of capitalism—self-interest, competition, commodification, and profit. They serve as flagships, operational arms, for capitalism's expanding domain, driving themselves and their values into every corner of society. As a result, societies change from *having* corporations to *being* corporate. And, inevitably, everything is economized.

We see the dynamic unfold, for example, in proclamations during the coronavirus pandemic that the economy should take precedence over saving lives. In that spirit, President Trump tweeted that "the cure cannot be worse (by far) than the problem," referring to proposals to restrict economic activity in order to slow the virus's spread. The message was essentially that, as Douglas Rushkoff describes it, "the economy is not here to serve human beings; human beings are here to serve the economy." That was the thinking behind Trump's announcement in mid-March that he would reopen the economy by Easter and also U.K. prime minister Boris Johnson's initial flirtation with not shutting down the economy at all. It's the thinking manifest in right-wing commentators' claims that economic values should trump saving lives—prompting the *Washington Post* columnist Max Boot to remark that "apparently, the right-wing devotion to life ends at birth . . . [with] the 'pro-life' movement . . . so willing to sacrifice the lives of the elderly and ailing in a sick attempt to restart the U.S. economy while we are struggling with more coronavirus cases than any other country."

It needs to be noted, however, that there's been a strong counternarrative to the "economy over lives" mantra. Boris Johnson quickly recanted his plans at the outset of the crisis. Trump purported to do the same, tweeting in late March, "The economy is No. 2 on my list. First, I want to save a lot of lives." More broadly, throughout the pandemic there was widespread commitment to the notion that economic growth and performance should give way to saving lives. "Imagine if blunt economic interest was, in fact, dictating our response," remarked Adam Tooze, a professor at Columbia University and author of *Crashed*. "Would we be shutting the economy down? . . . The big idea of the 1990s that 'the economy' will serve as a regulating superego of our politics is a busted flush." Be that as it may, by late April President Trump had again changed course, now calling for economies to reopen—and some states did that, against health experts' advice—and stirring up dissent against lockdowns.

Still, the real issue at play here—and not only for the United States—is that over the last few decades, economization has been deeply entrenched and institutionalized worldwide, a result of corporations pushing for more power and control. That will not be easily undone, whatever the postpandemic world brings. And helping to propel it forward has been, and will continue to be, the corporation's "new" persona. Now supposedly conscientious and publicly minded, companies claim they can do a better and more efficient job of governing than governments can. And governments have largely capitulated, off-loading to corporations control over key public domains—in other words, economizing them.

Back in Davos, at the JPMorgan Chase party, Bibop Gresta waits to talk to Jamie Dimon. He's being coached by Chase executive Sanjay Jain. "In 2009 [*sic*] when the financial crisis happened," Jain tells Gresta, "JPMorgan, and Jamie Dimon in particular, picked Detroit as the one city in the entire country we were gonna save. And so, you need to say to Jamie: 'I just want you to know that we are building a Hyperloop to Detroit. We care about Detroit as much as you do.' Got that script?"

"Got it," says Gresta.

"One-on-one, then, let's go," says Jain as he guides Gresta toward Dimon.

Spotting Gresta, Dimon calls out, "Hey, good to see you!" He pokes fun at Gresta's tuxedo (Dimon is in jeans and a blazer) and brings Tony Blair, who is standing next to him, into the fun. "I was telling Tony Blair you guys have something in common," Dimon says as Blair grins eagerly. "You were in a rock band, and he had his own rock band before he was prime minister!"

Once the banter stops, Gresta begins his pitch. "So I know what you've done for Detroit and all the effort that you did to save it. And it's not public yet," Gresta says, following the script Jain gave him, "but we signed a deal to actually build a Hyperloop to Detroit. You know, we are trying to contribute, following your example."

"That's great," says Dimon.

Jain chimes in that Hyperloop is "an amazing company" (which he apparently believes—he left Chase soon after Davos to become Hyperloop's chief strategy officer), and Dimon signals the meeting's end, turning sideways toward Sandra Navidi, who's been waiting to greet him. "I'll see you in a couple weeks," he tells Gresta, who then moves over to talk with fellow rock 'n' roller Tony Blair. Afterward, Gresta is excited about the meeting, not least by the prospect of working with someone he admires for initiating "programs that really try to improve society, like creating a special program for Detroit, to reconstruct it completely."

Gresta's not alone in praising Dimon and JPMorgan Chase for social commitment. The bank routinely ranks high on *For-*

tune magazine's Change the World list, and Dimon is widely lauded for public expressions of concern about inequality and also for his outspoken criticism of President Trump's racist and anti-immigration stances. As head of the Business Roundtable, he helped steer America's top CEOs toward "new" corporation ideas, spearheading the group's avowal to eschew narrow pursuit of profit and shareholder value and to embrace a "fundamental commitment to all our stakeholders [and to] the communities in which we work." JPMorgan Chase leads by example, running numerous purpose-driven programs, such as the Detroit initiative, which, the bank says, represents its philosophy of "private enterprise for public good" and "a new corporate responsibility model designed to create impact by focusing on some of the crucial drivers of inclusive growth."

Detroit truly needed help when the bank stepped in. Battered by deindustrialization through the 1990s and early 2000s, the city was driven to the brink of ruin by the 2008 crash and officially declared bankruptcy in 2013. By 2017, however, JPMorgan Chase was touting Detroit as "America's comeback city" and taking credit for the shift, having helped finance numerous initiatives. But the bank's work in Detroit is only "part humanity," says Dimon. "Obviously, it's good for the bank." As he recently reminded investors, "We are, just to make it clear, a for-profit institution, and we are making an *investment* in Detroit."

Indeed, Chase's model for urban renewal—"inclusive collaboration and public-private partnership," as the bank describes it—is highly profitable for it and its clients. Finding business opportunities in voids left by failed and inadequate public administration, the bank chooses what to do and how to do it on the basis of what will likely yield profit. Many of the opportunities involve privatizing the delivery of public goods and services, a practice JPMorgan Chase knows well as one of the world's leading privatization financiers. Its clients include private prison companies—though recently, under fire from protesters, it abandoned that sector—water companies, and corporate social service providers, among others. The bank is well positioned to help its clients reap large profits from Detroit, which has become a veritable gold mine for corporations wanting to take advantage of transferring public service provision—and therefore public revenue—to corporations.

When, for example, the city's public school system, already in crisis, effectively collapsed in the wake of 2008, for-profit operators swooped in to take control. By 2016, 80 percent of the city's numerous charter schools (Detroit has the nation's second-highest number of students in charter schools) were controlled by for-profit companies. Detroit's water system was also devastated by the city's collapse, not least because more than half of the $1 billion the city had raised through bond issues in 2011 and 2012 was claimed back by banks, including JPMorgan Chase, in the form of penalties for having defaulted on loans. Paying that pain forward, Emergency Manager Kevyn Orr (appointed by then governor Rick Snyder to take control of city finances after the bankruptcy) shut off water to households behind in their payments, thirty-three thousand of them in 2014, the first year of the program. Despite global criticism and a rebuke from the United Nations, the city persisted with the shutoff plan, depriving more than one hundred thousand households of water services to date. As the coronavirus ravaged Detroit, lack of water and sanitation services due to shutoffs exacerbated suffering and propelled the spread of the virus.

Though Detroit undoubtedly needed help when Dimon and JPMorgan Chase showed up, it has to be asked: In what kind of world—in what kind of *democratic* world—does a bank *save* a major American city?

Ten years before Dimon's JPMorgan Chase party at the World Economic Forum's 2008 gathering in Davos, CEOs from fourteen major corporations, Nike, Microsoft, Coca-Cola, and Merck among them, came together to declare society was at the dawn of "a new era in public-private partnership, a new frontier in corporate global citizenship," where corporations would take the lead in "building better governance systems and public institutions." Global ills were mounting and governments were failing to solve them, they said, as inequality widened, corruption spread, and the environment deteriorated. It was time for corporations to step in and help. They had the resources and reach to make a difference, and their newly minted characters made them good actors who could help solve the world's most pressing problems. Henceforth corporations should, and would, help govern society, the CEOs proclaimed, as partners with (and, implicitly, sometimes replacements for) governments.

In 2008, it was a novel notion that corporations should help *govern* society. By Davos 2018, it had become a central tenet of the "new" corporation movement. There, Richard Edelman told me that with "big changes in the reliability of business as a potential good actor," corporations are "now expected to be agents of change" and to "fill a void left by government." Michael Porter, whose "shared value" concept articulates the "new" corporation ethos, observed that "there's a real lack of faith in government, and companies are standing up and filling that void." And Davos chief Klaus Schwab, who first articulated the "new" corporation notion with his concept of "stakeholder capitalism," and whose WEF extols the philosophy of public-private partnership, told me, as noted above, that what's really needed to make the world right is a "permanent platform for public-private cooperation."

Such comments reflect a broad elite consensus, crystallizing over the decade since that 2008 CEO declaration in Davos, that corporations should *take over* from governments in various public domains.

Escalating privatization has been a tangible result of that consensus. Though having begun in earnest in the early 1980s, it faltered in the early 2000s as scandal-plagued companies lost public trust. A new rationale was needed for privatization to regain its previous momentum, and the "new" corporation provided it—much as it had for deregulation. Now caring and publicly minded, corporations claimed, they should be trusted, in place of governments, to deliver public goods and services. Not only could they "do well by doing good," but they could do *better* than governments, they said. Spurred on by that new rationale, privatization ramped up again, to the point that, today, corporations have become "voracious," as Diane Ravitch, the commentator and former assistant secretary of education, describes it, "in seeking to privatize almost everything."

They see major opportunities for profit and growth in public sectors from which historically they've been excluded, such as water systems, schools, libraries, social services, and the military. And with their new shiny personas helping overcome traditional reticence about for-profit delivery of public goods, corporations have rapidly infiltrated new areas and on a global scale. Take water services. Since 2000, multinational utilities and engineering firms such as Veolia, Thames, and Suez have tripled the number of people they serve worldwide, with an overall rise from 335 million to more than a billion (the increase is eightfold in the Global South). They've succeeded, in part, by presenting themselves as caring solution providers, promising to "solve environmental challenges and help customers reach their goals" (Veolia); "solve the world's most complex challenges related to water scarcity, quality, productivity, the environment and energy" (Suez); and "make a positive contribution to our customers, communities, and biodiversity on our land" (Thames).

The problem, however—and this is true not only for water but for all public goods that fall into private hands—is that decisions about who gets service, what kind of service they get, how much they pay, what kind of infrastructure is built, and how that infrastructure is maintained must always be driven by profit. Which means the underlying premise of public provision—that everyone gets "*equal* access to the basic necessities of life*," as Ravitch describes it—no longer governs. It's replaced by the profit imperative. Once privatized, water, like everything else, becomes a commodity, now bought and sold rather than provided as a human right.

Which is why Martin Riese thinks privatization is such a bad idea.

Riese is an unlikely defender of water as a human right. At least that's what I initially thought. As the world's leading water sommelier (yes, *water* sommelier), he peddles luxury bottled water to wealthy patrons at a posh Los Angeles restaurant. He's also created the world's most expensive bottle of water, priced at $100,000, which he personally delivers to anyone who orders it, anywhere in the world. The pricey bottle is endemic, I thought when I first heard of it, of how ridiculous it is to treat water as a commodity. I was surprised to learn Riese agrees. His $100,000 bottle of water, he says, is a kind of performance art piece, designed to "showcase how ridiculous we can get" in commercializing water. As for his day-to-day work selling luxury water to wealthy restaurant patrons, he sees it as educative, part of a broader life mission to teach people that "we should value water more—that it is not just water, but a human right."

Riese's passion for water developed at a young age—"I was just intrigued by the fact tap water tasted different in different places, fascinated it even had taste. When on vacation with my family, we'd come to a new city, and I'd literally run to the hotel tap and drink the tap water to see how it tasted." Once he was grown-up, tasting water became his vocation. He created the world's first water menu for a restaurant. He wrote a book about water. He became certified as a water sommelier. And in 2011, he assumed his current post as water sommelier for the Los Angeles Patina Restaurant Group. Through it all, Riese says, he has come to revere water, almost spiritually. "When I see water," he says, "I see life."

That reverence has made Riese critical of commodified water and the corporations that profit from it. Big-brand purified water—like Coke's Dasani, Pepsi's LIFEWTR, and Nestlé's Pure Life—is the "biggest scam on planet Earth," he says. It's just processed tap water—and "dead water" at that, he says, because the minerals have been extracted out of it. Purified water's production depletes aquifers (often in poor and water-stressed communities) and causes environmental harm, and contrary to its producers' much-advertised claims about health benefits, says Riese, citing a World Health Organization study, it's actually bad for people's health. "You should not drink it," he warns. "It will find minerals in your body, and suck them out and get rid of them."

Privatization, however, looms as an even larger worry for Riese than purified water. "I'm very, very scared to see this trend," he says. "Water should be state owned. It cannot be privatized. When you're privatizing water, corporations suddenly are in charge of a human right." Global experience with privatized water confirms his concerns, with disastrous results overall and especially for poor communities. After taking over public water systems, corporations typically maintain profits by neglecting maintenance where costs are high, boosting service fees, and diminishing service. They exclude communities that are unprofitable to serve by, for example, extending services only to those that already have expensive-to-build mains. And because the contracts between water corporations and public authorities typically guarantee minimum profits for corporations, governments end up paying the price for profit shortfalls, a disincentive to their challenging corporate-imposed rate increases and cost cutting.

In short, providing high-quality services to *everyone,* the essence of a human right, doesn't happen when corporations take over water systems. That's not what corporations do. Which is why people around the world have been pushing back against water privatization, beginning in the early 2000s when a water subsidiary of engineering giant Bechtel was driven out of Cochabamba, Bolivia, by a popular uprising (the story is featured in my first book and film, *The Corporation*). Since then, more than two hundred cities worldwide, including many in the United States, have de-privatized their water systems. Oscar Olivera, the leader of the Cochabamba uprising and now general coordinator at Fundación Abril, an organization devoted to "preservation and recovery of water for the common good," sees the trend, he recently told me, as evidence of a growing popular rejection of corporate campaigns to transform common goods into profitable commodities.

That may be so, but those campaigns continue nonetheless, not only in relation to water but in other areas, too, including children's education.

When Bill Gates took the podium at Davos 2008 to announce he was leaving Microsoft, he told the audience there was much he still wanted to accomplish. Global poverty had to be solved, he said, and the solution was to reprogram capitalism along "new" corporation lines. "The genius of capitalism," he said, "lies in its ability to make self-interest serve the wider interest." But despite having "improved the lives of billions," capitalism had to be remade so that it would better "serve poorer people." "Creative capitalism" was the name he gave his new concept. Its key was to "stretch the reach of market forces so that more people can make a profit, or gain recognition, doing work that eases the world's inequities"; to focus more of "the caring and innovation power, the resources, of corporations . . . on the needs of the poorest," he later explained in an interview. Governments still had roles to play, but mainly as facilitators of corporations, their job limited "to . . . creat[ing] market incentives for business activity that improves the lives of the poor."

That corporations should lend a helping hand while tapping the world's poor for profits was still a novel idea when Gates made his speech in 2008. Now it's a key strategy for all major brands, as previously noted—including Nestlé (with its pushcart program in Brazil), Coca-Cola (producing nutraceutical beverages in India), and Unilever (training beauticians in Bangladesh). First conceived by the economist C. K. Prahalad—who began in the 1990s talking about corporations serving the "bottom of the pyramid" as a way to make a profit and help the world's poor—the idea, an iteration of "doing well by doing good," lies at the heart of Gates's creative capitalism. And importantly for this discussion, it extends beyond consumer goods. When Gates calls for "stretching markets," for example, what he really means is broadening their reach, and that of their main operators, corporations, to include things previously excluded—mainly, public goods and services.

It's no surprise, then, that Gates has poured hundreds of millions of dollars into privatizing schools. His backing helps fuel the charter school movement in the United States and more recently in poor countries. He invested millions (alongside the

Chan Zuckerberg Initiative, the World Bank, Pearson, and others) in a for-profit company, Bridge International Academies, that owns and runs schools in Africa and Asia. The company's stated plan is to reach more than ten million children in some of the poorest parts of the world and make money from doing so. "Private schools for the poor is a $51 billion market," exclaims the company's cofounder Jay Kimmelman. "The biggest education market that no one's ever heard of, no one's even thought about."

Bridge is "a flagship of creative capitalism," Shannon May, Bridge International's cofounder and Kimmelman's wife, told me. "We're designed to solve a social problem, using capital markets and consumer need." Named Social Entrepreneurs of the Year at Davos 2015, May and Kimmelman are not shy about their ambition to make money from poor people. "We know our role is to create value," May says, "to be a good partner for our shareholders, and those who have entrusted us with their capital." The real question, however, is, how do you make money when your customers have so little of it?

Bridge deploys a business model inspired by other companies that sell low-priced products to low-income people. It targets mass markets—"as we're able to provide this service across tens of millions of children, there will be value," says May. It's seemingly affordable—"even people who are living in poverty are earning cash, and they're earning cash for a reason; they're earning it to be able to spend it on things they need in their lives." And it drives costs down as much as possible—"we take lessons from other global service providers, like McDonald's or Starbucks. We build to scale, we systematize, we standardize," says Kimmelman. "We call this vertically integrated platform our 'Academy in a Box.'"

Key to the business model are "word-for-word, action-by-action scripts delivered in real time to Android-based tablets," says Kimmelman. The tablet tells teachers exactly what to say and also, says May, "all of these different ways to behave: move away from the board, circulate in the classroom, visit each group, give them one-on-one coaching." Teachers don't have to plan lessons or make pedagogical choices, which allows Bridge to hire individuals with no experience, training, or government certification. Because everything is scripted, Bridge teachers don't have to be—*or be paid as*—trained professionals, no more than McDonald's workers have to be trained chefs. Pretty well anyone can do it, May told me. True, "you've gotta be able to read," she said. "It might seem like a low bar, but you have to start somewhere."

Using technology to de-professionalize teachers, and thereby reduce costs, is not unique to Bridge. It's become a veritable movement among education reformers worldwide. Bridge's tablets, and the pedagogical approach they represent, mirror a major trend. These days, the most vocal school privatization advocates come from the tech sector, and their express aim is to replace teachers with technology. Bill Gates, Mark Zuckerberg, and Reed Hastings are just a few of "The Silicon Valley Billionaires Remaking America's Schools," according to *The New York Times,* and a large part of their mission is to automate classrooms. As described by Emmett Carson, then a manager of many of these billionaires' philanthropic portfolios, what they are attracted to, and want to support, are "models [that] can produce better results . . . given the changes in innovation that are underway, with artificial intelligence and automation."

"In the tech industry's dream," says Ravitch, "if the teacher is removed from the equation, then you can cut costs dramatically." What the industry and its billionaire philanthropists want, she says, is "to have teacherless classrooms"—to develop and deploy technologies that, like Bridge's tablets, allow companies to hire nonprofessionals and sometimes replace teachers altogether. To that end, Google, Facebook, Apple, and Microsoft, among others, are developing a bevy of technologies—virtual classrooms, interactive teaching software, digital marketing strategies (to insert in online lessons), machine testing and continuous assessment, digital behavior management, and social and emotional development tools—that, together, constitute a rapidly expanding tech sector estimated to be worth more than $45 billion.

While many of the new technologies obviate the need for professionally trained teachers, others allow small numbers of instructors to reach large numbers of pupils remotely. Corporate-run virtual "schools," for example, provide students with computers on which they follow lessons at home. Now operating in numerous states—they are particularly widespread in Pennsylvania—"cyber-charters" have become cash cows for their corporate operators, because despite not having expenses associated with brick-and-mortar schools, per-student funding from public coffers remains the same. Cyber-charters are notorious for cheating scandals and enrollment inflation, among other kinds of scams and fraud, but the real problem, says Ravitch, is that they don't work, as reflected by "low test scores, terrible graduation rates, and tremendous attrition."

Conservative school reformers cheer alongside liberal Silicon Valley moguls like Gates and Zuckerberg as new technologies take over teaching. "New computer-based approaches to learning simply require *far fewer teachers per student*—perhaps half as many, and possibly fewer than that," say the conservative commentators John Chubb and Terry Moe in their book *Liberating Learning*. Which, an added bonus, dilutes the power of teachers' unions. "Technology," as Chubb and Moe explain, "is also destined to help resolve the *political* problem that has prevented reformers from taking effective action. To put it simply: the seepage of technology into the system—which cannot be stopped and will continue—works slowly but inexorably to undermine the political power of the teachers' unions. With their power to resist weakened over time, the floodgates will then be opened."

The stay-at-home schooling made necessary by the coronavirus pandemic is advanced by some conservative commentators as further support for their cause. "The resistance—led by teachers' unions and the politicians beholden to them—to allowing partial homeschooling or online learning for K–12 kids has been swept away by necessity," according to Katherine Mangu-Ward, editor in chief of *Reason* magazine. "It will be near impossible to put that genie back in the bottle in the fall." (Though Sonia Shah, the author of *Pandemic: Tracking Contagions, from Cholera to Ebola and Beyond,* counters that "the hype around online education will be abandoned, as a generation of young people forced into seclusion [by the pandemic lockdown] will reshape the culture around a [new] appreciation for communal life.")

The allure of teacherless classrooms may be strong for those who seek profits from education. But what they propose is questionable from pedagogical perspectives. Most education experts agree with Ravitch that "the very essence of education is the human interaction between the teacher and the student"—the sense among students that a human being cares about them, wants them to learn, empathizes and works to communicate with them, and respects them. No doubt not all teachers achieve that, sometimes because straitened conditions in schools make it impossible, other times because they're poorly trained or lacking talent. The solution, however, is not to de-professionalize and replace them with machines. It's to support them, help them develop their abilities as professionals, and provide conditions in schools that are conducive to teaching and learning.

In the end, that's what bothers Kenyan teachers' union leader Wilson Sossion most about Bridge and its tablets—that the model downgrades and dehumanizes teaching. "You cannot have teachers who behave as robots," he says, "to follow scripted curriculum that tell you walk three steps to the blackboard, walk around the classroom. A teacher ought to be a natural teacher." Bridge is endemic of what's wrong with the broader school privatization movement, adds Ravitch. The movement's "reformers" "don't want to reform schools," she says. "They want to replace them with privatized schools, in many cases for-profit or run by for-profit agencies," and then reduce costs and boost profits by automating teaching. It's a model of education, she says, that "lacks a human ideal of developing the individual and nurturing his or her talents."

But there's an even larger concern about Bridge, says Ravitch—"colonialism, pure and simple . . . Bridge is saying, 'Give us your education system, we will take care of it.' " That's a problem because education is not just training. It's about socializing children, instilling values, creating citizens. "You cannot rely on Mark Zuckerberg, Bill Gates, the World Bank—institutions from the prosperous side of the world—to take over and provide the education that you should be providing in your country," she says. "Education is not apolitical. You teach a set of values when you're teaching." When I asked Sossion whether he thinks Bridge is guilty of colonialism, he told me it's much worse than that. "What Bridge is doing is not mere colonialism," he said. "When you deny children the fundamental human right to access quality teachers, to access good education, and you utilize poor citizens of this world as a source of income—it's evil."

Yet utilizing poor citizens of this world as a source of income is precisely what Bill Gates advocates with his "creative capitalism." He wants corporations to play greater roles in providing public services in poor countries, in exchange for opportunities to extract profit, often from taxpayer funds. Social entrepreneurs and investors like May, Kimmelman, and Gates say market solutions are better than public ones (May told me, for example, that "when education is treated as a space that shouldn't have investment, it becomes a desert where there are no ideas, where people aren't pushing forward"), but there are profound limits inherent to those solutions. While it may "seem incredibly noble that they're saying business should serve a social purpose," as Anand Giridharadas describes it, "what they're also saying is that the kinds of change we ought to pursue are the kinds of change that kick something back to the winners." In other words, change is pursued to yield profit for investors and corporations, not on the basis of what citizens truly need. And while the two may sometimes align, they don't necessarily, and they often diverge.

By this point, the story should be clear—corporations are leveraging their new personas to replace governments in providing public goods and services. That's what Bill Gates's creative capitalism is really about. It's what Richard Edelman celebrates by claiming corporations, as "good actors," can fill voids left by governments. It's the idea implied by Klaus Schwab's notion of a permanent platform of cooperation between "new" corporations and governments. And it's the basis, among other things, of Jamie Dimon and JPMorgan Chase's promise to save Detroit, Shannon May and Jay Kimmelman's vow to save children in Africa, and Veolia's claim that it can solve water crises in poor communities. The overarching message? Corporations are good now. They can help lead society and solve its problems. They should replace governments in many roles.

That message's imperial ambition is difficult to discern behind the "new" corporation's gloss of good intentions. But sometimes it slips out. During my interview with Richard Edelman, for example, after he had told me how corporations were now good actors ready to fill voids left by governments, I asked him: "What are the consequences for democracy and citizenship if corporations take over government roles?"

"I'm not much of a believer in political citizenship," Edelman said. "I actually believe much more in the power of the marketplace." It was astonishing, and disturbing, to hear the world's leading business consultant, widely regarded as a thoughtful and committed advocate for social change, so casually dismiss "political citizenship"—in other words, *democracy*—out of a preference for markets. And even more a concern because the words he spoke articulate a broad antidemocratic sentiment pervasive among "new" corporation leaders.

Those leaders are, after all, the same people who over the last twenty years have fought to dismantle the social state. Jamie Dimon and JPMorgan Chase, for example, have championed and profited from, among other things, tax cuts for corporations and the rich (most recently in President Trump's tax bill), more privatization, trade deals that allow corporations to chase cheap labor, and anti-union laws. They've funded campaigns to elect politicians who could be trusted to implement those policies and doggedly lobbied for deregulation. As well, on Dimon's watch, JPMorgan Chase egregiously flouted financial laws and regulations, helping to cause the 2008 meltdown, for which the bank paid $13 billion in legal settlements.

Yet despite all that, Dimon and his bank publicly champion equality and avow commitments to social causes—like promising to save Detroit. It's an "amazing kind of two-step," says Giridharadas. "You first create conditions in which people in a city like Detroit are shattered by your speculation decisions, and then you have the gall to market yourself to those folks as their Christ." But it's not only Dimon and Detroit. That same two-step is being danced by the entire "new" corporation movement. Over the last two decades, corporations have promised to care about society and solve its problems, while pressuring governments to retreat from doing the same. "It's so remarkable," says Giridharadas, "the same folks, who actually pushed for government to do less, to not be able to solve social problems, now present themselves as the solution to the problems they engineered." Reaping profits all the while.

The process is sometimes described as "starve the beast"— the beast being government. First, corporations deny governments adequate resources to fund public services by avoiding taxes, pushing for tax cuts, and lobbying against spending. Crises inevitably ensue—failing schools, water systems, cities, prisons, and so on. And corporations step in saying they have the solution—privatization—and that they will do a better job than the government.

A central message of the "new" corporation movement is that "we don't need government very much anymore because socially responsible corporations will fill the void," says the commentator and former secretary of labor Robert Reich. It's "one of the biggest lies being told," he says, yet it's had great impact. The message (or lie) that "good" corporations can take over from governments has helped pave the way for industry's successful push to cut taxes, slash spending, and remove regulations. Which, in turn, deprives governments of the revenue they need to run quality public services. The result? Systems delivering public services falter and fail, and corporations swoop in to fill the void, boosting their profits and broadening their control over society.

In the meantime, citizens understandably give up on governments that have, at the behest of corporations, given up on them. "We feel so powerless and frustrated about the ability of our government systems to actually solve social problems that we start to sort of put our faith in corporations," says Stacy Mitchell of the Institute for Local Self-Reliance. "When citizens see a big corporation doing something positive, it creates a sense of hope, that maybe we can solve our biggest problems because these corporations have become sustainable and socially responsible." The catch, though, she adds, is that "in the process of doing that we're going further down the path that led us here. We're actually losing our ability to govern ourselves effectively and turning over power to a set of entities who are only really out for their own interests."

None of this denies that corporations sometimes do good. The question, as noted and addressed earlier, is how much and what kinds of good can they can do? And, perhaps more important, what are the larger consequences of allowing corporations to replace democratic governments as guardians of public interests? When "corporations 'do well by doing good,' they do what's easy, what's brandable," says Wendy Brown. "But that's not how you do democracy in a place that ostensibly cares about the public interest or the public good of all." Far from championing public policies aimed to promote social welfare, "new" corporations and their leaders actively fight against those policies. They fight to roll back workers' rights and unions, taxes on wealth and corporate profits, social spending and programs, and regulations that restrict offshoring, downsizing, mergers and acquisitions, and campaign financing. They spin a rhetoric of concern and benevolence, while working hard to destroy the social state—arguably harder than their "old" corporation counterparts did.

With the coronavirus pandemic, the ill consequences of that destruction have become shockingly obvious. Wealthy countries, and the United States in particular, were so intent on shrinking government over the last few decades—serving up tax breaks, spending cuts, and deregulation to big business—that they left themselves without the means to protect citizens. "What a small, shameful way for a strong nation to falter: For want of a

75-cent face mask, the kingdom was lost," wrote *New York Times* columnist Farhad Manjoo. The U.S. Department of Health and Human Services estimated 3.5 billion face masks were needed to fight the pandemic. Nearly 200 million, still just a fraction, had been part of a national strategic stockpile created in 2006. But half of those were used to fight the H1N1 flu pandemic in 2009. And they were never replaced. Nor did anyone give much thought to the implications of hospital protective gear manufacturing moving overseas—just two decades ago most of it was made at home. "Getting enough protective gear was among the cheapest, most effective things we could have done to slow the pandemic," said Manjoo. "That we failed on such an obvious thing reveals an alarming national incapacity to imagine and prepare for the worst."

The face mask debacle is just one result of a government shrunken to the point of severe inadequacy. A government war game–like simulation in 2019, code-named "Crimson Contagion," modeled a pandemic eerily similar to the coronavirus—it originated in China, spread quickly around the world through air travel, and was officially declared a pandemic a month and a half after first being detected. In the simulation, according to a draft report marked "not to be disclosed," more than 100 million Americans fell ill, nearly 8 million were hospitalized, and more than half a million died. The report further revealed a federal response that was underfunded, unprepared, uncoordinated, and overall "confused," confirming findings from similar exercises over the previous four years, all of which warned of severe shortages of vital medical equipment (including masks and ventilators), inadequate capacity to manufacture such equipment, too-slow responses in shutting down schools and public events, and dire consequences from limited testing capacity.

In light of Crimson Contagion and all the other knowledge at hand, it seems reasonable to view with some skepticism Trump's statement that: "Nobody knew there would be a pandemic or epidemic of this proportion. Nobody has ever seen anything like this before." As Hannah Beech and Ben Hubbard noted in *The New York Times*: "The work done over the past five years . . . demonstrates that the government had considerable knowledge about the risks of a pandemic and accurately predicted the very types of problems Mr. Trump is now scrambling belatedly to address."

Then there's the Trump administration's 2019 termination of Predict, a scientific program designed to predict and prevent pandemics (the program was temporarily extended when the coronavirus pandemic hit). For years, scientists have known that changes to ecosystems—including those resulting from climate change, as noted earlier—set off chains of consequences that can lead to new diseases and pandemics. Nonhuman animal habitat is lost, proximity between animals and humans increased, and pathogens jump from animals to humans. "Any emerging disease in the last few decades has come about as a result of encroachment into wild lands and changes in demography," as disease ecologist Peter Daszak describes it. Moreover, the number of emerging diseases has quadrupled over the last half decade due to such encroachment, with a new animal disease capable of infecting humans discovered on average every four months.

Predict's sole purpose is to help forecast and prevent pandemics through close study of likely "hot spots." In its race to detect pandemic threats over its ten-year existence, it collected more than one hundred thousand biological samples from animals, found over a thousand new viruses, trained thousands of people across Africa and Asia, and built dozens of research laboratories. "The fate of the next pandemic may be riding on the work of Predict," *The New York Times* reported in 2012.

Acceding to corporate demands for tax and spending cuts, governments have for years been shutting down and scaling back public health and social welfare programs. When the coronavirus pandemic hit, those earlier decisions determined who would suffer, how, and how much. Though no one was immune to the virus, what quickly became apparent as it swept across the globe was that poor and low-income people would be its main victims. Without savings, sick leave, and access to healthcare, their choices were limited. They had to go to work to survive, or because their employers demanded it, or because their service-industry jobs were deemed essential and could not be done remotely from home. They lived in often overcrowded residences, making isolating at home either impossible or a harsh sentence, as well as a breeding ground for further spread of the virus. They risked having water or electricity shut off, and many lacked Internet service to continue school or college. Absent well-functioning and equitable health and social systems, they were left to become sicker, die more, and fall into desperate straits. "The way in which the virus spreads and takes lives and cuts off access to basic needs, health care, food, shelter," as Wendy Brown told me, "brings into stark relief the economic, racial, and gender inequalities already deeply built into the system over the last four decades."

Yet "new" corporations have told us over those decades that the program they proffer—a shrunken social state and a leading role for big business—is the answer. The changes they pushed for concentrated wealth, beggared ordinary citizens, and made many people's lives perilous. Despite that, they continue to "talk an extraordinary game and also act an extraordinary game of trying to help out in an age of inequality," as Giridharadas describes it, "willing to do absolutely anything to help except by stepping off the backs of working people who have been screwed, and passed over by four decades' worth of change." The coronavirus pandemic is the perfect example, he says. Big corporations and wealthy people "pushed for public policies like not having paid sick leave, having health care tied to being employed, the Trump tax cut and tax cuts of all manner for the last many decades— their choices as a class over the last generation are literally why the crisis is playing out in the way it is here."

"New" corporation advocates promise that policies beneficial to them—like lower taxes and less regulation—will benefit everyone. A rising tide lifts all boats, wealth will trickle down. But that hasn't happened. And if history is any guide, it never will. As Nick Hanauer, a venture capitalist, describes it, "Trickle-down economics is simply the newest instantiation of the oldest con in human societies, which is the rich telling the poor that our relative positions are righteous and justified."

One undeniable result of big business's assault on the social state is spiraling inequality, now magnified by the devastating economic impact of the coronavirus pandemic. As corporations lined up for bailouts—having spent the cash they earned from record profits and tax cuts on stock buybacks to enrich their shareholders—tens of millions of ordinary citizens fell hard through the cracks, losing jobs, using up meager savings, lacking sick leave and in many cases medical insurance, and getting— if they were lucky—a one-time $1,200 check. "The imbalance is unbelievable," Robert Reich told me. "Socialism for the rich, corporate socialism, but the harshest form of capitalism for most working people and the poor." Which really just echoes policies of the last several decades that have boosted corporate profits and shareholder value while deepening inequality and destroying the middle-class.

In the United States and Canada, for example, from 1980 to

2016, the share of national income going to the top 1 percent jumped from 34 percent to 47 percent. Average household wealth more than doubled for that group (from $10.5 million to $26.4 million), while for the bottom 40 percent it decreased more than twentyfold (from $6,900 to a deficit of $8,900). In 1980, the top 1 percent and the bottom 90 percent owned roughly the same share of wealth in the United States—32 percent and 34 percent, respectively. In 2015, the respective proportions were 40 percent and 21 percent. Between 1980 and 2016, the ratio of CEO pay to that of the average worker in the United States grew ninefold, from 42 to 1 to 361 to 1 (thirty-three major U.S. companies have ratios above 1,000 to 1). And since the 1980s, workers' wages have fallen in lockstep with corporate-propelled drops in union density.

What the numbers reveal—and there are many more that tell the same story—is a growing chasm between rich and poor and a near collapse of the middle class. No longer can people depend on secure and well-paying jobs and the availability of free (or subsidized) social services to live decent-quality lives and to have hope for their, and their children's, futures. It's true that regimes of social provision and protection have never been perfect, far from it. They were (and continue to be) shot through with systemic inequalities and even at their best provide uneven and inadequate services. But "new" corporations don't aim to fix broken public systems and improve the social state. They aim to dismantle them, to jettison the very idea that the government's job is to promote equality, human welfare, and some measure of solidarity among citizens.

"Democracy doesn't require perfect equality," says the philosopher Michael Sandel, but "it does require that people from different walks of life and different class backgrounds encounter one another." People must feel cared for and protected by society, that they are part of it, not apart from it. And that requires more than just political citizenship—equal votes and equal treatment by law. It requires *social* citizenship as well—some measure of equality in relation to what's needed to live decent-quality lives. The "new" corporation program undermines social equality, and hence democracy, because it leaves the provision of many of those things to corporations and markets.

Even their staunchest defenders acknowledge markets are not about social equality. They're about competition and hierarchy. Individuals come and go with the resources they have, their power proportional to those resources. There's no sense of common fate or endeavor, no concern for others or the group as a whole. Indeed, there's "no such thing as society," as Margaret Thatcher famously stated, only individuals maximizing self-interest. And that vision of society—a kind of *anti*-society society—is where we're fast moving as "new" corporations continue their successful campaign to stretch markets and push back the social state.

We're "drifting, almost without realizing it, from having a market economy to becoming a market society," says Sandel. And while market *economies* are undoubtedly useful for organizing productive activity, market *societies,* Sandel continues, are places "where almost everything is up for sale." And that inevitably corrodes the commonality democracy requires. "If the only thing money governed were access to yachts and BMWs and fancy vacations, inequality wouldn't matter as much," he says. "But if money governs central aspects of the good life—decent health care, good education for your kids, living in a neighborhood that's secure and not wrought with violence—then inequality matters a great deal."

Which is why nations, beginning in the late nineteenth century, created the social state in the first place. Recognizing markets were ill-equipped to deliver social citizenship, they shifted things such as health care, education, security, transportation, communications, water, energy, recreation, housing, and old-age support out of markets and into public domains. Corporations now push for the opposite, to re-marketize what had been de-marketized. And they're succeeding, with the inevitable result that for things once believed too essential to leave to the market's unequal logic, it's now the case that "those who have the most get the most, and those who have the least have very little access, and very little prospect of rising," as Diane Ravitch describes it. As a result, "we lose our ability to provide a decent quality of life for everyone, become increasingly unequal, and we lose our democracy."

Growing inequality, fueled by the collapse of public provision, is causing what Sandel calls the "skyboxification" of society. As a young baseball enthusiast, he told me, he used to go to watch his Minnesota Twins play. At games he'd notice, from his perch in the stadium's cheap bleacher seats, the more expensive box seats behind home plate. The difference in ticket price was only a few dollars. "CEOs and mailroom clerks found themselves sitting side by side. Everyone had to eat the same soggy hot dogs and drink the same stale beer. And when it rained, everyone got wet." But today, he says, it's different. "The affluent and the privileged can watch the game from high above the common folk in the stands below."

If such segregation were happening only in sports stadiums, it wouldn't be a problem, says Sandel. "But something similar has been happening throughout our social life." More and more, "people of affluence and people of modest means live separate lives. We live and work and shop and play in different places. We send our kids to different schools." Affluent suburbanites ride commuter trains through devastated neighborhoods, barely registering, if at all, the decayed buildings, boarded-up stores, and palpable pain of racialized poverty. Well-to-do urbanites visit trendy restaurants and shops in safe and vibrant neighborhoods, oblivious to the carnage of drugs, violence, and poverty just a few blocks away. Comfortable rural dwellers enjoy pastoral surroundings, impervious to people's hardships in less well-off neighboring communities, many devastated by a raging opioid crisis.

This economic segregation (which is, of course, racialized) greatly threatens democracy, says Sandel. "The deepest corruption that the commercialization of everything has led to is the corruption of the commonality on which democracy depends." While those at the top enjoy unprecedented wealth and privilege, the vast majority of people are scrambling to make ends meet, to go to college, find decent and secure jobs, pay health bills and mortgages or rent, raise children, and have a dignified old age. They feel society's neglect, profoundly.

"You don't need a PhD in economics to know that your life sucks under capitalism," says Seattle City Council member Kshama Sawant. Especially young people, she says, "are waking up to this understanding that this world is not working for them, that they have nothing really to look forward to other than a life of low-wage jobs, being saddled with debt, never having any hope of retirement, and really an epidemic of depression and mental illness. They correctly view this society as deeply dysfunctional, and there's a really strong urge to change it."

For large numbers of people, there's no longer a question that change is needed. The only question is what kind of change they'll pursue. They "feel we've lived in this age incredibly abundant in innovation but short on people's lives getting better," says Giridharadas, "and it's only a matter of time before they want to shatter the system. But there's no guarantee when people rise up to shatter a system whether you get Medicare for all or a wall on the southern border."

And there lies the crux of the problem. While many today

call for a stronger and fairer social state, many others, across Europe and North America, are turning to hate and xenophobia, "roaring against immigrants and other imagined dark invaders of their nations," as Wendy Brown describes it, and demanding repressive measures against them.

The "new" corporation is partly responsible for this ugly turn.

Though "new" corporations and their leaders did not directly foment the current right-wing rebellion—indeed, many express revulsion and openly condemn it—they did help create the conditions that fostered it. The immediate impact of corporations' successful push to roll back taxes, regulations, and public provision was to devastate many lives and communities. People lost jobs and opportunities. They lost their homes. Unable to afford adequate health care, they lost health and lives. Some succumbed to opioid and other addictions, committed suicide, or were victimized by the violence of hollowed-out, decaying cities. Large numbers of people legitimately came to feel unjustly betrayed by a society that no longer cared for them nor had the means to help them. So they became angry and looked for someone to blame.

Today, as in past eras, some of that blame and rage gets tragically aimed in the wrong direction—at migrants and minorities, among others. "There are no examples in human history where this level of concentrated wealth and power didn't result in either a police state or a revolution or both," says Nick Hanauer, attributing the current right-wing upsurge to a "breakdown in the social cohesion that makes democracy and civil society possible, a breakdown created by forty years of rising economic inequality and the evisceration of the middle class."

Corporations neatly escape blame when new right-wing movements and the governments they elect single out "others," rather than big business, for having caused social conditions to deteriorate. And they also gain new allies in their fight against the social state, which both they and new right-wing movements aim to destroy. In much the same way corporations and Southern racists together cheered Reagan's deregulation push in the 1980s—the former because they objected to regulations' curbing profits and the latter because they saw federal civil rights legislation as an illegitimate curb on white supremacy—today's right-wing movements call for an end to "big government," complaining that civil rights protections and social spending unjustly disfavor white people and undermine the natural fairness of markets.

Those movements "completely agree with the free market fundamentalism of the new order, completely agree that democracy is the enemy," says Wendy Brown. Their bid is "not for democratic equality and social provision, not to restore the social state, restore the respect and dignity of working and middle-class people with public institutions, schools, libraries, and parks, and so forth," but to place their whiteness, traditional values, and nativism at the heart of the country's concerns—in other words, to restore their supremacy. Corporations seek a different kind of supremacy—economic supremacy—but, as history sadly shows, particularly the history of European fascist movements in the 1930s, corporate supremacy and racist supremacy can be synergistic.

Supremacy, of all kinds, is really the problem. Supremacy of white people. Supremacy of corporations. Supremacy of the rich. And the converging supremacies of all three, which is what currently energizes the political success of right-wing movements, including Trump's presidency. What's new about the mainstream Right is that nativism and racism are now openly embraced. What's not new are the ties to big business. Right-wing regimes, like Trump's, accelerate the corporate takeover of society, through both the kinds of personnel they bring into administrations and the policies they promulgate. They "represent a continuation of privatization, deregulation, of the destruction of welfare, undermining labor unions, global travel of corporations abroad," as the political theorist Michael Hardt describes it. "An increase in the rule of corporations that now have freer rein."

Democracy cannot tolerate the supremacy of particular groups, whether corporations, economic elites, or white people. As Supreme Court Justice Louis Brandeis is reputed to have said, with respect to corporations and economic elites, "We can have democracy in this country, or we can have great wealth concentrated in the hands of a few, but we can't have both." With respect to the supremacy of white people, if we've learned anything from history, it's obvious that neither it nor regimes that represent it have any place in a democratic, let alone a decent, society.

Democracy is about rule by "the people." Which means the idea of "the people" must be intelligible. There *must,* therefore, be a thing called society, to reverse Margaret Thatcher's phrase—a sense among citizens of common good, aspiration, and destiny. How do you create that in a complex, pluralistic, unequal, and divided society like ours? How do you ensure people, despite all their differences and inequalities, nonetheless feel like, and are, *equal* citizens, not just in theory but, at least to some extent, in their actual lives? How do you foster that commonality without which democracy cannot survive?

The answer over the last century has been the social state— the establishment through policy and law of obligations and entitlements that ensure that citizens contribute to caring for one another and are cared for by one another. That was the forged solution to the intrinsic conflict between democracy and markets. With markets structurally unequal and corporations institutionally self-interested, the idea was to remove the task of meeting people's basic needs from both and put it into democratic hands. Needless to say, that did not (and does not) result in perfect equality. But it at least nurtures an aspiration toward the kind of *social* equality democracy depends upon. What's needed is to build on that aspiration—to create social systems that meet people's basic needs and help them flourish. That doesn't mean making society homogeneous. It means fostering some sense of social solidarity and common destiny, while respecting and celebrating the differences among us—enabling people to flourish equally in light of those differences.

Ensuring aspirations of the social state and democracy are made real will take a lot of work. But that's not what's happening now. What's happening instead is that "new" corporations are working to destroy the whole project. They're throwing their power, influence, and money behind policies that divide society and put democracy at risk. They're leveraging the resulting devastation for profit and growth and then asking us to treat them as heroes for saving society. They're cooperating with right-wing regimes whose economic policies and ideologies align with their interests. It's an abject disaster for society and democracy. Yet "new" corporations escape blame, quietly slipping out the back door while they bemoan the dysfunctional state of affairs they've helped create.

And they've been able to do that because of a strange ideological synergy. On the one hand, corporations present themselves as "good actors," committed to social justice and a clean environment. On the other, right-wing movements present corporations as *not* the "bad guys," blaming "others" instead. Both ways, the corporation wins. Hidden by the intersecting narratives is the greedy and destructive corporate drive to remove every barrier to profit and growth, including the social state. And, of course, each narrative is patently false. Contrary to the first, corporations are not the "good actors" they claim to be (for all the reasons discussed above). Contrary to the second, corporations, not "others," *are* the problem (for the reasons just explored). With respect to the latter, it needs also to be emphasized: by focusing on conflicts *within* "the people" (among races, religions, sexes, and so on), right-wing movements truly miss, and obscure, the real conflict we all should be worried about—that *between* "we the people" and the corporations bent on ruling and exploiting us.

Crises bring change, often profound change. Wars and epidemics have a way of awakening senses of common destiny and shared fate in society; of making individualism, competition, and self-interest—the values of markets and corporations—seem small and wrong. Recall that those very values were the driving force behind a systematic hollowing out of the social state over the last forty years. Corporations led the charge, claiming governments should be scaled back, public programs cut, taxes and spending diminished, and their power and freedom increased. That aligned with an overarching "common sense" in society, that corporate capitalism is the only way, governments should slavishly serve it, economies must endlessly grow, and benefits will trickle down to everybody eventually.

The coronavirus pandemic casts all this in a new and unflattering light. The prevailing "common sense" suddenly looked suspect, if not depraved, as more people fell ill and died because of policies reflecting that way of thinking. And "new" corporations looked distinctly less noble as they lined up for bailouts (despite record profits, tax dodging, and stock buybacks), put employees at risk, and pushed for more tax cuts, deregulation, and privatization. As Robert Reich observes, "corporate social responsibility, again, is being shown by this crisis to be nice public relations, but a very, very thin veil." The decades-long refrain that corporations are our friends and governments our enemy rings hollow now. It's telling that even presidential contender Joe Biden has veered toward a progressive stance, invoking Roosevelt's New Deal, and insisting, for example, "that big corporations, which we've bailed out twice in twelve years, step up and take responsibility for their workers and their communities." More generally, there's a growing sense that people's lives and well-being should come first—that economies should serve people, not the other way around.

But still, there's the question: How do we get from where we are now to where we need to go?

6 DEMOCRACY UNBOUND

"THE GREATEST EXISTENTIAL CRISIS of our time is to at once understand the reality before us, and then to find the capacity to resist," observes the journalist and critic Chris Hedges. The previous chapters describe and analyze the "reality before us"—a pathologically self-interested institution that's causing harm and destruction, taking control of society, and undermining democracy while masquerading as benevolent. But what about the "capacity to resist"—what can we do to change that reality? What is the solution? In earlier chapters, I claimed corporations are the antagonists of the story, not the protagonists. So who, then, are the protagonists? I've implied throughout that they are us, "the people." Building on that notion here, I argue that our search for solutions has to begin with claiming real democratic power.

The pandemic has changed our moral and political landscape, perhaps permanently. Within a few short weeks, the economic values that dominated our lives and societies over the last forty years lost their luster. Caring for one's neighbor became more important than buying the latest gadgets. Nurses, doctors, and grocery store clerks emerged as heroes, taking the place of celebrity CEOs. Cooperation and coordination supplanted competition, and the entire economy was shut down to protect elderly and vulnerable people. All of a sudden, we realized we need government to protect our health and lives—that unnecessary death and suffering are the inevitable consequences of degrading public infrastructure.

There was a sense, even early in the pandemic, that big changes were afoot. "The Reagan era is over. The widely accepted idea that government is inherently bad won't persist after coronavirus," the historian Lilliana Mason remarked. "The coronavirus pandemic marks the end of our romance with market society and hyperindividualism," said the sociologist Eric Klinenberg. According to Joseph Stiglitz, the crisis revealed the "important role for government: health care for all, making sure everybody has access to a university education without getting into enormous debt, ensuring that we have a Green New Deal"—"progressive capitalism," he calls it, though, he says, it could equally be called "democratic socialism."

But how real is the prospect of change in the shifting political landscape of the pandemic? If history shows anything, it's that those who have power and wealth do not give it up easily. We should not expect big business to end its decades-long war on the social state and democracy, just like that. Corporations may have been set back by the crisis, as they were by the 2008 financial collapse. But despite similar prognostications after that crisis—that big business had been permanently humbled, that "big government" was back, that inclusion and equality were the new future—corporations barely missed a beat. They were bailed out, barely regulated (the few reforms put in place at the time have mostly been rolled back), and they doubled down on their push for deregulation, privatization, and tax cuts.

There are two lessons to be drawn from all this, and together they form the story of this chapter. The first is that we need to be realistic. Change doesn't happen automatically. Even when things are truly terrible, when we are faced with systems so unjust and morally bankrupt that they should fail, they persist nonetheless. Crisis awakens people's sense of outrage and helps them see what's wrong with prevailing systems. But outrage alone does not bring change. Action is also necessary—and not just any action, but action that's likely to be effective.

The second lesson is that calls for change need to begin with repurposing old institutions, particularly those of democratic governance, while also charting a course toward new and different ways to be together. We still need government—and indeed a socially robust version of it. But we also need something more. What the pandemic has shown is how quickly and easily people come together to help one another—young people in India and South Africa organizing to provide daily aid packages to the poor; volunteer drivers in Wuhan, China, creating a community fleet to transport medical workers when public transport closed down; people singing on rooftops in Italy or playing Bingo from their apartment balconies in Dublin; a quickly formed organization in the United States that connects health-care workers in need of support to people able to provide them meals and accommodation. "The horror films got it wrong," says the *Guardian* columnist George Monbiot. "Instead of turning us into flesh-eating zombies, the pandemic has turned millions of people into good neighbors." Such mutual aid and community initiatives are crucial moving forward, not, Monbiot notes, as "a substitute for the state, but an essential complement" to it.

And that's the key. Moving forward from this pandemic, we need both to reenergize the social capacities of the democratic state and build strong, sustainable, and caring communities. Importantly, what we cannot do is return to the previous "normal." Not only was that "normal" part of the reason for the virus's devastating impact, but it was already shot through with crises—climate change, spiraling inequality, and the evisceration of democracy. As the political philosopher Michael Hardt observes, "What we have to return to is not normal, but struggles against the crises that defined normal." That doesn't mean we need to reject everything from the previous "normal." But it does demand a change in values and priorities, and that we find ways to ensure governments robustly serve citizens' needs and protect the natural environment. That's no simple task, and it will require a fight. But we're not starting from scratch. As this chapter shows, there's a burgeoning new politics that's re-creating democratic governance. It's been gaining momentum for a decade, but its roots go back further than that.

It's August 28, 1963, and Martin Luther King, Jr., is standing at the podium in front of the Lincoln Memorial in Washington, D.C. A quarter of a million people crowd before him, having just marched against injustice and Congress's deadlock on the Civil Rights Act. King begins to speak, and about twelve minutes into his remarks Mahalia Jackson, who had introduced him with a stirring rendition of "I Been 'Buked and I Been Scorned," shouts from behind him, "Tell 'em about the dream, Martin, tell 'em about the dream!" He looks up from his notes and continues, never to glance at them again. "So even though we face the difficulties of today and tomorrow, I still have a dream. It is a dream deeply rooted in the American dream. I have a dream that one day this nation will rise up and live out the true meaning of its creed: We hold these truths to be self-evident: that all men are created equal."

Marshall Ganz was still a student when King gave his famous speech. Having witnessed firsthand the fallout from Nazi atrocities in Europe—he had lived in postwar Germany for three years while his father, a rabbi, was stationed there as a U.S. Army chaplain—he understood injustice and wanted to do something about it. In 1964, he left college and traveled to Mississippi to join the Mississippi Summer Project, one of hundreds of northern college students volunteering to help register African American voters. They and the local activists they worked with faced bombings, arson, murders, and kidnappings. National news coverage spurred outrage across the country and, among other things, helped break the deadlock in Congress to get the Civil Rights Act passed.

The 1964 Mississippi Summer Project would also shape the fate of Edwin Finley Taliaferro, a teenager living in Detroit who would later change his name to Chokwe Lumumba (in homage to the murdered Congolese revolutionary Patrice Lumumba). The Mississippi Summer Project, Lumumba recalled years later, was instrumental in "helping organize the Mississippi Freedom Democratic Party [which] in the early seventies had a profound effect on the state Democratic Party, [forcing it] to mandate that half of its delegates would have to be black and half be women." It "rocked the foundation of the white supremacist government and culture in the South," he said. In 1971, Lumumba put his legal studies on hold and moved to Jackson, Mississippi, to fight for racial justice as a member of the Republic of New Afrika (RNA), a revolutionary group seeking black self-determination in the South.

Racist repression was still rife in Mississippi when he arrived. "We still faced intimidation from right-wing forces—Klansmen populated police departments, discrimination on jobs was commonplace, and we were locked out of government completely, actually victims of government violence." Soon after Lumumba's arrival in Mississippi, FBI agents and local police raided RNA offices. A gun battle ensued, a police officer was killed, several FBI agents were injured, and eleven RNA members were arrested. Lumumba, away from the office during the altercation and arrests, returned to Detroit to finish law school. In the early 1980s, he again moved to Jackson, now to practice law (defending black activists in high-profile cases, among other things) and to continue working for African American self-determination. By then, "black people's movements had moved from the phase of just merely turning the other cheek in the face of attacks and egregious repression to actually declaring the right to self-defense, under the inspiration of Malcolm X," he says. "And that certainly was the position that we took. . . . We weren't going to be victimized. We came in peace, but we came prepared."

Marshall Ganz, in the meantime, had joined Cesar Chavez's United Farm Workers as an organizer in 1965. He stayed with that union for sixteen years, becoming its director of organizing and an elected member of its national executive board. After working with grassroots groups on organizing strategies and voter mobilization throughout the 1980s, he went back to school in the early 1990s to earn his PhD. Today, Ganz, a leading thinker on political organizing, is concerned, he says, by some of what he sees. Though there's no shortage of mobilizations, especially as digital communications and social media make it easy and cheap to get lots of people out for protests and rallies, "what such mobilization is *not* doing is bringing those people into relationship with each other." Instead, he says, there's an "aggregation of a lot of individual voices, through mouse clicks, or through presence at a rally, but it doesn't connect them to each other. The collective capacity necessary to really build power isn't built."

You can get "a bunch of people to turn out" for a protest, he says, but when "there's nothing behind it, no capacity to strategize and no infrastructure," there's no momentum to carry anything forward. People leave the rally or march as quickly as they show up, and "nothing happens," says Ganz. "Mobilizing is not the same thing as organizing." In contrast with many of today's mobilizations, he points to the 1963 March on Washington. That, he says, "was the result of ten years of organizing, of bringing people together at local levels, at state levels, and actually building the capacity through relationships, through organizational structure, leadership strategy, and all the rest."

Today, Ganz says, it's right-wing movements that seem to be best at organizing. The National Rifle Association, he notes, has fifteen thousand local gun clubs all over America, in every legislative district, in every state, "so they have really been organizing, they have an organized base of constituency that is the foundation for their political influence and their power." That's what's needed on the progressive side, he says, "organizing at the base and engaging people in real learning." And part of that, he says—again invoking the NRA (and the civil rights movement too)—is to develop strategies for working with government, from both outside and inside. Progressive activists neglect government at their peril, he says. Especially today, with Trump's "wrecking crew dismantling government when it comes to environment, education, corporate regulation, everything," progressives need "to come up with an account of why government is good, not bad, why corporations are not the solution to everything" (a point underlined by the current pandemic crisis, as noted earlier).

This is precisely what Chokwe Lumumba would end up doing in Jackson. In 2009, he ran for election to city council (with support from the Malcolm X Grassroots Movement he helped create) and won. Then, in 2013, he ran again, this time to become mayor, and won again, now firm in his belief that "one of the routes to self-determination is to use the governmental slots in order to accumulate the political power that we can, and then to demand more, and to build more." Gaining electoral power is "necessary" for progressives, he believes, albeit "not sufficient to win our struggle." On its own, political office can do little, he says. But in concert, and sometimes tension, with grassroots movements, it can be a potent part of progressive struggles.

Once he became mayor, Lumumba established the Jackson People's Assembly, so that citizens could "challenge government, ask government questions, get informed by government, and protest government when necessary." He also fostered links with activist organizations, particularly Cooperation Jackson, a group that, according to its website, aims to "organize and empower the structurally under- and unemployed sectors of the working class, particularly from black and Latino communities, to build worker-organized and -owned cooperatives," and ultimately to "replace the current socioeconomic system of exploitation, exclusion and the destruction of the environment with a proven democratic alternative." Cooperation Jackson has, among other things, bought vacant lots and abandoned buildings for a community land trust, created urban farms to provide jobs and affordable produce, built affordable and sustainable housing, and helped create solar and green energy cooperatives. The group was well-prepared and highly effective in creating mutual aid networks during the pandemic.

Lumumba saw his mayoralty as one piece, an important one, for "creating a positive, progressive movement across the borders of the United States and internationally," while he was also well aware of the limits of municipal politics. "We know that the problem is that too few people control too many of the resources that people live on, and that's why you have your big gap between haves and have-nots," he said. "We can have influence on trying to stop these corporations from discriminating on various different levels, but we don't have the ability to police that completely, because we're just a city."

When Lumumba died of a heart attack in February 2014, just months after taking office, his son Chokwe Antar Lumumba, who had worked with him closely, lost the special election held to replace him. But he won the next general election in June 2017 with 93 percent of the vote and vowed upon taking office to continue his father's work. The people's assemblies were key to his plan. "I don't believe that we're going to bring Jackson into a better place because I have all of the ideas, but because we're willing as an administration to listen to other people," he says. (Recently he held an assembly to determine whom he should endorse in the 2020 primary: the people chose Bernie Sanders, so that was his choice.) And he also made it a central aim to encourage the creation of cooperative businesses (in partnership with Cooperation Jackson). More generally, his goal was (and is) to make Jackson "the most radical city on the planet . . . a model for other cities" and "an example of what government for the people can be."

Jackson has become a beacon of hope with Lumumba as mayor. Despite being in the heart of the Deep South, with a horribly racist past (sometimes present) and high levels of poverty and crime, the city now is a hub for both grassroots organizing and refashioning democratic institutions to be participatory and inclusive. No one, least of all Lumumba, claims it's all perfect, and some activists have broken ranks, saying change is not sufficiently swift. Nonetheless, today's Jackson shows that a new kind of democracy is possible, even in an unlikely place.

In 2018, Mayor Lumumba signed a letter to support another politician trying to do democratic government differently. The letter was "to the people of Barcelona" and urged them to reelect Ada Colau, their progressive mayor. Mayor Lumumba had a special connection to Mayor Colau. He had visited Barcelona—in the run-up to his election and then after becoming mayor—to see how she and her party were running their government and also, he says, to "talk with her about the cooperative businesses they'd developed." Colau was clearly an inspiration for Lumumba, as she would have been for his father, who likely would have agreed with her that "the most revolutionary thing we can do is to have a real democracy."

It's July 2013 and Ada Colau stands in the ornate lobby of a Barcelona bank shouting through a megaphone to the crowd of activists she's led to occupy it. "The president of the bank can make decisions, and until he arrives, we're not leaving!" The president never shows up, and Colau is dragged out of the bank by police, who then arrest her. Already a household name in Spain—having called a representative of the Spanish Banking Association "a criminal" at a nationally televised parliamentary hearing—Colau headed an organization, *Plataforma de Afectados por la Hipoteca* (PAH; Platform for People Affected by Mortgages), formed to assist Spanish homeowners losing and being evicted from their homes in the wake of the 2008 financial crisis. In addition to occupying banks, PAH rallied citizens to go to eviction sites and physically block police from enforcing orders, an effective strategy that, by drawing attention to the issue, also helped support Colau's efforts to secure better policies. "It was a very tough fight," Colau says in retrospect, "to stop home evictions and force the banks to negotiate with these families so they could keep their homes or, at minimum, not have a debt for life."

Two years earlier, on May 15, 2011, Colau, heeding social media calls to "take the cities, take the squares," joined thousands of others in Barcelona to protest government corruption and austerity. Deteriorating social conditions and crises had become endemic—youth unemployment was at 50 percent, people were facing eviction from their homes, and government corruption was rife. Citizens had had enough and came out in the tens of thousands. "The roads were stopped, and a lot of people didn't get to work, everything was at a stop, and suddenly things that normally don't happen did happen, and we were in the center of the media and the political agenda, and everybody was talking about it," says Álvaro Porro, a friend of Colau's and a fellow activist.

The Spanish protesters were inspired by recent uprisings in the Middle East, where large numbers of people had taken to the streets in Tunisia, Egypt, Syria, Yemen, and Bahrain to protest against dictators, repression, and poverty and to demand democratic reform. Together known as the Arab Spring, the uprisings were notable for their common tactic of occupying squares, for weeks and even months. That was emulated by the protesters in Barcelona (and other Spanish cities) where, after the first day of protest, a small group lingered in the main square and set up camp for the night. They were violently evicted by police. A video of harsh police tactics went viral, prompting hundreds more to join the initial group in the square the next night. The police responded with force again, another video went viral, and this time thousands came to the square. Over the next few days, more and more people joined them and set up encampments, occupying the square until police forcibly broke up the encampments five months later. The movement called itself Los Indignados, or 15-M for short (because it had begun on May 15).

Micah White, a student and activist living in the United States at the time, watched closely as events unfolded in Spain. He was struck by two things about 15-M and the Arab Spring before it—the new tactic of occupying streets and squares, rather than marching through them; and the fact that participants weren't just protesting against the way things were but had a vision about how things should be—they believed "true democracy, something that seemed impossible, was in fact within their reach." This was a pivotal moment, White thought. Something like 15-M and the Arab Spring could happen in the United States. "We could spark some sort of spiritual introspection in America, strive for a democracy in this country that's not run by corporate capitalism." He, together with *Adbusters* magazine publisher Kalle Lasn, with whom he worked, came up with a plan.

They began by crafting a "tactical briefing" that they sent to magazine subscribers and more broadly over the Internet. "A worldwide shift in revolutionary tactics is underway right now that bodes well for the future," the briefing began. A "fusion of Tahrir [Square, in Egypt] with the acampadas of Spain," the shift went beyond mere protesting to imagining what a new kind of democracy would look like. "We talk to each other in various physical gatherings and virtual people's assemblies, we zero in on what . . . would propel us toward the radical democracy of the future." And then the tactical part: "We go out and seize a square of singular symbolic significance and put our asses on the line to make it happen. On September 17, we want to see twenty thousand people flood into lower Manhattan, set up tents, kitchens, peaceful barricades and occupy Wall Street for a few months." The final sentence made it clear that the stakes were high. "It's time for DEMOCRACY, NOT CORPORATOCRACY. We're doomed without it."

"The moment was so ripe," says White. "Within twenty-four hours, activists in New York City just took up the idea and ran with it, made it their own." Enraged by the corporate reckless-ness and greed that had led to the 2008 crisis, and the fact that banks had been bailed out and no one had gone to jail—while millions of ordinary citizens lost homes, savings, and jobs—people were primed to protest. Occupy Wall Street crystallized their anger and quickly spread through the United States and beyond. And the tactics, borrowed from M-15 and the Arab Spring, made it clear that this was no ordinary protest. "Most people understood that marching in the streets hadn't worked," says White. "So, with Occupy Wall Street, it was suddenly like, 'Oh, maybe camping in the streets would work. No one's ever tried that before. Let's do it!'" As Michael Hardt observes, contrasting Occupy to the early-2000s anti-globalization marches, the encampments "were sedentary, they stayed still, they refused to move, that was what they were all about."

What truly made Occupy different, however, says Hardt, was its vision of what a new society should look like. "Protest and resistance are never enough," he says. "They're super-important. Everyone should feel the right to fight, the importance of being in the streets, resisting. That's essential, but at a certain point, protest has to be transformed into proposition, an alternative form of life, an alternative social world, an alternative way of being together." In that spirit, it was important to White, who previously had been a student of Hardt's, that people knew what they were protesting *for* as much as what they were protesting against. "So much of our lives is about the stories we tell ourselves," he says. "And corporations have done a very effective job at defining the limits of possibility and defining basically what we can expect out of life." With Occupy, he wanted to "wake people up," to "get them to dream again."

Occupy encampments were "participatory democracies in miniature," says Hardt. "That's why they felt so magical to everyone who participated." Decision-making was broadly distributed, social services provided—free medical care, food, child-care, and counseling—and lectures and seminars on offer. "They were trying to transform urban space into something we shared, to discover ways of managing it collectively," says Hardt. "They had general assemblies, often awkward, but partially successful ways of making collective decisions in relatively large groups." As one participant described it, Occupy was "a model for a new society, not a protest in the sense of being against something, but a way to formulate something new."

It was inevitable Occupy would come to an end. Several months after it started, encampments in cities around the world were broken up by police, often violently and sometimes brutally. For White, it was a difficult time, but also a moment of epiphany. Throughout his life, he says, he had been told and believed a story, that "if you can get large numbers of people into the streets, largely unified around a central demand, then you will achieve social change because your government will have to listen to you." At the end of Occupy, he "woke up and realized, This story is not true," recognizing, as Marshall Ganz insists, that mobilizing people, even in very large numbers, does not itself create social change. Occupy had millions of people in the streets, in eighty-two countries, protesting against economic injustice and imagining democratic alternatives. It was, says White, "the perfect example of the story line that we had been telling and were being told as activists, and it didn't create social change." There was an important lesson to be learned, he says.

Occupy was "a *constructive* failure," says White. "It failed to achieve the revolutionary change that we set out to achieve, but it taught us something very important—that we should not create social movements that just try to get people into the streets. We need to pair protests with gaining sovereignty, with winning elections."

White points to Spain's 15-M as a sharp reminder of that lesson. The timing of the movement was tied, in part, to the 2011 Spanish general election. A key belief of the protesters was that all parties running in the election, even the progressive ones, were part of the same corrupt order. None truly represented the people's will and needs. The movement's slogan, "They do not represent us," captured that notion and helped fuel a nation-wide boycott of the election. Widely observed, with large numbers of people staying home (or in the squares) on voting day, the boycott unwittingly helped Spain's main right-wing party win a landslide victory. "When the movement dissipated," says White, "a lot of activists in Spain realized, 'Oh, wow. I think we made a strategic blunder there!'"

Ada Colau agrees.

While she was occupying the square in Barcelona, Colau believed the 15-M slogan, "They do not represent us." "We were coming from a point of civil resistance in the face of the 2008 crisis," she says, and the slogan captured her sense that representative democracy was failing. "We shouted in the square that things could be different, it is all a matter of will," she says. Yet as the occupation dragged on and nothing changed—except that a right-wing party won the election—the whole experience of "collective power among citizens" in the square began to feel like "an experience of the limits of citizen empowerment." The thought nagged at her as she pursued her activist work on evictions after 15-M. And she began to wonder whether the next step might be "to achieve political power, to step forward and regain control of the public administration and recover what's ours, to control public resources to serve the interests of the people and make politics more democratic."

So she organized other activists, most of whom were skeptical about and had no experience in electoral politics, to try to "achieve in government what was being shouted in the streets, which was to make a deeper democracy possible." The group was joined by others—small-business owners, environmentalists, feminists, anarchists, socialists, immigration activists, and ordinary citizens—to form a new municipal political party, Barcelona en Comú. With loose ties to a national party, Podemos, also formed by 15-M activists (and currently part of Spain's governing coalition), Comú was to be like no other party, Colau says: "a diverse group of people," united by progressive inclinations and a strong desire "to change things, to make a different kind of politics, to fight corruption, open up government institutions, make them transparent and participatory, and create a more democratic process." The party ran a slate of candidates in the 2015 Barcelona election and Colau won, becoming Barcelona's first woman mayor.

From the start, Mayor Colau's plan was to break historic ties between Barcelona's government and the city's corporate elites, who had determined priorities and shaped policy for years. She was helped in that plan by the fact that she and her party had no such ties. She knew no one from corporate quarters, didn't have their numbers in her phone, didn't meet them for lunch or dinner, she told me. "I was never invited to their parties." She and her eleven Comú council members were "intruders" in the eyes of elites, she told me, which meant she could build relationships on a clean slate, without owing any debts or favors. And that's what she and her group did, approaching corporate interests not as subordinates, or even as equal partners with government, but from a premise of democratic sovereignty, one where "government decides the rules of the game, and leadership is in the public sector."

Equally important to diminishing business's influence over

government, says Colau, was increasing that of citizens and grassroots movements. "Active and critical citizens keep the government in check, demanding and mobilizing to change things. If there is more social pressure, we will get better. We need social pressure." It's a balance, she says. As mayor, she has to govern for the whole city and can't simply advance agendas of movements that helped put her in office. Which can be frustrating for members of those movements. "There are citizens who want more changes and want them faster, but we have a lot of limits. We are not going to have the revolution in two days in Barcelona." Still, she says, "we have been able to do things" and proudly lists off examples—disaster-relief measures for victims of austerity; weekly neighborhood town halls; refugee assistance programs; being first among Spanish cities in stopping home evictions and investing in social programs; reducing emissions and promoting green energy alternatives.

There's much more to do, says Colau. And the fight continues, in Barcelona and everywhere, between "those who want a democracy and the well-being of the majority with human rights as a priority, and those who want to make economic profit the grand mantra." But she's hopeful. "I will always have hope," she told me. "If I did not have hope, I would not be in politics. With these people—my people—I have seen we are capable of doing things others said were impossible; I will always carry this force in my heart."

In June 2019, Colau was reelected mayor of Barcelona for a second term. During her campaign, more than two hundred progressive luminaries from around the world—including Noam Chomsky, Vandana Shiva, Thomas Piketty, and Mayor Chokwe Antar Lumumba (as noted above)—had jointly penned an open letter to the people of Barcelona to endorse her candidacy. "Barcelona has become a beacon of hope," they wrote, "proving that we don't have to be afraid of standing up to corporate power. That there is another way of doing politics that puts people at the center."

Kshama Sawant, a leading voice in Occupy Seattle, found herself, like Colau, pondering the limits of protest when police cracked down on and ended the occupation she was part of. Fellow activists were bereft and didn't know what to do next, she says. "Let's just work for Obama now," many told her. "We have nothing else." Feeling that was a profound waste of the radical energy Occupy had sparked, she began thinking, again like Colau, that what was needed was "our own political voice in the halls of government." So she ran for city council with the aim of charting a new path in electoral politics, one that unambiguously broke ties with big business and was truly inclusive of all citizens and grassroots movements. With her signature issue, the $15 minimum wage, she was elected in 2013 (then reelected in 2016 and again in 2019).

Soon after her first election victory, Sawant says, two of her fellow council members came to her office and told her that while it was all well and good that she had roused the rabble and won the election, they and every other council member would oppose the $15 minimum wage plan. Sawant responded by organizing a grassroots campaign that brought together workers, unions, social justice advocates, and ordinary citizens to fight for the plan. And it worked. By the time her proposal was put to a vote, council members' unanimous opposition had shifted to unanimous support, and the $15 minimum wage became law. It's a lesson, Sawant says, in the importance of staying connected to the grass roots and using political office "as a sort of amplified voice for the movement." Though corporations had fought vociferously against the $15 minimum wage, "we won," she says, "because we changed the balance of power by building the grassroots campaign," thus proving, as history shows time and again, "that it's only a collective organized effort that can move mountains and make things happen."

Lobbyists from Seattle-based Amazon make a lot of visits and phone calls to the city council, says Sawant, "but never to my office." That's because, she says, they know where she stands. She has been a strong critic of the company, particularly its demands for regulatory and tax breaks from the city. No surprise, then, that Amazon spent $1.5 million to oppose Sawant's 2019 bid for reelection. She won anyway.

It's not easy, says Sawant, to run against the corporate grain of electoral politics. You need a strong political backbone to remain true to the people you represent—"the black and brown people who are impacted by police brutality, women who are impacted by sexual harassment in the workplace, the enormous numbers of workers who are struggling with poverty and homelessness through no fault of their own." You have to stand up not only to the corporate lobbyists but also to your political colleagues, the men and women sitting next to you on the dais, many of whom are influenced by those lobbyists. "And that can be uncomfortable." But there are great possibilities for electoral politics when de-linked from corporations and striving for broad participation, she says. People, especially young people, want change, she told me, and when they see that it can happen—that a $15 minimum wage, health care, mass transit, and affordable housing are political possibilities—they'll join the fight for that and more. "It raises their sights toward a different kind of society."

Until quite recently, at least in the United States, "activists shied away from electoral politics," observes the broadcast journalist Juan González, cohost of *Democracy Now!* "They saw themselves as perennial critics of the system but without assuming responsibility for implementing policies that would transform the system." Now that's changing, at least at the municipal level, and it's not just Lumumba, Colau, and Sawant. A wave of progressive victories is sweeping across the United States and beyond—a "new urban renaissance," as González describes it, that includes New York City, Newark, Chicago, Paris, Madrid, Montreal, Puerto Rico, Pittsburgh, Boston, Vancouver, Seattle, Minneapolis, Philadelphia, and, recently, Montgomery, Alabama. Typically, the party that comes to power is new, not expected to win, and openly committed to breaking cozy ties with corporations and using government authority and power to tackle inequality and other social and environmental ills.

"What's different about this movement," González says, "is not only that progressives have seen the necessity to actually capture office, but that once they get into office, they understand the necessity for continuing to be connected to the grassroots movements that got them there." In that spirit, Colau told me, while "traditional political parties tend to see social movements as a threat, I understand them as one of the city's main assets, one of its main treasures. It is with their demands and criticism, their demonstrations, and pressure in the streets, from outside of the government, that democracy has historically advanced. I shall listen to those engaged in activism in the city, because they are fighting for the common good, the rights of all of us."

Deep relationships between politicians and grassroots movements are a defining feature of the new model of democracy emerging in local politics. Activist politicians understand the limits of their positions as elected officials and welcome, rather than resist, pressure from movements and an active citizenry. As Colau observes, government "is just one part, in a series of parts, for bringing about change, and social movements are therefore needed, now more than ever." This is especially so, she says, because as mayor, she "cannot be an activist—I represent the city, and must manage the city, with all its limits and contradictions." As mayor, she has to work, for example, with banks and corporations rather than protest against them. And in that capacity, she says, she *needs* pressure from citizens and social movements, as it provides fuel for her efforts to ensure that "these business relationships ultimately advance public interests."

Micah White sees these new local experiments in participatory democracy as initial forays into what could become a revolutionary movement. "Revolutions always surprise us," he says. "I think the next wave of revolutions really is going to be this kind of strange thing where we wake up and we're like, 'Oh my gosh! There's this social moment! They're in the streets, but they're running election campaigns? They have candidates? And they're winning!?'" Cities, Colau believes, are the best place to start that revolution, because of the proximity between citizens and governments. "If democratic customs have to change, if the voice of the citizen must be heard," she says, "the place to do it is the city."

The "urban renaissance" shows a path forward as we consider how to rebuild in the wake of the pandemic crisis. It shows that existing democratic institutions can be made to work truly democratically and in synch with community forces at the grass roots—severed from corporate influence, prioritizing social concerns and environmental sustainability, ensuring public interests are protected and promoted, responsive to criticism, open to genuine participation by citizens, and accountable to them. As we pick up the pieces of a fractured economy, and ongoing climate and social crises, we can look to the successes of progressive city governments, noncorporate and activist in their orientations, as models for moving forward. No doubt there are limits on what city governments can do, given budgetary and legal constraints, yet, as Sawant says, "you've got to start somewhere"—though she also hopes "something similar could be possible on a larger scale."

Is it possible on a larger scale?

Chris Barrett is a thirtysomething tech entrepreneur living in a small New Jersey town near New York City. I first met him in the early 2000s as a character in the film I wrote and cocreated, *The Corporation.* He and his friend Luke McCabe had just made a media splash by seeking a corporation to sponsor their lives. "We saw Tiger Woods on TV with a hat with a Nike logo on it," Luke recounted in the film, "and we figured, you know, he probably gets like millions of dollars just to wear the hat at a press conference—we can do that for someone and hopefully get money so we can go to school." The two sent bids to different corporations, got a bite from First USA, and inked a deal with the bank that obliged it to pay their college tuition in exchange for, as Barrett describes it, "giving First USA a good name in the media, including them in our news stories, and giving them as much advertising as we can." The story was an apt metaphor for what would become a complete corporate takeover of our lives.

When recently I caught up with Barrett, he told me he hadn't realized "the magnitude of what we were doing" until he saw *The Corporation.* "My mind just kind of exploded," he says. "It opened my eyes." By then, he and Luke had cut ties with First USA, feeling the bank had treated them badly—by, for example, not making tuition payments—which only confirmed, Barrett says, "how psychopathic First USA was." The experience, along with the film, led him to develop "a progressive and anti-corporate mindset," he says. That in turn drew him, in 2008, to Barack Obama's campaign. "I saw this man speak and it was incredible. I'd never witnessed anything like that in my entire life."

But Barrett was ultimately disappointed by Obama, like so many progressives during and after his presidency. While Obama did do some important things in office and was always a beacon of grace and intelligence, he ultimately failed to challenge, and indeed fully embraced, the market- and corporate-led orthodoxy of previous decades. Surrounding himself with Wall Street and Silicon Valley magnates and for the most part following their advice, he allowed during his presidency corporations to get bigger, economic power to become more concentrated, the rich to get richer, and the poor to get poorer. He did little to curb monopolies (particularly in tech, airlines, big food, pharma, and agriculture), and his centerpiece health-care policy, the Afford-able Care Act, stopped short of replacing private insurance mar-kets with a public system. He championed privatization and market solutions for education and for environment and climate issues, favoring, for the latter, carbon trading and offsets.

"There was an opportunity in 2008 when Obama was elected," says Farhad Manjoo. "The market had crashed, it was an oppor-tunity to reeducate the public about government. Obama chose not to do that. He went in a different direction. And I think it was a missed opportunity." People were losing homes and jobs at rates and in numbers reminiscent of the Great Depression. "Obama might have found widespread public appetite for the sort of aggressive, interventionist restructuring of the Ameri-can economy that Franklin D. Roosevelt conjured with the New Deal," says Manjoo. But, "rather than try for a Rooseveltian home run, he bunted." Reflecting the cant of a Democratic Party that had long abandoned its historical (at least during the twen-tieth century) mission to fight concentrations of economic power and promote social good for ordinary people, Obama embraced the "new" corporation catechism of small government and big markets rather than its New Deal opposite.

Disappointed by Obama, Barrett looked for a 2016 candidate who truly reflected his progressive values. "I was having lunch with my grandfather, and I asked him who should the Democratic nominee be. And he told me Bernie Sanders looks pretty good," Barrett recalls. "I hadn't really heard of him, so when I went home and researched his platform, I realized that I align with a lot that Bernie says." Barrett went to New Hampshire, where the primary campaign was in full swing, joined People for Bernie, and became an assistant fundraising manager. He'd noticed how in that state drivers would often pay for the person waiting behind them at tollbooths. He found it "mind-blowing," and it gave him an idea. "I came up with 'Bern It Forward,' where people could donate one dollar on behalf of their friends directly to Bernie Sanders's campaign." He created a sub-Reddit platform for donations based on that model and raised more than $10 million for the campaign.

What moved Barrett most during Sanders's campaign, he says, was how inspired and mobilized people were around progressive ideas and values. Like Lumumba, Colau, and Sawant, Sanders built on Occupy and other social movements to offer a progressive vision of society rooted in socially proactive government that meets people's needs and reins in corporate power. He flat-out rejected the market-led policies and diminishment of government of previous decades, and, drawing on Occupy's public criticism of corporate greed, he called out banks and big business, clearly tagging them as the problem, not the solution. His platform represented a massive and unambiguous rejection—unprecedented in post–World War II America—of market-led policy. That, and also inspiring a wave of progressives to run for office—including Chris Barrett—will be his legacies, regardless of losing to Hillary Clinton in 2016 and to Joe Biden in 2020. "It's common to say now that the Sanders campaign failed," as Noam Chomsky describes it. "That's a mistake. . . . It was an extraordinary success, completely shifted the arena of debate and discussion. Issues that were unthinkable a couple years ago are now right in the middle of attention."

Barrett had been devastated by Sanders's loss in 2016. "I needed to regroup," he says. "We thought we were in control of our future, and that was just ripped away from us." However, he says, "I didn't want to just sit back and let the evil powers in this world take control." Sanders, almost immediately after losing, began encouraging his followers to seek political office—to get on ballots for elections at all levels, local school boards, city councils, state legislatures, and so on. Barrett was one of the thousands who heeded the call. "I met a local political organizer in my hometown of Collingswood, New Jersey," he says. "He was putting together a slate of progressive candidates to run against the current Democratic county committee members in our town. I thought that was a brilliant idea, exactly what Bernie wanted us to do. I signed the form, we were running for office, and I won."

Barrett told me he could never have realized when he was seeking a corporate sponsorship and being filmed for *The Corporation* that fifteen years later he would be an elected official in New Jersey. He finds political office challenging and is coming to understand its limits as well as its possibilities. "Being on the inside is not easy," he says, echoing Lumumba, Colau, and Sawant. He is hopeful change will come but believes it will take time. "It's a long-term play for us," he says. "It might not be in the next election, but at some point we will have a progressive president. The Democratic Party will be the progressive party of the future. The next wave is happening."

Understanding what's currently ailing democracy helps shine a light on what needs to be done to change things. In particular, it helps us see why widening and deepening democracy, as Barrett, Lumumba, Sanders, Colau, Sawant, and so many others are trying to do, is not only possible but necessary. Within weeks of the coronavirus pandemic hitting the shores of the United States and other advanced capitalist societies, the profound injustices and inadequacies of current systems became painfully clear. Medical systems struggled. Poor people and precarious workers suffered disproportionately. Corporations that had avoided taxes, cut workers, fought unions, cheated consumers, and squandered record profits on stock buybacks got bailouts. And governments, which had responded to corporations' calls over the last forty years to retreat from robust roles in protecting public interests, found themselves woefully ill-prepared to deal with the crisis.

The shock of the pandemic put in plain view the precariousness of democratic institutions. But it's important to remember—things were already precarious before it hit.

Over the last decade, right-wing political movements gained power and traction around the world as citizens elected demagogues who openly flouted constitutional democracy, professed racism and xenophobia, and strengthened ties between governments and big business. Now pundits wring their hands—especially in the United States, with a president and supporters, including the Senate majority, seemingly blind to basic constitutional principles—and they wonder how it is that so many people can be so unconcerned about, and indeed complicit in, what appears to be a massive assault on democracy.

One answer, as I suggest in the previous chapter, is that people are angry, and legitimately so. Their lives have deteriorated badly over the last forty years. They've been neglected and left behind as a result of corporate-instigated rollbacks of job protections and social programs. Frustrated by shrinking resources, less social security, and greater vulnerability, some are swayed by hate-spouting demagogues, while others, perhaps not drawn by the hate, nonetheless tolerate it, believing that only "strong" and "non-elite" leaders can deliver the change that's needed. In the meantime, core principles of constitutional democracy lose their purchase, overshadowed by people's struggles to make ends meet, and their angry sense of being beaten down and betrayed.

The "new" corporation movement bears some responsibility for this. Recall the ideas and programs that it's pressed. Corporations should fill voids left by retreating governments. They are efficient, effective, caring, and conscientious, able to meet people's needs, protect the environment, and solve the world's problems. Governments are, on the other hand, inept, corrupt, bloated, paralyzed by partisanship, and unresponsive. Over the years, these messages, nicely wrapped in conscientious rhetoric, have helped corporations push for and justify rollbacks of public oversight and provision of social goods. The effect on the ground has been to diminish government's presence and relevance in people's daily lives and its capacity to deal with their needs, including during times of crisis.

Which suggests another reason, beyond anger, why people have become disenchanted with democracy in recent years. When governments retreat as they have done, when they no longer care about people, it's logical people would stop caring about them. Why should we worry about lofty constitutional principles—whether, for example, it's all right for a president to ask a foreign power to dig up dirt on a political rival—when those principles, and the governments they bind, have no apparent bearing on our lives? The point is, a reason people are giving up on democracy—supporting patently antidemocratic, and even autocratic, movements and governments—may be that democracy has given up on them. This is not a happy thought. Indeed, it's truly unsettling. But on the positive side, it provides clues for how to move forward.

By corollary to the above, it seems reasonable to suggest that for democracy to work, it has to be working for people, tangibly. While democratic principles and institutions are necessary, they are not sufficient. Democracy needs a *social* element too, a positive, proactive, and protective presence in people's lives. "The system that we have now isn't really working for anybody, as huge inequalities harm people in so many ways," says the legal scholar Ray Madoff. "We need a reason to fall in love again with government, and with the things that government can do." And that, I suggest, is where solutions lie. Not to have less government. But to have more. In other words, infusing democracy with a social element may be necessary for its very survival. That seems to be the lesson from the precarious place it's now in.

What's needed, then, is a new and deeper kind of democracy than what we have become used to—the participatory, inclusive, and social kind discussed above. Government has to be made more relevant in people's lives, more open to their participation, and more responsive to their needs and demands. "We need to get back to what my mom taught me about when I was little, which is how FDR saved society with his New Deal," says Elizabeth May, former leader of the Green Party of Canada. "An engaged citizenry in a democracy can change policy, change society; if we want equity, if we want social justice, and if we want to avoid global average temperature increase getting above 1.5 degrees Celsius, we have to take control of the levers of power, take them away from corporations." The good thing is, that's starting to happen. Until recently, social movements were more interested in building power in the streets and neglected running for office. But now "they are starting to see the nature of power, where it lies, and the reason to contest it," as the commentator Jonathan Tasini describes it. "There has not been in a long time this kind of progressive energy, the kinds of numbers of people who want to run for office, want to become involved in movements, who understand that there's a crisis."

It's telling that just over half of American millennials say they're skeptical about capitalism, while 61 percent report responding positively to the word "socialism." More generally, 43 percent of Americans agree that socialism would be good for the country (among Democrats, that number is 57 percent), and polls consistently show majority support for health care as a right, free college tuition, and a tax system that doesn't benefit the rich. All of which helps explain Vice President Mike Pence's felt need to cajole conservative youth in a recent address to resist the "siren song of socialism" and Jamie Dimon's warning that socialism "would be a disaster for our country" and that it "inevitably produces stagnation, corruption, and often worse."

The point is, progressive politics are trending strongly in the United States. There are local electoral successes like those canvassed above. Sanders's broad support in 2016 and 2020 (despite the outcomes). Election victories in congressional districts (like those of Representatives Alexandria Ocasio-Cortez, Rashida Tlaib, Ilhan Omar, Ayanna Pressley, and Katie Porter). And more than one hundred democratic socialists currently holding office in the United States, across school boards, city councils, and state legislatures (importantly, the latter as *democratic* socialists, who reject central planning and accept markets and for-profit corporations but prescribe strong oversight by regulators and unions and provision of public goods by government).

It's difficult to predict where it all goes. But what seems clear is that progressive energy has become a force for creating new ways to do democracy, ones that have that needed *social* element. The coronavirus pandemic has underlined just how important that element is, and it may be propelling us toward it. In the United States, the moment hearkens back to Franklin D. Roosevelt fighting concentrated wealth and corporate power during the Great Depression. No surprise, then, that Representative Ocasio-Cortez would call her sweeping plan for change a Green New Deal (GND), an obvious homage to Roosevelt's New Deal. Like its predecessor, Ocasio-Cortez's plan is all about breaking the stranglehold of market-led policy and championing the kind of socially proactive government we so clearly need.

The GND includes, among other things, rights to high-quality health care; affordable, safe, and adequate housing; economic security; clean water and clean air; healthy and affordable food; access to nature; and quality education. It supports and protects unions and guarantees good jobs. It demands respect for the sovereignty, land, and treaties of indigenous peoples and aspires to end historic oppression of "frontline and vulnerable communities." It calls for eliminating pollution, achieving net-zero greenhouse gas emissions, restoring and protecting natural ecosystems, and relying 100 percent on clean and renewable energy. Finally, it proposes participatory and inclusive democratic processes and collaboration with grassroots groups. It's as much a new paradigm for democratic governance as it is a program of policies and principles.

At this point, the Green New Deal is only a plan. The real question is how to make it, or something like it, real.

The last decade has seen a remarkable rise of resistance to corporate rule and values, fueled by visions of deeper democracy, greater equality, and true environmental sustainability. The 2011 movement of the squares (including Occupy), indigenous movements for self-determination, Black Lives Matter, Me Too, Idle No More, anti-austerity movements around the world, progressive electoral victories and momentum, protests against pipelines and other extractive megaprojects, teachers' strikes against privatization, water de-privatization movements, student strikes against climate change, and on and on—nearly everywhere, people are pushing back against corporate rule and impunity.

This chapter argued that protest is not enough, that electoral movements are needed to put sovereign power behind the values and energy people express in the streets. The pandemic crisis underlines the importance of socially proactive government. But none of that means protest and other kinds of action outside of government—such as mutual aid, community building, and grassroots organizing—aren't also necessary. Grand Chief Stewart Phillip, who has led marches, vigils, occupations, and blockades for indigenous self-determination and environmental justice, told me that what happens in the streets and in grassroots movements is "an essential part of the democratic process." But it's not enough, he said. "We also need more direct engagement in formal political processes."

Strong and active social movements, involved in organizing, educating, and protesting, are crucial for broadening support and pressuring governments. Electoral politics must also be a key site of struggle, however. As already noted, in decades past, activists tended to shy away from such politics, viewing government as part of the problem, not the solution. That's why the new wave of progressive electoral movements is notable, exciting, and necessary. It's the reason I focused on those movements. But in no way does that deny the need for the hard work of organizing for change at the grass roots.

Both activism and electoral politics are necessary. Neither is sufficient. It's the synergy between them that holds great promise and gives reason for hope.

AFTERWORD

No matter that men in the hundreds of thousands disfigured the land on which they swarmed, paved the ground with stones so that no green things could grow, filled the air with fumes of coal and gas, lopped back all the trees, and drove away every animal and every bird: spring was still spring.

—Leo Tolstoy, *Resurrection,* 1899

TODAY, AS I WRITE THESE WORDS, the sun shines brightly outside. Flowers crowd against fences, grasses push up through sidewalk cracks, bees buzz, and songbirds sing (though more quietly than last year). The coming of spring, Leo Tolstoy wrote in words following the above passage, is testament to nature's resilience against industrialism's destructive force. But Tolstoy went on to warn that that unnatural force could ultimately prevail, not least because people too often "consider sacred and important . . . not the spring morning . . . not the beauty which inclines the heart to peace and love and concord . . . [but] their own devices for wielding power over their fellow men."

This book examined one such device, the publicly traded business corporation, and revealed that its destructive push to dominate and exploit is rooted in a pathologically self-interested nature. That it's seduced us to believe it is conscientious and benevolent. That we've dropped our guard as a result. And that, like fog rolling into a city, corporations and their values have crept into the cores of our lives and societies. With disastrous results.

The solution I proposed, to reinvigorate and deepen democracy—to ensure it controls corporations rather than being controlled by them—is hardly precise. My purpose is to suggest a path forward that is promising and realistic, not a detailed and exact plan. History shows that attempts at the latter typically fail, and sometimes horrifically. Ultimately, "the people" must decide what our collective fate and future should be. My job, along with that of so many others, is to provide insights and ideas that may help along the way. And I hope I've done that. The coronavirus pandemic adds special urgency to the book's arguments, which connect to and are illustrated by its every dimension—its causes and origins in environmental degradation, its harsher effects on poor and vulnerable people, the woefully inadequate responses from government, and also, of course, the broad questioning of corporate rule and values it has inspired.

"So much of our lives is about the stories we tell ourselves," Micah White told me. "Corporations have done a very effective job at defining the limits of possibility, defining what we think, what we can expect out of life." The corporation is capitalism's main vehicle for telling, and bringing to fruition, its overarching story, which goes something like this: Human beings are self-interested and competitive. We find happiness and worth in what, and how much, we own and consume. Corporations should be free to pursue profit as they wish. They are accountable to their shareholders and bound by market dictates. Governments should stay out of their way—they are neither needed nor wanted as regulators (though welcome, of course, when they help advance corporate agendas).

"New" corporations tell an attractive version of the story, one that features concerns about people and planet. But it's really just a veneer, as I've shown. And its ultimate effect, as I've also shown, is to sustain the same old ideas and practices. However, there is some hope in the fact that "new" corporations feel they *have* to tell that story. Though it obscures truth and justifies expanding the corporation's domain, the fact that so many people *want* the story to be told reveals the broad appeal of its values. People may mistakenly believe corporations can genuinely serve those values, but that's a problem of analysis, not of heart and soul. The fact that they want to work for, buy from, and manage and invest in corporations that care about humanity and the planet says something. They may be following the wrong star, going in the wrong direction. But there's hope in their quest.

Throughout all of history's bloodshed and horror, we, as human beings, have striven for higher purpose, some truth about what it means to be human. Across societies, in every era, through art, music, literature, religion, and the teachings of great leaders, poets, and philosophers, the same story is told and retold. That we try to be good to one another, struggle against corruption and injustice, work together to create communities where everyone can flourish, believe it's better to share than to take, to care for than exploit, to nourish the Earth rather than extract from it, to be compassionate rather than competitive. That story is, of course, the opposite of corporate capitalism's story, contradicted on every count.

As Grand Chief Stewart Phillip told me, four hundred million indigenous people around the world share a common spiritual belief that is "diametrically opposed to the corporate values of capitalism." They believe, he said, that "we have universal responsibilities to protect and defend Mother Earth, and to protect our people, not to exploit for profit until there's nothing left." Pope Francis similarly extols the "relationship of mutual responsibility between human beings and nature" and blames current world ills on the fact that "economic powers continue to justify the current global system where priority tends to be given to speculation and the pursuit of financial gain," while people too often view themselves as "masters, consumers, and ruthless exploiters." Mayor Ada Colau told me we have to resist corporations' story that "human beings are self-interested, that 'man is a wolf to man,' a subliminal message to make us accomplices in a determined state of things."

What unites those who fight for change today is refusal to be those accomplices and also the belief that a different way is possible. Change tends to happen, Micah White told me, when things appear to be at their worst, when "people are all disappointed, getting discouraged. Revolutions always come as a surprise." The political commentator Heather McGhee recounted how in recent history, her ancestors were enslaved, people routinely died on the job, unions were illegal, and women couldn't vote. Yet over time, movements of ordinary people rose up and fought successfully for change. "I think we are in the midst of another one of those movements right now," she says. Michael Hardt told me that "even when you think nothing is happening, nothing is possible, something beautiful and inspiring comes up; people aren't going to stop imagining better futures and fighting for them. People always fight."

No doubt in today's world there's plenty of cause for pessimism and despair. But pessimism is surrender, and despair defeat. Which is why Mayor Colau is right when she says, "The most revolutionary thing to do today is to have hope."

Yet as Colau well knows, hope is not enough. Work is also necessary. That was Marshall Ganz's point. Social change doesn't happen without the hard work of organizing. Mobilizing is never enough. Nor is protest. There also has to be a proposition—a vision of a better society—as Michael Hardt reminds us. And, as Micah White insists, our ambitions should be to create and be a part of government, not just to protest what governments do. By emphasizing stories about activists who chose to go into politics, like Colau and others, I do not in any way diminish all the other ways through which people resist corporate rule—the organizing, protesting, litigation, union activism, activist art and literature, teaching, researching, alternative media, and so on. These are all vitally necessary. But they're not enough. For systemic change to happen, we, "the people," need to gain the sovereign power democracy theoretically bestows upon us.

And that requires, at a minimum, breaking the monopoly on power currently held by corporations and economic elites. You can't do that by letting "new" corporations take the lead as change agents. That only boosts their power and diminishes democracy—and it doesn't work anyway, as I've argued throughout. The solution has to be political—to organize, campaign, work in social movements and unions, form new political parties and change existing ones, register people to vote, and run for office. No doubt creating a just and sustainable world is going to take a lot of work. But that's what being a citizen demands. And it's within our grasp.

Those are the final words in the manuscript I submitted to my publisher in early 2020. By the time I got the copyedited version back, everything had changed. Over those six weeks, a coronavirus epidemic had become a global pandemic, millions of people were ill, many had died, and the world and its economy were shutting down. All of which leads me to this final thought: Change is not only within our grasp. It's crucial for our survival.

What we have been doing to one another and to the planet cannot go on. The terrible truth is that corporate capitalism, especially that of the last forty years, is killing us. It's killing whole species. Killing the air, water, and earth. Killing compassion and justice. Killing our human values and democracy. The pandemic and its effects are a particular form of this killing, part of the larger cascade of crises that are currently unfolding.

Corporations may have propelled innovation over the last century, making lives better through new technologies, medical discoveries, transportation advances, and the like. But for the last forty years they have overplayed their hand. They pushed to scuttle the social state, leaving vast numbers of people struggling daily to survive. They pushed for impunity to fuel climate change, pollute the air, clog oceans with plastics, and destroy forests and species (increasing the risk of deadly pandemics, among other things). They pushed back against democracy on every front and fostered a new wave of authoritarianism. And they did all these things because, institutionally, that's what they're designed to do. It's no surprise they've done what they have. The tragedy is that we let them.

Humanity and the planet are on a perilous path as a result. Indeed, we're likely careening toward destruction. The coronavirus crisis is a sample of what's to come if we don't change things, and fast. It's a wake-up call, at least for those who need to be woken to the fact that we're in crisis. For most of humanity, that's old news. Crisis is their normal. Whether because they are displaced from homes by climate change–driven floods, fires, or hurricanes or by foreclosing banks, or they had no home to begin with. Or they're sick without medical insurance or paid leave. Or because of air pollution, or poisoned water, or the vicissitudes of hard lives. Or they're impoverished and malnourished, whether in wealthy or poor countries. Or they lack access to water, electricity, education, and decent housing. Or they're victims of violence, because they are women, or racialized, or indigenous, or sexual minorities. Crisis upon crisis, a chronic presence. That was the lot for most people on the planet before the pandemic hit.

Change was urgently needed then. And now we need to make it happen in the pandemic's wake. Crisis can no longer be denied, not even by those whose privilege shielded them from it before. The pandemic has taught us that borders do not contain crises— not borders of countries, nor of wealth and privilege. The health and well-being of everyone determines that of everyone else. The state of the natural environment and climate impacts everyone. All the technology in the world cannot stave off global catastrophe. Self-interest, individualism, competition, and commoditization must be tempered rather than exalted. Collective and cooperative action is needed to solve the world's problems. Our fates and futures are common and interdependent. Social solidarity is imperative, not optional.

Everyone is scared about this pandemic, everyone impacted. Everyone is saying, "Something needs to be done, now, to stop this!" And that's true. Something does need to be done. But it has to be something more than just solving the current crisis, as important as that is. Going back to the previous "normal" is not an option. For humanity to survive, let alone flourish, we need to fight for larger change, to create a different and better world.

On May 25, 2020, George Floyd was killed at the hands of four police officers in Minneapolis. This book was on its way to the printer, but I was able to add these final thoughts.

———

The fight to create a different and better world gains new urgency as citizens across the globe pour into the streets to protest racial injustice. Though ignited by the brutal police killing of George Floyd, these protests are about much more. Modern corporate capitalism is rooted in racist oppression and colonialism. Its rise reflected the prevailing idea at the time that nonwhites are less than fully human—the same twisted logic advanced to justify slavery, genocidal policies, and land grabs from indigenous peoples, and slave-like conditions for workers in colonial territories. The great corporate fortunes of early capitalism—imperial companies like the Dutch East India Company and the Hudson's Bay Company, as well as slave traders, banks, and industrial empires—were thus forged from white supremacist beliefs and practices.

The fact is, modern corporate capitalism was built on foundations of dehumanizingly racist doctrines and practices. In the United States and other places, for example, "the original capital was provided by the labor of slaves," as Angela Davis notes. "The Industrial Revolution, which pivoted around the production of capital, was enabled by slave labor." And the echoes of that past, and colonialism more generally, reverberate ever-louder today.

The same racialized groups who, not so long ago, were enslaved, dispossessed, and brutally exploited, including African Americans in the United States, now are overrepresented among the underpaid and underemployed, more likely to be threatened and unsafe in their lives and work, poorer, less healthy, ill-housed, deprived of basic necessities, exploited by multinational companies seeking cheap and exploitable labor, and toiling as migrant workers in slave-like conditions. They're over-incarcerated, over-policed and criminalized, too often slain by police and military, inordinately made ill and killed by industrial and workplace pollution, and most vulnerable to the ravages of climate change. Indigenous peoples around the world suffer from all of that, as well as being evicted from their territories to make way for extractive projects that waste their lands.

The ongoing worldwide protests sparked by George Floyd's unjust death are helping lay bare the systemic roots of racism. As outrage spreads, movements like Black Lives Matter build upon past movements and are, in turn, built upon by new movements across the globe. Racist horrors and injustices, lived and suffered by racialized peoples for centuries, are thrust powerfully into the light of public scrutiny.

Most "new" corporations have joined in, proclaiming solidarity with protesters and social movements. And while their leaders' avowals and promises to help are likely sincere, the fact remains (as I've argued throughout) that corporations can only do such *good* as will help them do *well*—a profound limit on how (and how much) good they do. And even worse, an obfuscation of their predilection to do *bad*—to, in this case, promote racial *in*justice.

Just look at what corporations do. They campaign for cuts to taxes, regulation, and spending and thus undermine policies designed to foster racial equality—human rights protections, antipoverty programs, workers' rights, job and income security, social services, public schools, health care and housing, pay equity, and anti-discrimination measures. They lobby for laws that facilitate exploitation of migrant workers. They push for megaprojects—mines, pipelines, oil fields, and industrial farms—that dispossess indigenous peoples and destroy their lands and ways of life, campaign for trade deals that facilitate harsh exploitation of workers in the Global South and the abandonment of those in the Global North, lobby to ensure pollution and climate-altering emissions (both of which inordinately impact the racialized poor) are weakly regulated, if at all. Through such actions, "new" corporations foster new forms of colonialism, ones that converge synergistically with old forms of racism.

That is the world in which George Floyd was killed. Minneapolis, like other large American cities, is beset with increasing—and increasingly racialized—poverty, a product, in large part, of those market-led policies that corporations have promoted for years. Such poverty inevitably foments social crisis. And rather than addressing that with robust social provision—the route corporations steadfastly oppose—harsher policing has been the answer. "Public schools, public hospitals, public libraries, all of the things that make a city function . . . have been systematically defunded, increasingly privatized," notes the Princeton University professor and commentator Dr. Keeanga-Yamahtta Taylor. "And the way that cities manage the inevitable crises that arise from that, when combined with unemployment . . . poverty . . . evictions and all of the insecurities that we see wracking cities across this country: the police are used to manage that crisis." Racialized poverty is thus criminalized.

Today's protests are challenging that and the broader dynamics of injustice informing it. They are puncturing myths and seeking change. "This is America's moment of reckoning," as the Harvard University professor and commentator Dr. Cornel West describes it. "The catalyst was certainly Brother George Floyd's public lynching, but the [broader context is the] failure of the predatory capitalist economy to provide the satisfaction of the basic needs of food and health care and quality education, jobs with a decent wage. . . . [It's a system] obsessed with money, money, money, domination of workers, marginalization of those who don't fit." The current wave of protests is widening the flow of global movements for changing that and quickening its pace. Rooted in justifiably rebellious rage, it holds promise for something larger. "All of this rebellious energy, it's got to be channeled through organizations rooted in a quest for truth and justice," says West. "Rebellion is not the same thing as revolution. What we need is a nonviolent revolutionary project of full-scale democratic sharing—power, wealth, resources, respect, organizing—and fundamental transformation."

Amen to that.

ACKNOWLEDGMENTS

MANY HELPED ME WRITE THIS BOOK, in so many different ways. My deepest gratitude to all of you. Rebecca Jenkins, my soul mate, muse, and trusted editor was with me every step of the way, her love a constant support, her wisdom a guiding light, her editing deepening the ideas and prose. Myim Bakan Kline improved the work with insights from his formidable intellect and inspired me with his steadfast belief in the power of ideas and reason. Sadie Jenkins Wade's deep intelligence and empathy showed that the solidaristic vision underlying this work is realizable. Paul Bakan offered research and sage advice on drafts, along with love and confidence. He, along with my deceased mother, Rita Bakan, were intellectual mentors, teaching me to value what's important in life and to be skeptical but never cynical. Marlee Kline gifted me with her love and so much else, including the knowledge that intellectual work is not an end in itself but a means for creating a better world.

My editor at Vintage, Andrew Weber, improved the book

with his writerly instincts, fierce intelligence, and strong sense of what's right, both in writing and life. Diane Turbide, my Canadian editor, strongly supported the project from the start and encouraged me throughout. My agent, Jonathon Lyons, recognized the book's importance early on and worked tirelessly to persuade others of that view.

Family members (other than those already mentioned) offered love, support, and encouragement: Laura Bakan and Derryck Smith, Michael Bakan and Megan Bakan, Pauline Westhead, Marilyn Jenkins, Carol and Terry Kline, Eleanor Feirestein, John and Glenna Jenkins, Ellen and Peter Colley, Carol Jenkins and Philip Tietze, Lucia Jenkins and Bob Cox, Ruth Jenkins, Ronnie Kline and Ruth Buckwold, Sandy Kline, Danny and Nina Bakan, Reg Eddy, Markus Wade, and Ric Chin, all my nieces and nephews: Isaac and Leah, Adina and Zevi, Adam, Jackie, Sandy, Morgan, and Martha, Celina and Naomi. Sky (aka "Bunty"), my canine companion, bolstered my spirits with her love and loyalty.

Peter Roeck, who edited the companion film, provided friendship and support, and contributed, along with my codirector, Jennifer Abbott, to the ideas and research. The film's producers, Betsy Carson and Trish Dolman, gave logistical support, as did other members of the production team: Adam McKay, Ian Kerr, Kate Kroll, and Larry DiStefano. Several researchers did invaluable work: Grace Nosek, Catherine Higgens, Alexandra Chapman, Andrew Williamson, Stefan Labbe, Rachel Judkins, and Sophie Woodrooffe. Friends read drafts, offered insights, discussed ideas, and helped in other ways: John Fellas, Ken and Reva Davidson, Andrew Petter, Maureen Maloney, Sarah Polley, David Sandomierski, Patrick Macklem, Bruce Ryder, David Schneiderman, Julie DiLorenzo, and Peter Dauvergne. The many people interviewed for the book and film were generous with their time and ideas, which greatly enriched both works.

Mark Achbar deserves special mention, as it was with him that this project, and its predecessor, got started.

The Allard School of Law, University of British Columbia (UBC), and especially Dean Catherine Dauvergne and other cherished colleagues, supported me in numerous ways. Writing residencies at the Rockefeller Foundation's Bellagio Center, the Virginia Center for the Creative Arts, and the Oñati International Institute for the Sociology of Law afforded friendship, stimulation, and tangible support. The UBC Public Humanities Hub awarded me a much-needed teaching release. Bruno, staff, and regulars at the Corner Café provided a friendly place to write and fuel (coffee) to keep me going.

Parts of chapters one to three are based on ideas appearing in my 2015 article "The Invisible Hand of Law: Private Regulation and the Rule of Law" in the *Cornell International Law Journal*.

NOTES

Introduction

4 **wages stagnated:** Wages for the top 1 percent grew by nearly 150 percent, while for the bottom 90 percent wages grew by 15 percent. CEOs make nearly three hundred times what average workers make, compared with thirty times as much in 1980. For these and other measures of inequality, see Lawrence Michell, Elise Gould, and Josh Bivens, "Wage Stagnation in Nine Charts," Economic Policy Institute, January 6, 2015, https://www.epi.org/publication/charting-wage-stagnation/.

4 **worse off than their parents:** See Joe Myers, "Millennials Will Be the First Generation to Earn Less Than Their Parents," World Economic Forum, July 19, 2016, https://weforum.org/agenda/2016/07/millennials-will-be-the-first-generation-to-earn-less-than-their-parents/.

4 **mortality rates . . . began rising in 2014:** See Stephen Bezruchka, "Increasing Mortality and Declining Health Status in the USA: Where Is Public Health?," *Harvard Health Policy Review,* October 11, 2018, http://hhpronline.org/articles/2018/10/8/increasing-mortality-and-declining-health-status-in-the-usa-where-is-public-health/.

4 **"deaths of despair" . . . at all-time highs:** See "Long-Term Trends in Deaths of Despair," United States Congress, Senate Joint Economic Committee, September 5, 2019, https://jec.senate.gov/public/index.cfm/republicans/2019/9/long-term-trends-in-deaths-of-despair/.

1. The New Corporation

11 **the focus of Davos 2020:** Press release, "Stakeholder Capitalism: A Manifesto for a Cohesive and Sustainable World," World Economic Forum, January 14, 2020, https://www.weforum.org/press/2020/01/stakeholder

-capitalism-a-manifesto-for-a-cohesive-and-sustainable-world/; and press release, "Measuring Stakeholder Capitalism: World's Largest Companies Support Developing Core Set of Universal ESG Disclosures," World Economic Forum, January 22, 2020, https://www.weforum.org/press/2020/01 /measuring-stakeholder-capitalism-world-s-largest-companies-support -developing-core-set-of-universal-esg-disclosures/.

16 **more than 80 companies and CEOs:** The Plug, "Statements Made by Top Tech Companies on Racial Justice, BLM, and George Floyd," May 31, 2020, tpinsights.com (https://docs.google.com/spreadsheets/d/1OZx-_tm3 PPyx6-ZJAST1xxOJRfn7KfYDjDT6JedrTfs/htmlview?pru=AAABcpDw Plo*0eM2IAJlXf1FA_0Msfkq8A#gid=0).

20 **The recent coronavirus pandemic is a case in point:** See Anne Gearan, "Corporate Executives Play an Outsize Role at Trump's Coronavirus Briefings," *Washington Post*, March 31, 2020, https://www.washingtonpost.com /politics/corporate-executives-play-an-outsize-role-at-trumps-coronavirus -briefings/2020/03/30/3d0cd72c-729f-11ea-a9bd-9f8b593300d0_story .html?utm_campaign=wp_post_most&utm_medium=email&utm_source =newsletter&wpisrc=nl_most; and Blake Morgan, "50 Ways Companies Are Giving Back During the Coronavirus Pandemic," *Forbes*, March 17, 2020, https://www.forbes.com/sites/blakemorgan/2020/03/17/50-ways -companies-are-giving-back-during-the-corona-pandemic/#1d74c0ed4723. See also Jane Borden, "The Curious Case of the Coronavirus Commercial," *Vanity Fair*, April 22, 2020, https://www.vanityfair.com/hollywood /2020/04/coronavirus-advertising-brands-commercials.

24 **deep cuts to environmental protection and other regulatory areas:** Tara Golshan, "Trump's 2020 Budget Proposal Seriously Cuts the Nation's Safety Net," Vox, March 11, 2019, https://www.vox.com/policy -and-politics/2019/3/11/18259789/trumps-2020-budget-proposal-cuts/.

25 **$32 billion combined savings of top U.S. banks:** See Yalman Onaran, "Trump Tax Cut Hands $32 Billion Windfall to America's Top Banks," Bloomberg, January 16, 2020, https://www.bloomberg.com/news/articles /2020-01-16/trump-tax-cut-hands-32-billion-windfall-to-america-s-top -banks/.

26 **securing new exemptions that reduced to almost nothing:** Jesse Drucker and Jim Tankersley, "How Big Companies Won New Tax Breaks from the Trump Administration," *New York Times*, December 30, 2019, https://www.nytimes.com/2019/12/30/business/trump-tax-cuts-beat-gilti .html?searchResultPosition=1.

26 **allowing some of them . . . to abandon elaborate offshore tax- avoidance schemes:** See Toby Sterling, "Google to End 'Double Iris, Dutch Sandwich' Tax Scheme," Reuters, December 31, 2019, https://www .reuters.com/article/us-google-taxes-netherlands/google-to-end-double -irish-dutch-sandwich-tax-scheme-idUSKBN1YZ10Z/.

27 **America's superrich boosted their collective fortune:** Chuck Collins, Omar Ocampo, and Sophia Paslaski, "Billionaire Bonanza 2020: Wealth Windfalls, Tumbling Taxes and Pandemic Profiteers," Institute for Policy Studies, April 23, 2020, https://mronline.org/wp-content/uploads /2020/04/Billionaire-Bonanza-2020-April-21.pdf.

29 **"harness the power of purpose" because that will "drive performance and profitability"**: Valerie Keller, "The Great Search for the Corporate Soul," *Thrive Global,* September 28, 2017, https://www.thriveglobal.com /stories/13540-the-great-search-for-the-corporate-soul/.

29 **Michael Porter says his "shared value"**: Michael E. Porter and Mark R. Kramer, "Creating Shared Value: How to Reinvent Capitalism and Unleash a Wave of Innovation and Growth," *Harvard Business Review,* January–February 2011, 2–17, http://www.creativeinnovationglobal.com.au/wp -content/uploads/Shared-value-Harvard-business-review.pdf, at 5 and 16. In another article, Mark Kramer uses the phrase "doing well by doing good" to describe what "shared value" is truly about. Mark Kramer, "CSR vs. CSV—What's the Difference?," FSG, February 18, 2011, https://www .fsg.org/blog/csr-vs-csv-what's-difference/.

29 **Honeywell's . . . "clean energy generation"**: "KidSmartz/Corporate Citizenship Honeywell," Honeywell.com, January 2015, https://www.honey well.com/en-us/newsroom/news/2015/01/kidsmartz-corporate-citizenship -honeywell/.

29 **JPMorgan Chase investing in a renewal program in Detroit**: See "*Advancing* Cities: Detroit," JPMorgan Chase, https://www.jpmorganchase .com/corporate/Corporate-Responsibility/detroit.htm/. More generally, for commentary on the growth of impact investing (investments that are intended to generate environmental and social impact alongside financial returns), see J. Haskell Murray, "Social Enterprise and Investment Professionals: Sacrificing Financial Interests?," *Seattle University Law Review* 40, no. 2 (2017): 774–77; and Tom C. W. Lin, "Incorporating Social Activism," *Boston University Law Review* 98 (2018): 1535, https://www.bu.edu/bulaw review/files/2019/01/LIN.pdf.

30 **Coca-Cola mounting youth empowerment programs**: "Thirsty for More: Coca-Cola's Shared Value Approach with Communities Across Brazil," Shared Value Initiative, https://www.sharedvalue.org/resources/thirsty -more-coca-cola's-shared-value-approach-communities-across-brazil/.

30 **Doing good can also build positive reputations**: This is key to Bill Gates's concept of "creative capitalism," discussed in more depth below, which advocates that corporations can reap benefits by serving the poor, sometimes in the form of profit, other times through "recognition." He says: "Recognition enhances a company's reputation and appeals to customers; above all, it attracts good people to the organization. As such, recognition triggers a market-based reward for good behavior." Bill Gates, "Bill Gates—2008 World Economic Forum—Creative Capitalism," Bill & Melinda Gates Foundation, January 24, 2008, https://www.gates foundation.org/media-center/speeches/2008/01/bill-gates-2008-world -economic-forum. For a more general discussion of reputational and other benefits gained by corporations through "doing good," see Lin, "Incorporating Social Activism."

30 **social license to operate**: Definition at "Social License to Operate," Learning for Sustainability, 2017, https://learningforsustainability.net/social -license/.

30 **Honeywell built a LEED . . . gold-certified production plant in Kan-**

sas City: James Dornbrook, "Energy Secretary: KC's New NNSA Facility a Model for U.S.," *Kansas City Business Journal,* August 22, 2014, https://www.bizjournals.com/kansascity/news/2014/08/22/national-security-campus-nnsa-kansas-city.html.

30 **Shareholder value is maximized, and corporate interests are served:** For scholarly and other commentary elaborating on this point, see Lin, "Incorporating Social Activism"; John Mackey and Raj Sisodia, *Conscious Capitalism* (Boston: Harvard Business Review Press, 2014); Shuili Du, C. B. Bhattacharya, and Sankar Sen, "Maximizing Business Returns to Corporate Social Responsibility (CSR): The Role of CSR Communication," *International Journal of Management Reviews* 12, no. 1 (2010); and Justin Fox and Jay W. Lorsch, "What Good Are Shareholders?," *Harvard Business Review,* July–August 2012.

31 **the law *demands* corporations do well:** See Joel Bakan, *The Corporation: The Pathological Pursuit of Profit and Power* (New York: Free Press, 2004).

31 **Merrick Dodd and Adolf Berle:** The articles are A. A. Berle, Jr., "Corporate Powers as Powers in Trust," *Harvard Law Review* 44 (1931): 1049; and E. Merrick Dodd, "For Whom Are Corporate Managers Trustees?," *Harvard Law Review* 45, no. 7 (1932): 1145.

31 **Professor Lynn Stout:** Professor Stout makes her argument at length in Lynn Stout, *The Shareholder Value Myth: How Putting Shareholders First Harms Investors, Corporations, and the Public* (San Francisco: Berrett-Koehler Publishers, 2012).

32 **in Canada, for example, where the Supreme Court recently held:** The case is *BCE Inc. v. 1976 Debentureholders,* 2008 SCC 69, 3 SCR 560. In an excellent discussion of the case's implications, Professor Carol Liao argues forcefully that it pushes Canadian law away from narrow reliance on shareholder value and thus distinguishes it further from U.S. corporate law. Carol Liao, "A Canadian Model of Corporate Governance," *Dalhousie Law Journal* 37, no. 2 (2014): 559–600. As I argue below, however, claiming some room for managers and directors to consider nonshareholder values does not displace the "best interests" test, nor its primary orientation toward the short- and long-term interests of shareholders.

32 **creating wealth for shareholders remains the corporation's *fundamental* mandate:** For scholarly commentary confirming this point, see Joel Bakan, "The Invisible Hand of Law: Private Regulation and the Rule of Law," *Cornell International Law Journal* 48, no. 2 (2015): 279–300; Steven L. Schwarcz, "Misalignment: Corporate Risk-Taking and Public Duty," *Notre Dame Law Review* 92 (2016): 1–50; Leo E. Strine, Jr., "Our Continuing Struggle with the Idea That For-Profit Corporations Seek Profit," *Wake Forest Law Review* 45 (2012): 135; and Aaron K. Chatterji and Barak D. Richman, "Understanding the 'Corporate' in Corporate Social Responsibility," *Harvard Law & Policy Review* 2 (2008): 33–52.

32 **it "would be foolish":** Jeffrey Bone, "The Supreme Court Revisiting Corporate Accountability: BCE Inc. in Search of a Legal Construct Known as the 'Good Corporate Citizen,'" *Alberta Law Review* (2010).

33 **the *Financial Times* reports:** Robert Armstrong, "Warren Buffett on

Why Companies Cannot Be Moral Arbiters," *Financial Times,* December 29, 2019, www.ft.com/content/ebbc9b46-1754-11ea-9ee4-11f260415385/.

2. Still Crazy After All These Years

41 **reduce waste, save energy, recycle resources, and prevent pollution:** From Koch Industries' website, "Responsibility Is Our Highest Priority," from *Five Steps We Take,* https://www.kochind.com/responsibility/.

41 **British American Tobacco:** British American Tobacco, "Sustainability: Why It Matters," *Sustainability Summary* (2012): 1–2, http://www.bat.com /group/sites/uk__9d9kcy.nsf/vwPagesWebLive/DO9DCL3P/$FILE/med MD95XPJA.pdf?openelement.

41 **the World Health Organization:** Paragraph 27 of *Guidelines for Implementation of Article 5.3 of the WHO Framework Convention on Tobacco Control* (3d Sess., FCTC/COP3[7], November 2008) states: "The corporate social responsibility of the tobacco industry is, according to WHO, an inherent contradiction, as industry's core functions are in conflict with the goals of public health policies with respect to tobacco control." On that basis, the document explicitly recommends against private regulation, with paragraph 21(3.3) stating: "Parties should not accept, support or endorse any voluntary code of conduct or instrument drafted by the tobacco industry that is offered as a substitute for legally enforceable tobacco control measures." Accessed at http://www.who.int/fctc/guidelines/adopted/article_5_3/en/.

41 **FedEx claims:** See FedEx, "Our People," http://www.fedex.com/sc/about /our-people/index.html; Michael Sainato, "FedEx Mounts Big-Money Push to Head Off Unionization by U.S. Workers," *The Guardian,* January 14, 2020, https://www.theguardian.com/us-news/2020/jan/14/fedex-anti -union-campaign-teamsters; Rachel Abrams and Jessica Silver-Greenberg, " 'Terrified' Package Delivery Employees Are Going to Work Sick," *New York Times,* March 21, 2020, https://www.nytimes.com/2020/03/21/business /coronavirus-ups-fedex-xpo-workers.html.

41 **Google vaunts:** Irina Slav, "Why Big Tech Is Backing Oil," OilPrice.com, January 6, 2020, https://oilprice.com/Energy/Energy-General/Why-Big -Tech-Is-Backing-Big-Oil.html.

41 **Amazon promises:** Edward Ongweso, Jr., "Brave: Corporations Stand in Solidarity with the Communities They Exploit," *Vice,* June 4, 2020, https://www.vice.com/en_us/article/bv8nv3/brave-corporations-stand-in -solidarity-with-the-communities-they-exploit.

42 **Procter & Gamble:** From "Pampers + Sustainability," https://www.pampers .com/en-us/about-us/sustainability/article/reducing-environmental-impact/.

42 **a product widely believed to be unsustainable:** Disposable diapers make up 30 percent of nonbiodegradable waste in landfills. It is not yet known how long it will take for diapers in landfills to decompose, but it could conceivably be thousands of years. See "Why Disposable Diapers Are Dirty and Dangerous," Small Footprint Family, https://www.smallfootprint family.com/dangers-of-disposable-diapers/.

42 **Coca-Cola uses renewable and recyclable plant-based plastics to make**

its bottles: Coca-Cola has branded the plant-based technology "PlantBottle." PlantBottles contain up to 30 percent plant-based materials. See "What Is the Difference Between PlantBottle Packaging and Traditional PET Plastic Bottle?," Coca-Cola Co. Product Facts, https://www.coca-colaproductfacts .com/en/faq/packaging/plantbottle-packaging-and-traditional-pet/.

42 **"represents the very antithesis of what sustainability means":** Luke Upchurch, "Can Bottled Water Ever Really Be Sustainable?," *The Guardian,* June 6, 2013, http://www.theguardian.com/sustainable-business/can -bottled-water-be-sustainable/.

42 **benefits to themselves and their shareholders:** For similar conclusions, see Charles Eisenstein, "Let's Be Honest: Real Sustainability May Not Make Business Sense," *Sustainable Business* (blog), *The Guardian,* January 8, 2014, http://www.theguardian.com/sustainable-business/blog/sustainability -business-sense-profit-purpose; Megan Bowman, "The Limitations of Business Case Logic for Societal Benefit & Implications for Corporate Law: A Case Study of 'Climate Friendly' Banks," August 29, 2014, paper presented at the Conference on Empirical Legal Studies (CELS), University of California, Berkeley, November 6–8, 2014, http://papers.ssrn.com/sol3/papers. cfm?abstract_id=2489116; Markus J. Milne, Helen Tregidga, and Sara Walton, "Words Not Actions! The Ideological Role of Sustainable Development Reporting," *Accounting, Auditing & Accountability Journal* 22, no. 8 (2009): 1211–57; Crawford Spence, "Social and Environmental Reporting and Hegemonic Discourse," *Accounting, Auditing & Accountability Journal* 20, no. 6 (2007): 855–82; Andrew Hoffman, "Climate Change Strategy: The Business Logic Behind Voluntary Greenhouse Gas Reductions," *California Management Review* 47, no. 3 (2005): 21–46.

42 **CEOs themselves report:** See "United Nations Global Compact-Accenture CEO Study on Sustainability 2013: Architects of a Better World," Accenture, September 2013, 1, 4, and 11, https://www.unglobal compact.org/docs/news_events/8.1/UNGC_Accenture_CEO_Study_2013 .pdf. Despite these survey results, the idea that business rather than government should take the lead in solving social and environmental problems continues to have much resonance among business leaders and commentators. See, for instance, Marc Gunther, "Corporate Executives Gather at the UN for a Go at Fixing Sustainability," *The Guardian,* November 21, 2014, www.theguardian.com/sustainable-business/2014/nov/21/future -corporation-united-nations-regulation-government/.

43 **"The world needs to go through an energy transition":** See Samantha Raphelson, "Energy Companies Urge Trump to Remain in Paris Climate Agreement," *All Things Considered,* NPR, May 18, 2017, https:// www.npr.org/2017/05/18/528998592/energy-companies-urge-trump-to -remain-in-paris-climate-agreement/.

43 **"meet the goals of the Paris Agreement on Climate Change":** See "Leading Investors Back Shell's Climate Targets," Royal Dutch Shell, December 3, 2018, https://www.shell.com/media/news-and-media-releases/2018 /leading-investors-back-shells-climate-targets.html/.

43 **"take some credit":** For certain of the accord's provisions, see the statement by Shell's climate change adviser, as reported by Kate Wheeling in

"How Oil Companies Are Still Undermining the Paris Agreement," *Pacific Standard,* December 11, 2018, https://psmag.com/environment/did-royal-dutch-shell-help-write-the-paris-agreement/. For a similarly scathing review of Shell's claims to have helped write the Paris Agreement, see Kate Aronoff, "Shell Oil Executive Boasts That His Company Influenced the Paris Agreement," *The Intercept,* December 7, 2018, https://theintercept.com/2018/12/08/shell-oil-executive-boasts-that-his-company-influenced-the-paris-agreement/.

43 **defended the accord:** Various companies (including Shell, Walmart, and Unilever) wrote to the president ahead of his decision to withdraw the United States from the Paris Agreement in 2017, highlighting the way in which they believed the United States would benefit from continued participation in the agreement. See "Letter to the President of the United States," April 26, 2017, https://c2es.org/site/assets/uploads/2017/04/business-letter-white-house-paris-agreement-final-04-26-2017-1.pdf.

44 **could alone defeat Paris targets:** See "Climate on the Line," Oil Change International, January 2017, http://priceofoil.org/content/uploads/2017/01/climate_on_the_line_FINAL-OCI.pdf.

44 **The accord contains no legally binding emission targets:** For the limitations of the Paris Agreement, see Raymond Clémençon, "The Two Sides of the Paris Climate Agreement: Dismal Failure or Historic Breakthrough?," *Journal of Environment & Development* 25, no. 1 (2016): 4, 6, 18, and 19, https://journals.sagepub.com/doi/pdf/10.1177/1070496516631362/.

44 **the Paris accord is toothless:** Raymond Clémençon, "The Two Sides of the Paris Climate Agreement: Dismal Failure or Historic Breakthrough?," *Journal of Environment & Development* 25, no. 1 (2016): 29, https://journals.sagepub.com/doi/pdf/10.1177/1070496516631362/.

44 **Scientists have already sounded the alarm:** See "Global Warming of 1.5°C," special report, Intergovernmental Panel on Climate Change, 2018, https://www.ipcc.ch/sr15/download/. See also Jonathan Watts, "We Have 12 Years to Limit Climate Change Catastrophe, Warns UN," *The Guardian,* October 8, 2018, https://www.theguardian.com/environment/2018/oct/08/global-warming-must-not-exceed-15c-warns-landmark-un-report/.

45 *The Economist* **notes "a single, jarring truth":** See "The Truth About Big Oil and Climate Change," *The Economist,* February 9, 2019, https://www.economist.com/leaders/2019/02/09/the-truth-about-big-oil-and-climate-change/; and "The Shale Boom Has Made America the World's Top Oil Producer," *The Economist,* October 20, 2018, https://www.economist.com/business/2018/10/20/the-shale-boom-has-made-america-the-worlds-top-oil-producer/.

46 **"The real danger," as the youth environmental activist Greta Thunberg described:** Chris D'Angelo, "Greta Thunberg Blasts 'Creative PR' in Her Climate Speech," *Wired,* December 12, 2019, https://www.wired.com/story/greta-thunberg-blasts-creative-pr-in-her-climate-speech/; Emily Holden, "How the Oil Industry Has Spent Billions to Control the Climate Change Conversation," *The Guardian,* January 8, 2020, https://www.theguardian.com/business/2020/jan/08/oil-companies-climate-crisis-pr-spending/.

46 **In his 2020 letter to CEOs, for example, Larry Fink:** Larry Fink, "A

Fundamental Reshaping of Finance," January 2020, https://www.blackrock .com/uk/individual/larry-fink-ceo-letter/; Patrick Greenfield, "World's Top Three Asset Managers Oversee $300bn Fossil Fuel Investments," *The Guardian,* October 12, 2019, https://www.theguardian.com/environment /2019/oct/12/top-three-asset-managers-fossil-fuel-investments/; Jillian Ambrose, "BlackRock Lost $90bn Investing in Fossil Fuel Companies, Report Finds," *The Guardian,* July 31, 2019, https://www.theguardian.com /environment/2019/jul/31/blackrock-lost-90bn-investing-in-fossil-fuel -companies-report-finds/; and Ian McGugan, "BlackRock's Green Investing Strategy Is Not a Moral Awakening," *Globe and Mail,* January 15, 2020, https://www.theglobeandmail.com/investing/markets/inside-the-market /article-blackrocks-eco-investing-strategy-is-not-a-moral-awakening/.

47 **The fossil fuel industry continues to boost production:** See, for example, Nicholas Withers, "10 Major Oil & Gas Projects to Watch in 2020," *EngineeringPro,* January 8, 2020, https://www.fircroft.com/blogs/10 -major-oil-and-gas-projects-to-watch-in-2020-08816193115.

48 **a heightened risk of deadly pandemics:** See Bryn Nelson, "The Next Coronavirus Nightmare Is Closer Than You Think," *Daily Beast,* February 20, 2020, https://www.thedailybeast.com/get-ready-for-more-corona virus-nightmares-thanks-to-climate-change; and Jim Robbins, "The Ecology of Disease," *New York Times,* July 14, 2012, https://www.nytimes .com/2012/07/15/sunday-review/the-ecology-of-disease.html.

48 **Displacement of human beings as a result of climate change:** See Hannah Beech and Ben Hubbard, "Unprepared for the Worst: World's Most Vulnerable Brace for Virus," *New York Times,* March 26, 2020, https:// www.nytimes.com/2020/03/26/world/asia/coronavirus-refugees-camps -bangladesh.html.

49 **Nestlé . . . rebranded itself as a "nutrition, health and wellness company":** Nestlé has recently appointed the former head of a German health-care provider as CEO, in line with its desire to transform the business toward health and wellness. See Reuters, "Here's How Nestle's New CEO Is Going to Transform the Company," *Fortune,* June 28, 2016, http://fortune .com/2016/06/28/nestle-ceo-schneider/. See also "Q&A: Nestlé's Work to Become a 'Nutrition, Health and Wellness Company,' " Sustainable Brands, June 13, 2018, https://sustainablebrands.com/read/organizational-change /q-a-nestle-s-work-to-become-a-nutrition-health-and-wellness-company/; 3BL Alerts, "Publication of the 2016 Nestlé in Society Creating Shared Value and Meeting Our Commitments Report," 3BL Media, March 7, 2017, https://www.3blmedia.com/News/Publication-2016-Nestle-Society -Creating-Shared-Value-and-Meeting-Our-Commitments-Report/.

49 **Unilever's Sustainable Living Plan:** See Unilever, "Improving Health and Well-Being," https://www.unilever.com/sustainable-living/improving -health-and-well-being/.

50 **creating new markets for products:** The strategy is rooted in the ideas of the economists C. K. Prahalad and Stuart L. Hart, who proposed in the late 1990s and early 2000s that corporations could and should seek profits by targeting the world's poorest, the "bottom of the pyramid." Their ideas, which they wrapped in the term "inclusive capitalism," were in line with

"new" corporation ideas. They wrote in an article titled "The Fortune at the Bottom of the Pyramid": "For companies with the resources and persistence to compete at the bottom of the world economic pyramid, the prospective rewards include growth, profits, and incalculable contributions to human-kind. Countries that still don't have the modern infrastructure or products to meet basic human needs are an ideal testing ground for developing envi-ronmentally sustainable technologies and products for the entire world." See article at https://www.strategy-business.com/article/11518/.

50 **"a winning position":** From "2016 Full Year Results Conference Call Transcript," at 6, Nestlé, February 16, 2017, https://www.nestle.com/sites /default/files/asset-library/documents/investors/transcripts/2016-full-year -results-investor-call-transcript.pdf.

50 **Nestlé created a direct-sales force of pushcart vendors:** The cus-tomers of Nestlé's door-to-door vendors, only recently victims of hunger and malnutrition, are now part of a widespread obesity epidemic in Brazil and sufferers of related illnesses like diabetes and heart disease. Andrew Jacobs and Matt Richtel, "How Big Business Got Brazil Hooked on Junk Food," *New York Times,* September 16, 2017, https://www.nytimes.com /interactive/2017/09/16/health/brazil-obesity-nestle.html.

50 **between 2011 and 2016:** Ibid.

50 **"the most successful sector":** Alice Street, "Food as Pharma: Market-ing Nutraceuticals to India's Rural Poor," *Critical Public Health* 25, no. 3 (2014): 361–62, https://www.tandfonline.com/doi/full/10.1080/09581596 .2014.966652/; and Smitha Verma, "Nutraceutical in India: How Big Is the Market? Are They Really Beneficial?," *Financial Express,* September 2, 2018, https://www.financialexpress.com/lifestyle/nutraceutical-in-india -how-big-is-the-market-are-they-really-beneficial/1299759/.

51 **"clear case of 'doing well by doing good'":** Street, "Food as Pharma: Marketing Nutraceuticals to India's Rural Poor," 362.

51 **Vitingo:** See "Know Vitingo," Coca-Cola Co., https://www.coca-colaindia .com/brands/know-vitingo/.

51 **Nestlé markets the meal-replacement beverage Boost:** See "Product Details of Boost High Protein," Nestlé, https://www.nestlehealthscience .us/brands/boost/boost-high-protein/.

51 **Horlicks:** See "Horlicks," GSK Products, Horlicks, https://india-consumer .gsk.com/en-in/products/horlicks/; and "Unilever to Acquire Horlicks and Other Consumer Healthcare Nutrition Products from GSK," Unilever, December 3, 2018, https://www.unilever.com/news/press-releases/2018 /unilever-to-acquire-horlicks-and-other-consumer-healthcare-nutrition -products-from-gsk.html.

51 **"just tall claims":** Arun Gupta, as quoted by Smitha Verma, "Nutraceuti-cal in India: How Big Is the Market? Are They Really Beneficial?"

52 **diverts from roots and causes:** Alice Street, "Food as Pharma: Marketing Nutraceuticals to India's Rural Poor."

53 **Warren Buffett's skeptical assessment:** Ben Winck, "This Is the Share-holders' Money: Billionaire Warren Buffett Argues That Companies Should Stop Making Decisions Based on Their Social Beliefs," *Business Insider,* January 2, 2020, https://markets.businessinsider.com/news/stocks/warren

-buffett-companies-should-prioritize-profitability-over-social-causes-esg
-2020-1-1028791675/.

53 **For Volkswagen, this is the perfect day to release an Internet video:**
English version on file with the author. Spanish version available online at
https://www.youtube.com/watch?v=BE8M7Oj-EFM/.

54 **"no other automobile and transportation manufacturer":** Andrew
Burger, "Volkswagen Lays Out Vision of 'Sustainable Mobility' in 2013
Sustainability Report," *Triple Pundit,* May 26, 2014, http://www.triple
pundit.com/2014/05/volkswagen-lays-vision-sustainable-mobility-2013
-sustainability-report/.

54 **a scandal of breathtaking scope and cynicism:** Despite the "long tradition of scandal and skullduggery in the auto industry," *The New York Times*
reported at the time, "few schemes appear as premeditated as Volkswagen's
brazen move to circumvent United States emissions standards." James B.
Stewart, "Problems at Volkswagen Start in the Boardroom," *New York
Times,* September 24, 2015, https://www.nytimes.com/2015/09/25/business
/international/problems-at-volkswagen-start-in-the-boardroom.html/.

54 **forty times more pollutants:** See "Volkswagen AG Agrees to Plead Guilty
and Pay $4.3 Billion in Criminal and Civil Penalties," U.S. Department
of Justice, January 11, 2017, https://www.justice.gov/opa/pr/volkswagen
-ag-agrees-plead-guilty-and-pay-43-billion-criminal-and-civil-penalties
-six/; and Karl Mathiesen and Arthur Neslen, "VW Scandal Causes Nearly
1M Tonnes of Extra Pollution, Analysis Shows," *The Guardian,* September 23, 2015, https://www.theguardian.com/business/2015/sep/22
/vw-scandal-caused-nearly-1m-tonnes-of-extra-pollution-analysis-shows/.

54 **directly causing . . . illness and thousands of deaths:** See International
Institute for Applied Systems Analysis, "5,000 Deaths Annually from
Dieselgate in Europe," *Science Daily,* September 18, 2017, https://www
.sciencedaily.com/releases/2017/09/170918093337.htm; and Jennifer Chu,
"Study: Volkswagen's Excess Emissions Will Lead to 1,200 Premature
Deaths in Europe," *MIT News,* March 3, 2017, http://news.mit.edu/2017
/volkswagen-emissions-premature-deaths-europe-0303/.

54 **The presiding judge:** Judge Sean F. Cox of the U.S. District Court for the
Eastern District of Michigan.

54 **a slice of the $25 billion in fines and settlements:** Other lawsuits and
settlements within and outside the United States pushed the company's
ultimate liability to more than $30 billion. In addition, half a dozen
Volkswagen executives were charged by U.S. authorities, and five of them
remained in Germany to avoid arrest. The sixth, Oliver Schmidt, who had
been the executive in charge of compliance with U.S. law, made the mistake
of traveling to Miami for a vacation. He was arrested there, convicted, and
sentenced to seven years in prison as a "key conspirator, responsible for the
cover-up in the United States," according to Judge Sean F. Cox. See Margaret Cronin Fisk and Stephen Raphael, "VW Executive Sentenced to 7 Years
in Prison for Diesel Role," Bloomberg, December 6, 2017, https://www
.bloomberg.com/news/articles/2017-12-06/vw-executive-sentenced-to-7
-years-in-prison-for-diesel-role. The company apologized in a statement,
claiming it "deeply regrets the behavior that gave rise to the diesel crisis"

and that it "is not the same company it was 18 months ago." Share prices jumped after the court's decision against the company and its executives, with "first-quarter results . . . surprisingly good," according to *The Economist* in spring 2017, and investors "in a chirpy mood," partly because "the bill for Diesel-gate is now clear." See "Road Map: Volkswagen," *Economist Espresso,* May 10, 2017, https://espresso.economist.com/5c7a3b81a677c 639c76989610183c0e0/.

55 **"distinguished company"**: Johnson & Johnson is on the AAP list of "distinguished companies that have demonstrated their invaluable commitment to the AAP." American Academy of Pediatrics, "Corporate Friends of Children Fund Members," accessed October 10, 2019, https://www .aap.org/en-us/about-the-aap/corporate-relationships/Pages/Friends-of -Children-Fund-President%27s-Circle.aspx/.

55 **Tylenol and Motrin:** McNeil-PPC Inc., a wholly owned subsidiary of Johnson & Johnson, was directly responsible. See press release, "McNeil-PPC Inc. Pleads Guilty in Connection with Adulterated Infants' and Children's Over-the-Counter Liquid Drugs," U.S. Department of Justice, March 10, 2015, https://www.justice.gov/opa/pr/mcneil-ppc-inc-pleads -guilty-connection-adulterated-infants-and-childrens-over-counter-liquid/.

55 **off-label use by elderly patients:** See press release, "Johnson & Johnson to Pay More Than $2.2 Billion to Resolve Criminal and Civil Investigations," U.S. Department of Justice, November 4, 2013, https://www.justice.gov /opa/pr/johnson-johnson-pay-more-22-billion-resolve-criminal-and-civil -investigations/.

55 **marketing campaigns of opioids:** See Jan Hoffman, "Johnson & Johnson Ordered to Pay $572 Million in Landmark Opioid Trial," *New York Times,* August 26, 2019, https://www.nytimes.com/2019/08/26/health/oklahoma -opioids-johnson-and-johnson.html/.

55 **talc-based products:** Anjelica Cappellino reports that "lawsuits allege that the company's talc products are contaminated with asbestos," in "Latest Talc Verdict Against Johnson & Johnson Sets Tone for 2019 Litigation," Expert Institute, April 4, 2019, https://www.theexpertinstitute.com/latest -talc-verdict-against-johnson-johnson-sets-tone-for-2019-litigation/?utm _source=email&utm_medium=email&utm_content=blog-latest-J&J -talc-verdict-2019&utm_campaign=4.4.19-mini-2/; and Larry Bodine, "Behind a $55 Million Talc Verdict: J&J Knew About Cancer Risks Since the 1970s," Expert Institute, November 29, 2016, https://www.theexpert institute.com/behind-55-million-talc-verdict-jj-knew-cancer-risks-since -1970s/. And in relation to the marketing campaign that focused on African American women, see Chris Kirkham and Lisa Girion, "As Worries About Baby Powder Safety Mounted, J&J Focused Its Pitches on Minority, Overweight Women," Reuters, April 9, 2019, https://www.reuters.com /investigates/special-report/johnsonandjohnson-marketing/.

56 *big-tech companies*: See Jonathan Chew, "7 Corporate Giants Accused of Evading Billions in Taxes," *Fortune,* March 11, 2016, http://fortune.com /2016/03/11/apple-google-taxes-eu/.

58 **diagnosis of psychopaths:** American Psychiatric Association, "General Criteria for a Personality Disorder: DSM-5 Criteria Revised June 2011,"

https://www.psi.uba.ar/academica/carrerasdegrado/psicologia/sitios_catedras
/practicas_profesionales/820_clinica_tr_personalidad_psicosis/material
/dsm.pdf.

3. The Corporate Liberation Movement

59 **"fairly direct class hatred"**: Pat Rogers, "The Waltham Blacks and the
Black Act," *Historical Journal* 17, no. 3 (1974): 465–86.

60 **"unqualified good"**: E. P. Thompson, *Whigs and Hunters: The Origin of
the Black Act* (Harmondsworth, U.K.: Penguin Books, 1977), 267–68.

61 **"misuse of private economic power"**: For the entire Roosevelt quote and
further discussion, see my *The Corporation: The Pathological Pursuit of Profit
and Power* (New York: Free Press, 2004), 86.

61 **"Corporations' freedom detracts from our freedom, and it's a zero-
sum game"**: The entire quote from the *Guardian* columnist George Monbiot: "If [a corporation is] free to pollute the river or the atmosphere, other
people are not free from the impacts of that pollution. In fact, that pollution
can be a terrible imposition on the lives of other people. . . . So [their] freedom detracts from our freedom, and it's a zero-sum game."

62 **Trump's attack on the regulatory system:** See Eric Lipton and Binya-
min Appelbaum, "Leashes Come Off Wall Street, Gun Sellers, Polluters
and More," *New York Times,* March 5, 2017, https://www.nytimes.com/2017
/03/05/us/politics/trump-deregulation-guns-wall-st-climate.html/.
For more detailed analyses and information on the Trump administration's deregulation record, all accessed on October 11, 2019, see the Climate Deregulation Tracker at the Sabin Center for Climate Change Law,
Columbia Law School, http://columbiaclimatelaw.com/resources/climate
-deregulation-tracker/; the Regulatory Rollback Tracker at the Environmental and Energy Law Program, Harvard Law School, http://environment
.law.harvard.edu/policy-initiative/regulatory-rollback-tracker/; a list of regulations repealed under the Congressional Review Act, from the Center for
Progressive Reform, http://www.progressivereform.org/assaultscratargets
.cfm; and the Brookings Deregulatory Tracker at the Brookings Institution, https://www.brookings.edu/blog/up-front/2018/10/18/explaining
-the-brookings-deregulatory-tracker/. See for: **public lands**—Jim Robbins, "Open for Business: The Trump Revolution on Public Lands," *Yale
Environment 360,* October 8, 2019, https://e360.yale.edu/features/open
-for-business-the-trump-revolution-on-public-lands/; **coal-fired power
plants**—Jennifer A. Dlouhy, "Trump Makes His Biggest Move Yet to Try
to Save Coal Plants," Bloomberg, June 18, 2019, https://www.bloomberg
.com/news/articles/2019-06-18/trump-s-biggest-move-to-end-war-on
-coal-won-t-rescue-industry; **offshore drilling**—Coral Davenport, "Interior
Dept. Loosens Offshore-Drilling Safety Rules Dating from Deepwater Horizon," *New York Times,* May 2, 2019, https://www.nytimes.com/2019/05/02
/climate/offshore-drilling-safety-rollback-deepwater-horizon.html/; **automobile tailpipe emissions**—Coral Davenport, "U.S. to Announce Rollback of Auto Pollution Rules, a Key Effort to Fight Climate Change,"
New York Times, March 30, 2020, https://www.nytimes.com/2020/03/30

/climate/trump-fuel economy.html; **numerous other environmental protection rules**—Nadja Popovich, Livia Albeck-Ripka, and Kendra Pierre-Louis, "95 Environmental Rules Being Rolled Back Under Trump," *New York Times,* December 21, 2019, https://www.nytimes.com/interactive /2019/climate/trump-environment-rollbacks.html; **investor and consumer protection**—GoBanking Rates, "Trump Is Deregulating Banks: Here's What That Means for You," Nasdaq, February 12, 2019, https://www .nasdaq.com/articles/trump-deregulating-banks-heres-what-means-you -2019-02-12/; and Emily Stewart, "Trump Is Tearing Up the System That Protects Ordinary Americans from Financial Scams," Vox, February 26, 2018, https://www.vox.com/policy-and-politics/2018/2/26/17008864/trump-cfpb -mulvaney-investor-consumer-protections/; and **work and employment standards**—David Madland, Karla Walter, Alex Rowell, Zoe Willingham, and Malkie Wall, "President Trump's Policies Are Hurting American Workers," Center for American Progress Action Fund, January 26, 2018, https://www.americanprogressaction.org/issues/economy/reports/2018/01 /26/168366/president-trumps-policies-hurting-american-workers/; **"infection control" requirements in nursing homes**—Jesse Drucker and Jessica Silver-Greenberg, "Trump Administration Is Relaxing Oversight of Nursing Homes," *New York Times,* March 14, 2020, https://www.nytimes .com/2020/03/14/business/trump-administration-nursing-homes.html.

63 **"Regulation has gone out of fashion"**: Jeff Wise, "When the Rules Disappear: How the American Fervor for Deregulation Contributed to the 737 Max Crashes," *Slate,* March 21, 2019, https://slate.com/news-and -politics/2019/03/boeing-737-max-crash-faa-regulations.html.

64 **"trust[s] in the responsible company"**: From a speech made by Gordon Brown, November 28, 2005, full text published in *The Guardian* online, https://www.theguardian.com/business/2005/nov/28/economicpolicy .budget2006/.

64 **the Defense Production Act**: See Myah Ward, "White House Officials Push Back on Calls to Activate DPA for Critical Medical Supplies," *Politico,* March 26, 2020, https://www.politico.com/news/2020/03/26/dpa-white -house-coronavirus-medical-supplies-150583; Michael C. Bender and Mike Colias, "Trump Orders General Motors to Make Ventilators," *Wall Street Journal,* March 27, 2020, https://www.wsj.com/articles/trump-lashes -out-at-general-motors-over-ventilators-11585327749; James E. Baker, "It's High Time We Fought This Virus the American Way," *New York Times,* April 3, 2020, https://www.nytimes.com/2020/04/03/opinion /defense-protection-act-covid.html.

65 **In the meantime, the American Petroleum Institute**: See Michael J. Sommers, "Letter from API to President Trump," March 20, 2020, https:// www.api.org/~/media/Files/News/Letters-Comments/2020/3202020-API -Letter-to-President-Trump.pdf; Rachel Frazin, "Oil Industry Group Asks Trump Administration to Lessen Regulations Amid Coronavirus," *The Hill,* March 23, 2020, https://thehill.com/policy/energy-environment/489128 -oil-industry-group-asks-trump-administration-to-lessen-regulations; Susan Parker Bodine, "Memorandum: COVID-19 Implications for EPA's Enforcement and Compliance Assurance Program," United States Environ-

mental Protection Agency, March 26, 2020, https://www.epa.gov/sites/production/files/2020-03/documents/oecamemooncovid19implications.pdf; Oliver Milman and Emily Holden, "Trump Administration Allows Companies to Break Pollution Laws During Coronavirus Pandemic," *The Guardian*, March 27, 2020, https://www.theguardian.com/environment/2020/mar/27/trump-pollution-laws-epa-allows-companies-pollute-without-penalty-during-coronavirus?fbclid=IwAR11nzMjxanGk4Vd YJAbQziY6ag0-SAGGknejlJkcdaYEU8StOtpCjcCo9I.

65 **Banks also attempted to leverage the coronavirus crisis:** Renae Merle, "Big Banks Want Regulation Eased Because of Coronavirus. Experts Call It Opportunistic," *Washington Post*, March 3, 2020, https://www.washington post.com/business/2020/03/03/banks-lobby-coronavirus/.

66 **Earlier deregulation had fueled easy access to credit:** See Ruchir Sharma, "This Is How the Coronavirus Will Destroy the Economy," *New York Times*, March 16, 2020, https://www.nytimes.com/2020/03/16/opinion/coronavirus-economy-debt.html; Peter Eavis, Niraj Chokshi, and David Gelles, "Take Government Aid? We'll See, Some Businesses Say," *New York Times,* April 3, 2020, https://www.nytimes.com/2020/04/03/business/economy/coronavirus-business-bailouts.html?referringSource=article Share; Jonathan O'Connell, "Congress to Bail Out Firms That Avoided Taxes, Safety Regulations and Spent Billions Boosting Their Stock," *Washington Post*, March 25, 2020, https://www.washingtonpost.com/business/2020/03/25/still-too-big-fail-us-is-primed-bail-out-corporations-again/. Tim Wu, "Don't Feel Sorry for the Airlines," *New York Times,* March 16, 2020, https://www.nytimes.com/2020/03/16/opinion/airlines-bailout.html; Joseph Zeballos-Roig, "Airlines Go Begging for a Bailout but They've Used 96% of Their Cash Flow on Buybacks Over the Last 10 Years," *Markets Insider*, March 17, 2020, https://markets.businessinsider.com/news/stocks/airline-bailout-coronavirus-share-buyback-debate-trump-economy-aoc-2020-3-1029006175.

66 **asked the Trump administration to make cuts:** A copy of the letter asking for these cuts can be accessed online. See "A Letter from the Chair of the Smart Regulation Committee, Business Roundtable," February 22, 2017, https://www.documentcloud.org/documents/3480299-10-Examples-Industries-Push-Followed-by-Trump.html#document/p54/a341316/, at 54.

67 **turning global governance on its head:** For some key scholarly articles on the ideas in this paragraph, see Andreas Georg Scherer and Guido Palazzo, "The New Political Role of Business in a Globalized World: A Review of a New Perspective on CSR and Its Implications for the Firm, Governance, and Democracy," *Journal of Management Studies* 48, no. 4 (June 2011): 899–931, https://ssrn.com/abstract=1824946; Cary Coglianese and Jennifer Nash, "Motivating Without Mandates: The Role of Voluntary Programs in Environmental Governance," in LeRoy C. Paddock, Robert L. Glicksman, and Nicholas S. Bryner, eds., *Decision Making in Environmental Law* (Cheltenham, U.K.: Edward Elgar Publishing, 2016), http://scholarship.law.upenn.edu/faculty_scholarship/1647/; Charles Perrow, "Cracks in the Regulatory State," *Social Currents* 2, no. 3 (2015): 203–12,

at 204; and Neil Gunningham and Darren Sinclair, "Smart Regulation," in Peter Drahos, ed., *Regulatory Theory: Foundations and Applications* (Canberra: Australian National University Press, 2017), 133–48. See also Joel Bakan, "The Invisible Hand of Law: Private Regulation and the Rule of Law," *Cornell International Law Journal* 48 (2015): 279, https://www.lawschool.cornell.edu/research/ILJ/upload/Bakan-final.pdf.

67 **corporate decision-makers:** Cary Coglianese and Jennifer Nash, in "Motivating Without Mandates," describe the motivations for firms joining voluntary programs as "to stave off the costs of regulatory compliance, appeal to customers and other external interests, and fulfill managers' own values" (at 3, 15); see also D. McCarthy and P. Morling, "Using Regulation as a Last Resort? Assessing the Performance of Voluntary Approaches," Royal Society for the Protection of Birds: Sandy, Bedfordshire, 2015, at 9. See also Bakan, "The Invisible Hand of Law: Private Regulation and the Rule of Law."

68 **Trump recently revised the ratio to thirteen to one:** Paul Bedard, "Deregulation Explodes Under Trump, 13 Regulations Killed for Every New One, $33B Saved," *Washington Examiner,* July 22, 2019, https://www.washingtonexaminer.com/washington-secrets/deregulation-explodes-under-trump-13-regs-killed-for-every-new-1-33b-saved/.

68 **"working through the list as needed for the 2-for-1 offsets":** This statement is recorded in the minutes as being made by Lirio Liu, executive director of the Office of Rulemaking in the Federal Aviation Administration. The minutes are included in reporting by Marisa Garcia, "Did Trump Executive Orders Further Weaken FAA Oversight?," *Forbes,* March 18, 2019, https://www.forbes.com/sites/marisagarcia/2019/03/18/did-trump-executive-orders-further-weaken-faa-oversight/#24ec7c763ca7/.

68 **the FAA Reauthorization Act of 2018:** For reporting on the evolution of the bill, see Natalie Kitroeff and David Gelles, "Before Deadly Crashes, Boeing Pushed for Law That Undercut Oversight," *New York Times,* October 27, 2019, https://www.nytimes.com/2019/10/27/business/boeing-737-max-crashes.html. For commentary on one of the lawsuits that is currently under way against Boeing following the crash of the second plane, see Alec MacGillis, "The Case Against Boeing," *New Yorker,* November 11, 2019, https://www.newyorker.com/magazine/2019/11/18/the-case-against-boeing/.

68 **"put the interests of business ahead of aviation safety":** See Garcia, "Did Trump Executive Orders Further Weaken FAA Oversight?"

68 **"people are killed":** Reported by Thomas Kaplan in "After Boeing Crashes, Sharp Questions About Industry Regulating Itself," *New York Times,* March 26, 2019, https://www.nytimes.com/2019/03/26/us/politics/boeing-faa.html?module=inline/.

68 **FAA oversight had already been largely eviscerated:** The FAA has, for years, increasingly delegated authority to Boeing to certify the safety of its own planes (citing lack of funding and resources as justification). Dominic Gates, "Flawed Analysis, Failed Oversight: How Boeing, FAA Certified the Suspect 737 MAX Flight Control System," *Seattle Times,* March 17, 2019, https://www.seattletimes.com/business/boeing-aerospace/failed-certification-faa-missed-safety-issues-in-the-737-max-system

-implicated-in-the-lion-air-crash/; see also Jeff Wise, "When the Rules Disappear," *Slate,* March 21, 2019, https://slate.com/news-and-politics /2019/03/boeing-737-max-crash-faa-regulations.html; Kitroeff and Gelles, "Before Deadly Crashes, Boeing Pushed for Law That Undercut Oversight"; and Kaplan, "After Boeing Crashes, Sharp Questions About Industry Regulating Itself."

69 **insufficient oversight by the FAA of MCAS certification:** Finding F5.1-B of the report submitted to the associate administrator for aviation safety, "Joint Authorities Technical Review: Observations, Findings, and Recommendations," U.S. Federal Aviation Administration, October 11, 2019, https://www.faa.gov/news/media/attachments/Final_JATR_Submittal _to_FAA_Oct_2019.pdf.

69 **"responsibility for finding compliance":** Ibid. For recent revelations of Boeing employees mocking the FAA, see Natalie Kitroeff, "Boeing Employees Mocked F.A.A. Employees and 'Clowns' Who Designed 737 Max," *New York Times,* January 9, 2020, https://www.nytimes.com/2020/01 /09/business/boeing-737-messages.html?smid=nytcore-ios-share/.

70 **"open lines of communication":** "Joint Authorities Technical Review: Observations, Findings, and Recommendations," recommendation R5.

71 **He borrowed the idea from the United Kingdom:** See "The Coalition: Our Programme for Government," HM Government, May 2010, https:// www.gov.uk/government/uploads/system/uploads/attachment_data/file /78977/coalition_programme_for_government.pdf.

71 **"one-in, three-out rule":** See press release, "Government Going Further to Cut Red Tape by £10 Million," Gov.uk, March 3, 2016, https://www .gov.uk/government/news/government-going-further-to-cut-red-tape-by -10-billion/.

71 **the government said no:** The All-Party Parliamentary Fire Safety and Rescue Group (chaired by Ronnie King) wrote a letter to the minister for communities, calling for the government to rethink its approach to the "cost-effectiveness" of fitting fire sprinklers in tower blocks. The letter points out that there were an estimated four thousand older tower blocks missing this system in the United Kingdom. "Can we really afford to wait for another tragedy to occur before we amend this weakness?" "Letter from the All-Party Parliamentary Group on Fire Safety and Rescue to Stephen Williams, Minister for Communities," March 12, 2014, http://news.bbc.co.uk/2/shared/bsp /hi/pdfs/19_6_17_sprinklers.pdf. See also Peter Apps, "PM's Chief of Staff Did Not Act on Multiple Warnings About Fire Safety in Months Before Grenfell, New Letters Show," *Inside Housing,* June 13, 2019, https://www .insidehousing.co.uk/news/pms-chief-of-staff-did-not-act-on-multiple -warnings-about-fire-safety-in-months-before-grenfell-new-letters-show -61883/. For more analyses and reporting on Grenfell, see Kevin Rawlinson, Harriet Sherman, and Vikram Dodd, "Grenfell Tower Final Death Toll: Police Say 71 Lives Lost as Result of Fire," *The Guardian,* November 16, 2017, https://www.theguardian.com/uk-news/2017/nov/16/grenfell-tower -final-death-toll-police-say-71-people-died-in-fire/; "Grenfell Tower: 80% of Families Homeless as Inquiry Begins," *The Week,* December 11, 2017, http:// www.theweek.co.uk/grenfell-tower/90337/grenfell-tower-80-of-families

-homeless-as-inquiry-begins/; and Sarah Knapton and Hayley Dixon, "Eight Failures That Left the People of Grenfell Tower at the Mercy of the Inferno," *The Telegraph,* June 16, 2017, http://www.telegraph.co.uk/news/2017/06/15 /eight-failures-left-people-grenfell-tower-mercy-inferno/.

71 **Brandon Lewis claimed:** Hansard, February 6, 2014, https://publications .parliament.uk/pa/cm201314/cmhansrd/cm140206/halltext/140206 h0002.htm.

71 **"only as a last resort":** King, "give three up to get it," quoted in Beth Bell, "London Fire: A Tale of Two Tower Blocks," June 16, 2017, BBC News, http://www.bbc.com/news/uk-england-40290158/. The British government's rejection of the cladding was officially recorded in the Hansard record of debates in Parliament (when discussing calls to change building regulations in 2014).

71 **a fire broke out:** Details of the tragic events that unfolded at Grenfell Tower can be found in "London Fire: What Happened at Grenfell Tower?," BBC News, July 19, 2017, http://www.bbc.com/news/uk-england-london -40272168/.

71 **"The whole system of regulation":** Dame Judith Hackitt, "Building a Safer Future: Independent Review of Building Regulations and Fire Safety: Interim Report," Ministry of Housing, Communities, and Local Government, December 2017, at 5 and 70, https://www.gov.uk/government /publications/independent-review-of-building-regulations-and-fire-safety -interim-report/.

72 **"even when it was recommended and accepted":** "UK Government Urged to End Health and Safety Deregulation Following Grenfell Tower Blaze," British Safety Council, June 21, 2017, https://www.britsafe.org /about-us/press-releases/2017/uk-government-urged-to-end-health-and -safety-deregulation-following-grenfell-tower-blaze/.

72 **cut corners on process safety:** Anthony Ladd describes how BP applied its corporate pressure to anti-regulation throughout the second half of the twentieth century, up until the *Deepwater Horizon* spill (107–11). Anthony E. Ladd, "Pandora's Well: Hubris, Deregulation, Fossil Fuels, and the BP Oil Disaster in the Gulf," *American Behavioral Scientist* 56, no. 1 (2012): 104– 27, http://journals.sagepub.com/doi/abs/10.1177/0002764211409195/.

72 **"rail companies are allowed to regulate themselves":** As quoted in CTV.ca News Staff, "Deregulation a Disaster for Rail Safety: Report," CTV News, https://www.ctvnews.ca/mobile/deregulation-a-disaster-for-rail -safety-report-1.242963?cache=yesclipId104062?clipId=104066/.

72 **Willem Buiter:** The quote is from Willem Buiter, "Lessons from the Global Financial Crisis for Regulators and Supervisors," 13, paper presented at the twenty-fifth anniversary workshop, "The Global Financial Crisis: Lessons and Outlook," of the Advanced Studies Program of the Kiel Institute for the World Economy, May 8–9, 2009, http://eprints.lse.ac.uk/29048/1 /Lessons_from_the_global_financial_crisis.pdf.

73 **"Voluntary approaches deliver little or no improvement":** See Coglianese and Nash, "Motivating Without Mandates: The Role of Voluntary Programs in Environmental Governance." The authors continue: "Improvements that can be attributed solely to voluntary programs tend to be

small—nearly indistinguishable in most cases from what might well have happened anyway in the absence of these programs." Another wide-ranging investigation of self-regulation similarly concludes: "The impact of most voluntary schemes is limited; [they] are rarely if ever an effective substitute for regulatory . . . measures in seeking to achieve public policy objectives." McCarthy and Morling, "Using Regulation as a Last Resort? Assessing the Performance of Voluntary Approaches," 13, 23.

73 **the Trump administration's rollback of climate regulations:** The figure is found in a report prepared by the State Energy & Environmental Impact Center that was released at a gathering of the National Association of Attorneys General in Washington, D.C. See Reuters, "Trump Climate Deregulation Could Boost CO2 Emissions by 200 Million Tonnes a Year: Study," *U.S. News & World Report,* March 5, 2019, https://www.usnews.com/news/top-news/articles/2019-03-05/trump-climate-deregulation-could-boost-co2-emissions-by-200-million-tonnes-a-year-study/.

75 **smaller-scale grocers:** See Erica Pandey, "Walmart Is Winning the Antitrust Wars," Axios, October 9, 2019, https://www.axios.com/walmart-antitrust-amazon-competition-fdd557b9-987a-4eb5-b989-e65d76e8b128.html/.

75 **it's all right to buy more and more:** See Tala Schlossberg and Nayeema Raza, "The Great Recycling Con," *New York Times,* September 12, 2019, https://www.nytimes.com/2019/12/09/opinion/recycling-myths.html/; Oliver Franklin-Wallis, " 'Plastic Recycling Is a Myth': What Really Happens to Your Rubbish?," *The Guardian,* August 17, 2019, https://www.theguardian.com/environment/2019/aug/17/plastic-recycling-myth-what-really-happens-your-rubbish/; Roland Geyer, Kara Lavender Law, and Jenna Jambeck, "Production, Use, and Fate of All Plastics Ever Made," *Science Advances,* July 2017, https://www.researchgate.net/publication/318567844_Production_use_and_fate_of_all_plastics_ever_made/link/5970b8570f7e9bb1f4b94826/download/; Jonathan Clark, "Everything You Know About Recycling Is Wrong: Well, Most Everything," *Medium,* May 11, 2019, https://medium.com/@jonathanusa/everything-you-know-about-recycling-is-wrong-well-most-everything-f348b4ee00fe/; Matt Wilkins, "Most Recycling Won't Solve Plastic Pollution," *Scientific American,* July 6, 2018, https://blogs.scientificamerican.com/observations/more-recycling-wont-solve-plastic-pollution/.

76 **"more than two-thirds of global emissions":** See Tess Riley, "Just 100 Companies Responsible for 71% of Global Emissions, Study Says," *The Guardian,* July 10, 2017, https://www.theguardian.com/sustainable-business/2017/jul/10/100-fossil-fuel-companies-investors-responsible-71-global-emissions-cdp-study-climate-change/.

77 **"Improve lives with every purchase":** See Fair Trade Certified online, https://www.fairtradecertified.org/.

78 **"passive parts of the system":** To take an example, Greenpeace launched a campaign to convince Procter & Gamble to stop sourcing palm oil from shady suppliers whose practices were destroying forests and peat lands. Procter & Gamble could easily comply, and after some early resistance it did.

It simply had to be more selective and vigilant about its suppliers and ensure they were certified by the prevailing World Wildlife Fund–led certification regime. The campaign fell within the limits of what an NGO can demand of a corporation. But what if, Dauvergne hypothesizes, Greenpeace asked Procter & Gamble to completely change its business model, in terms of the amount of resources it extracts, the amount of energy it uses, and the amount of waste it produces? "That's not in the realm of acceptable criticism," he says, "because there's no way that Procter & Gamble could respond."

79 **B Lab, a nonprofit created by three American entrepreneurs:** See B Lab website and particularly information about funders, https://bcorporation .net/about-b-lab/funders-and-finances/.

80 **despite B Lab's attempts to entice:** Nevertheless, a handful of publicly traded companies make use of B Lab's assessment tools, most prominently Unilever and Danone, and have certified some of their subsidiaries, like Unilever's Ben & Jerry's and Danone's Happy Family.

80 **"erode true legal reform":** Quotes from Dennis Tobin and Carol Liao in Christine Dobby, "B.C. Joins Growing Trend to 'Benefit Companies' That Do Business in Responsible, Sustainable Manner," *Globe and Mail,* December 31, 2019, https://www.theglobeandmail.com/business/article-bc-joins -growing-trend-to-benefit-companies-that-do-business-in/.

80 **Elizabeth Warren proposes:** There's a second part to Warren's proposal, which is to require companies with more than $1 billion in annual revenue to allow their employees to elect 40 percent of the members of boards of directors. This is the model used in Germany, for companies like BMW, Bayer, Siemens, SAP, and Volkswagen. And while it may have some positive impacts—codetermination, as it's called, has been linked to less long-termism in corporate decision-making, more pay equality, and lower remuneration for CEOs—the track records of German companies, notoriously Bayer (which owns Monsanto) and Volkswagen, suggest it's no antidote to corporate abuse and impunity.

82 **"CheatNeutral offsets your cheating":** A report by *New Statesman* quotes the CheatNeutral website to highlight the irrationality of offsetting: "CheatNeutral is a joke. Carbon offsetting is about paying for the right to carry on emitting carbon. The carbon industry sold £60m of offsets last year, and is rapidly growing. Carbon offsetting is also a joke." Pete May, "Offset Your Infidelity?," *New Statesman,* May 14, 2007, https://www .newstatesman.com/society/2007/05/cheatneutral-offsetting/.

83 **take the place of legal limits:** See Kathleen McAfee, "Green Economy and Carbon Markets for Conservation and Development: A Critical View," *International Environmental Agreements: Politics, Law and Economics* 16, no. 3 (2016): 333, 334.

83 **just pay to offset your harm:** For commentary on the UN Climate Change video and its removal, see Megan Darby, "Keep Calm and Carry On Flying and Eating Steak: UN Climate Change Ad Criticized," *Climate Home News,* August 29, 2018, https://www.climatechangenews.com/2018/08/29/keep -calm-carry-flying-eating-steak-un-climate-change-ad-criticised/.

83 **only 2 percent of offset projects:** Martin Cames, Ralph O. Harthan, Jürg

Füssler, Michael Lazarus, Carrie M. Lee, et al., "How Additional Is the Clean Development Mechanism?," Öko-Institut e.V., March 2016, at 11, https://ec.europa.eu/clima/sites/clima/files/ets/docs/clean_dev_mechanism_en.pdf.

84 **an estimated 750 million extra tons a year:** Gilles Dufrasne, "Withdrawn UN Advert Shows Why Carbon Offset Scheme Should Be Scrapped," Carbon Market Watch, August 31, 2018, https://carbonmarketwatch.org/2018/08/31/withdrawn-un-advert-shows-why-carbon-offset-scheme-should-be-scrapped/.

84 **the project has now been de-registered:** The project was removed from the United Nations Clean Development Mechanism in 2016, prior to entering commercial operation. See Camilo Mejia Giraldo, "Panama's Barro Blanco Dam to Begin Operation, Indigenous Pleas Refused," Mongabay, March 24, 2017, https://news.mongabay.com/2017/03/panamas-barro-blanco-dam-to-begin-operation-indigenous-pleas-refused/. On the decision to remove the dam from the UNCDM, see "In Landmark Decision, Panama Withdraws UN Registration for Barro Blanco Hydrodam Project," Carbon Market Watch, November 10, 2016, https://carbonmarketwatch.org/2016/11/10/press-statement-in-landmark-decision-panama-withdraws-un-registration-for-barro-blanco-hydrodam-project/.

84 **a "green" waste dump in a poor black area:** See Kate Ervine, "Trading Carbon: Offsets, Human Rights, and Environmental Regulation," in Kate Ervine and Gavin Fridell, eds., *Beyond Free Trade: Alternative Approaches to Trade, Politics and Power,* International Political Economy Series (London: Palgrave Macmillan, 2015), 247–48.

85 **"replace every drop of water we use":** As quoted in Christine MacDonald, "Coke Claims to Give Back as Much Water as It Uses. An Investigation Shows It Isn't Even Close," *The Verge,* May 31, 2018, https://www.theverge.com/2018/5/31/17377964/coca-cola-water-sustainability-recycling-controversy-investigation/.

85 **"for every drop we use, we give one back":** The same advertisement can be found at https://www.coca-colacompany.com/packages/ad-for-every-drop-we-use-we-give-one-back.

86 **"not always to the aquifer from which the water was originally sourced":** From "Collaborating to Replenish the Water We Use," Coca-Cola Company, August 29, 2018, https://www.coca-colacompany.com/news/collaborating-to-replenish-the-water-we-use.

86 **best estimates are that it is about half the time:** *Corporate Citizenship* reports that Bea Perez (Coke's chief sustainability officer) "said only half the water replenished is done so directly at the source used by the company. The other half is returned through partnerships where the need is greatest." See Richard Phillips, "Taking the Fizz out of Coca-Cola's Water Replenishment Claims," *Corporate Citizenship* (blog), September 19, 2016, https://corporate-citizenship.com/2016/09/19/taking-fizz-coca-colas-water-replenishment-claims/. See also Will Sarni, "Claiming You're 'Water Neutral' Can Damage Your Brand," *Harvard Business Review,* November 23, 2009, https://hbr.org/2009/11/claiming-youre-water-neutral-c/.

86 **plant in Mehdiganj:** See "Indian Officials Order Coca-Cola Plant to Close for Using Too Much Water," *The Guardian,* June 18, 2014, https://www

.theguardian.com/environment/2014/jun/18/indian-officals-coca-cola
-plant-water-mehdiganj/.

86 **Coca-Cola bottling plant in Tamil Nadu:** See "Campaigners Defeat Coca-Cola Plant in South India," *The Ecologist,* April 21, 2015, https://the ecologist.org/2015/apr/21/campaigners-defeat-coca-cola-plant-south-india/.

87 **99 percent of the water used to make it:** See MacDonald, "Coke Claims to Give Back as Much Water as It Uses. An Investigation Shows It Isn't Even Close."

87 **increases the amount of safe drinking water available in one area:** A 2013 report highlights that in the majority of cases, improved sanitation and water access actually results in an increase in local water use. Joe P. Rozza, Brian D. Richter, Wendy M. Larson, Todd Redder, Kari Vigerstol, et al., "Corporate Water Stewardship: Achieving a Sustainable Balance," *Journal of Management and Sustainability* 3, no. 4 (2013): 47, https://www .coca-colasrbija.rs/content/dam/journey/rs/sr/private/pdfs/Coca-Cola-Water -Replenish-Peer-Reviewed-Paper.pdf.

87 **actually increasing erosion:** See MacDonald, "Coke Claims to Give Back as Much Water as It Uses. An Investigation Shows It Isn't Even Close."

88 **clearly ignored its own warning:** The concept paper was produced for Coca-Cola by experts and included Coca-Cola Company officials, including its lead author, Greg Koch. Winnie Gerbens-Leenes, Arjen Hoekstra, Richard Holland, Greg Koch, Jack Moss, et al., "Water Neutrality: A Concept Paper," November 20, 2007, http://www.indiaresource.org/campaigns/coke /2008/Waterneutrality.pdf.

88 **"Coke is symptomatic of the economy that is ecologically unsound":** Bartow Elmore, as quoted in MacDonald, "Coke Claims to Give Back as Much Water as It Uses. An Investigation Shows It Isn't Even Close."

4. California (Bad) Dreaming

92 **"on behalf of the future, I ask you of the past to leave us alone":** As reported by Steven Johnson in "The Political Education of Silicon Valley," *Wired,* July 24, 2018, https://www.wired.com/story/political-education -silicon-valley/. See also Farhad Manjoo, "Silicon's Valley's Politics: Liberal, with One Big Exception," *New York Times,* September 6, 2017, https:// www.nytimes.com/2017/09/06/technology/silicon-valley-politics.html/.

92 **government authority transferred to the tech industry:** See "BIL2012— Mencius Moldbug: How to Reboot the US Government," YouTube, October 20, 2012, https://www.youtube.com/watch?v=ZluMysK2B1E&feature =youtube/. Also, Justine Tunney, a Google engineer, created a petition to appoint Eric Schmidt as CEO of America. She suggested her Twitter followers read Mencius Moldbug. For more on the works of Mencius Moldbug, see "Mencius Moldbug Unqualified Reservations," https://www.unqualified -reservations.org/.

92 **Balaji Srinivasan:** Watch him making this point at https://www.youtube .com/watch?v=cOubCHLXT6A. See also Marcus Wohlson, "Silicon Valley's Elite Don't Want to Secede. They Just Want to Stay on Top," *Wired,* December 9, 2013, https://www.wired.com/2013/12/balaji-srinivasan-joins-a16z/.

92 **Seasteading:** See https://www.seasteading.org/.

92 **Peter Thiel:** See Noam Cohen, "The Libertarian Logic of Peter Thiel," *Wired,* December 27, 2017, https://www.wired.com/story/the-libertarian -logic-of-peter-thiel/.

92 **agreed upon by the Valley's liberals and libertarians . . . government regulation is bad:** The notion that Silicon Valley tycoons are heroic geniuses who epitomize the virtues of free enterprise—"people who do really good things and kind of help a lot of other people, and . . . get well compensated for that," as Mark Zuckerberg describes it—neglects to clarify that innovations, like Facebook, depend on technologies, like the Internet, that were created through massive state intervention and taxpayer dollars. See Kate Aronoff, "Mark Zuckerberg's Plea for the Billionaire Class Is Deeply Anti-Democratic," *The Guardian,* October 21, 2019, https://www .theguardian.com/commentisfree/2019/oct/21/mark-zuckerberg-plea -biillionaire-class-anti-democratic/.

93 *Standard Oil Co. of New Jersey v. United States*: For citation and source of quote, see https://supreme.justia.com/cases/federal/us/221/1/.

94 **synergies between lax regulation and business models based on monopoly:** It's worth noting that change seems to be in the air. Earlier in 2019, the House Judiciary Committee announced it would conduct a broad antitrust investigation into big tech, and oversight of Apple, Amazon, Facebook, and Google was split between the two top federal antitrust agencies. Speaker Nancy Pelosi later tweeted, "The era of self-regulation is over." See Cecilia Kang and Kenneth P. Vogel, "Tech Giants Amass a Lobbying Army for an Epic Washington Battle," *New York Times,* June 5, 2019, https://www.nytimes.com/2019/06/05/us/politics/amazon-apple-facebook -google-lobbying.html/.

94 **Google, Apple, and Facebook have made similar moves:** Though their platforms are different, Google's and Facebook's business models are similar—collect data from masses of users and use the information to develop ever more effective and precisely tailored advertising strategies to generate advertising revenue. The success of these companies is based on the massive amounts of data they can draw to feed algorithms to increase prediction and the mass numbers of viewers whose attention they can sell to advertisers. They effectively auction off ad space, their customers being advertisers, not users. Anything that increases the number of users and the amount of time they spend at the site increases potential revenue and the value of the company. To that end, Google has added email, document management, Google Home, Google Earth, and so on to its basic search engines. A slew of legal cases against the company underlines how they push into people's private domains—for example, taking pictures of people's homes and property for Google Earth without asking permission—without concern for law, exhausting adversaries in the many cases that are launched against them or settling and paying fines. As Shoshana Zuboff describes it, "This modus operandi is that of incursion into undefended private territory until resistance is encountered." Zuboff reports that Google has faced legal opposition and social protest in relation to claims of (1) the scanning of email, including those of non-Gmail users and those of students using its

educational apps; (2) the capture of voice communications; (3) the bypassing of privacy settings; (4) unilateral practices of data bundling across its online services; (5) the extensive retention of search data; (6) the tracking of smartphone location data; and (7) its wearable technologies and facial recognition capabilities. These contested data-gathering moves face substantial opposition in the European Union as well as in the United States. See Shoshana Zuboff, "Big Other: Surveillance Capitalism and the Prospects of an Information Civilization," *Journal of Information Technology* 30 (2015): 75–89, https://papers.ssrn.com/sol3/papers.cfm?abstract_id=2594754.

94 **are among the capital's top lobbyists:** See Kang and Vogel, "Tech Giants Amass a Lobbying Army for an Epic Washington Battle."

95 **"reduce human labor to almost nil":** Analytics Vidhya content team, "10 Real World Applications of the Internet of Things (IoT)—Explained in Videos," Analytics Vidhya, August 25, 2016, https://www.analyticsvidhya .com/blog/2016/08/10-youtube-videos-explaining-the-real-world -applications-of-internet-of-things-iot/.

95 **"the rule of law":** Zuboff, "Big Other: Surveillance Capitalism and the Prospects of an Information Civilization."

96 **"commoditizing behavior for profit":** Ibid.

96 **"real-time records":** Ibid.

97 **Triangle Shirtwaist Factory fire:** For further discussion, see my *The Corporation: The Pathological Pursuit of Profit and Power,* 73–74.

97 **Corporations opposed worker protection laws from the start:** For examples of tactics against unions, see "Union-Busting Playbook," Communications Workers of America, https://unionbustingplaybook.com.

98 **Google is taking no chances:** See Noam Scheiber and Daisuke Wakabayashi, "Google Hires Firm Known for Anti-Union Efforts," *New York Times,* November 20, 2019, https://www.nytimes.com/2019/11/20/technology /Google-union-consultant.html/; and Sean Hollister, "Google Is Accused of Union-Busting After Firing Four Employees," *The Verge,* November 25, 2019, https://www.theverge.com/2019/11/25/20983053/google-fires-four -employees-memo-rebecca-rivers-laurence-berland-union-busting -accusation-walkout/.

98 **Amazon training video:** See Janet Burns, "Report: Amazon's Anti-Union Training Is Revealed in Leaked Video," *Forbes,* September 27, 2018, https:// www.forbes.com/sites/janetwburns/2018/09/27/amazons-anti-union -training-strategy-revealed-in-leaked-video/#5ce828ae6068. The video itself can be found at https://www.youtube.com/watch?v=uRpwVwFxyk4/. See also Annie Palmer, "Senators Ask Jeff Bezos for Answers on Fired Coronavirus Whistleblowers," CNBC, May 7, 2020, https://www.cnbc.com /2020/05/07/senators-ask-jeff-bezos-for-more-info-on-amazon-firings.html.

98 **union density rates:** "Economic New Release: Union Members Summary," Bureau of Labor Statistics, U.S. Department of Labor, January 18, 2019, https://www.bls.gov/news.release/union2.nr0.htm/; Doug Henwood, "Why Bosses Hate Unions," *Jacobin,* January 27, 2015, https://www .jacobinmag.com/2015/01/union-membership-2014-bls/.

98 **Cowlar:** For more on the Cowlar, see https://www.cowlar.com/.

99 **The results are Kafkaesque:** James Bloodworth, who worked for Ama-

zon for a month in 2016 for his book, *Hired: Six Months Undercover in Low-Wage Britain,* as reported by Emine Saner, "Employers Are Monitoring Computers, Toilet Breaks—Even Emotions. Is Your Boss Watching You?," *The Guardian,* May 14, 2018, https://www.theguardian.com /world/2018/may/14/is-your-boss-secretly-or-not-so-secretly-watching -you/; also see Emily Guendelsberger, *On the Clock: What Low-Wage Work Did to Me and How It Drives America Insane* (New York: Little, Brown, 2019), as reported in Eric Spitznagel, "Inside the Hellish Workday of an Amazon Warehouse Employee," *New York Post,* July 13, 2019, https://nypost .com/2019/07/13/inside-the-hellish-workday-of-an-amazon-warehouse -employee/.

99 **"expectation of being treated like human beings":** Emily Guendelsberger, as reported by Eric Spitznagel, "Inside the Hellish Workday of an Amazon Warehouse Employee." See also Saner, "Employers Are Monitoring Computers, Toilet Breaks—Even Emotions. Is Your Boss Watching You?," where James Bloodworth describes how he couldn't keep up with the productivity targets, finally quit, and says of his time at Amazon that it didn't feel "that you were really treated as a human being." See also, Louis Matsakis, "Amazon Workers Face High Risks and Few Options," *Wired,* March 27, 2020, https://www.wired.com/story/coronavirus-amazon -warehouse-workers-risks-few-options/.

99 **poor sanitation at warehouses:** See Jay Greene, "Amazon Workers Test Positive for COVID-19 at 10 U.S. Warehouses," *Washington Post,* March 25, 2020, https://www.washingtonpost.com/technology/2020/03/24/amazon -warehouse-workers-coronavirus-positive/.

99 **a report coauthored by the economist Beth Gutelius:** Cited in Matt O'Brien, "As Robots Take Over Warehousing, Workers Are Pushed to Adapt," *Globe and Mail,* January 1, 2020, www.theglobeandmail.com /business/international-business/us-business/article-as-robots-take-over -warehousing-workers-pushed-to-adapt/. See Beth Gutelius and Nik Theodore, "The Future of Warehouse Work: Technological Change in the U.S. Logistics Industry," Center for Labor Research and Education, UC Berkeley Institute for Research on Labor and Employment, October 22, 2019, http://laborcenter.berkeley.edu/future-of-warehouse-work/. For more on the Amazon warehouse video game, see Carl Velasco, "Amazon Is Making Employees Treat Tedious Warehouse Work Like a Video Game," *Tech Times,* May 23, 2019, https://www.techtimes.com/articles/243665/20190523 /amazon-is-making-employees-treat-tedious-warehouse-work-like-a-video -game.htm/.

100 **Technologies that monitor and control workers' behavior:** Employee surveillance is a veritable industry today, with numerous apps and software available to employers to count keystrokes, track website visits, monitor social-networking activities, and record audio and video of employees. See Rob Marvin, "The Best Employee Monitoring Software for 2019," *PC Magazine,* September 27, 2019, https://www.pcmag.com/roundup/357211/the -best-employee-monitoring-software/; and Theodore Kinni, "Monitoring Your Employees' Every Emotion," *MIT Sloan Management Review,* Septem-

ber 15, 2016, https://sloanreview.mit.edu/article/tech-savvy-monitoring -your-employees-every-emotion/.

100 **an employee ID badge . . . biomeasuring wristwatch:** Thomas Heath, "This Employee ID Badge Monitors and Listens to You at Work—Except in the Bathroom," *Washington Post,* September 7, 2016, https://www .washingtonpost.com/news/business/wp/2016/09/07/this-employee-badge -knows-not-only-where-you-are-but-whether-you-are-talking-to-your -co-workers/.

100 **a Chinese company collects data . . . from brain-wave-scanning sensors:** Saner, "Employers Are Monitoring Computers, Toilet Breaks—Even Emotions. Is Your Boss Watching You?"

101 **Fausto Luna:** See Tyler Pager and Emily Palmer, "Uber Driver's Death Marks Seventh For-Hire Driver Suicide Within a Year," *New York Times,* October 7, 2018, https://www.nytimes.com/2018/10/07/nyregion/uber -driver-suicide-for-hire-taxis-new-york.html/.

101 **an extra $3 billion for the company:** The source of information in this paragraph is Hubert Horan, "Uber's Path of Destruction," *American Affairs,* 3, no. 2 (Summer 2019): 108–33, https://americanaffairsjournal.org/2019/05 /ubers-path-of-destruction/.

102 **the public is left with an unregulated alternative:** See Ginia Bellafante, "Why Your Uber Ride Can Cost as Much as a Plane Ticket," *New York Times,* January 3, 2020, https://www.nytimes.com/2020/01/03/nyregion/uber-lyft -price.html?smid=nytcore-ios-share/. See also Horan, "Uber's Path of Destruction."

102 **Amazon Flex:** See Amazon Flex online, https://flex.amazon.com.

102 **The system is rife with abuse:** See Caroline O'Donovan and Ken Bensinger, "Amazon's Next-Day Delivery Has Brought Chaos and Carnage to America's Streets—but the World's Biggest Retailer Has a System to Escape the Blame," BuzzFeed News, September 6, 2019, https://www.buzz feednews.com/article/carolineodonovan/amazon-next-day-delivery-deaths/; see also Brittain Ladd, "Amazon Is Hell on Wheels for Delivery Drivers," *Forbes,* September 13, 2018, https://www.forbes.com/sites/brittainladd/2018 /09/13/hell-on-wheels-what-its-like-to-be-a-delivery-driver-for-amazon /#1161b0d5219a/; and Hamilton Nolan, " 'We Are Treated Like Animals,' Say Amazon Flex Drivers," *Splinter News,* April 18, 2019, https://splinternews .com/we-are-treated-like-animals-say-amazon-flex-drivers-1834142643/. The hardships of drivers are revealed in the film *Sorry We Missed You,* directed by Ken Loach (released March 6, 2019).

102 **"The digital economy will sharply erode":** Arun Sundararajan, "The Future of Work," *Finance and Development* 54, no. 2 (June 2017), https:// www.imf.org/external/pubs/ft/fandd/2017/06/sundararajan.htm/. See also E. Tammy Kim, "The Gig Economy Is Coming for Your Job," *New York Times,* January 10, 2020, www.nytimes.com/2020/01/10/opinion/sunday /gig-economy-unemployment-automation.html?smid=nytcore-ios-share/.

104 **strategic cultivation of addiction . . . targeting of ever-younger children:** I discuss these issues at length in Joel Bakan, *Childhood Under Siege: How Big Business Targets Children* (New York: Free Press, 2011).

5. Being Corporate

110 "Study Finds That Diverse Companies": Anna Powers, "Study Finds That Diverse Companies Produce 19% More Revenue," *Forbes,* June 27, 2018, https://www.forbes.com/sites/annapowers/2018/06/27/a-study-finds -that-diverse-companies-produce-19-more-revenue/#54f1b4b6506f/.

110 "Sustainability Is 'Good for Humanity'": Libby Kane, "NYU Stern Professor: Sustainability Is 'Good for Humanity, but It's Better for Business,'" *Business Insider,* June 27, 2018, https://www.businessinsider.com /sustainability-good-for-humanity-better-for-business-2018-6/.

110 "Childhood Poverty Costs U.S. $1.03 Trillion in a Year": Neil Schoenherr, "Childhood Poverty Costs U.S. $1.03 Trillion in a Year, Study Finds," *Source,* Washington University in St. Louis, April 16, 2018, https://source .wustl.edu/2018/04/childhood-poverty-cost-u-s-1-03-trillion-in-a-year -study-finds/.

111 the economy should take precedence over saving lives: See Douglas Rushkoff, "We Wish to Inform You That Your Death Is Highly Profitable," *Gen,* March 25, 2020, https://gen.medium.com/we-wish-to-inform-you -that-your-death-is-highly-profitable-22c73744055c; Max Boot, "Now We Know: The Conservative Devotion to Life Ends at Birth," *Washington Post,* March 27, 2020, https://www.washingtonpost.com/opinions/2020/03/27 /now-we-know-conservative-devotion-life-ends-birth/; Eduardo Porter and Jim Tankersley, "Shutdown Spotlights Economic Costs of Saving Lives," *New York Times,* March 24, 2020, https://www.nytimes.com/2020/03/24 /business/economy/coronavirus-economy.html.

112 Adam Tooze: See Adam Tooze, "Coronavirus Has Shattered the Myth That the Economy Must Come First," *The Guardian,* March 20, 2020, https:// www.theguardian.com/commentisfree/2020/mar/20/coronavirus-myth -economy-uk-business-life-death.

114 "fundamental commitment to all our stakeholders": As reported by GuruFocus, "Jamie Dimon Throws Milton Friedman Under the Bus," Yahoo! Finance, August 23, 2019, https://finance.yahoo.com/news/jamie -dimon-throws-milton-friedman-193813409.html.

114 "private enterprise for public good": See Jamie Dimon, "Private Enterprise for Public Good," https://www.jpmorganchase.com/corporate /Corporate-Responsibility/cr-2016-2-private-enterprise.htm.

114 "a new corporate responsibility model": JPMorgan Chase, "America's Comeback City: The Rebirth of Detroit," *Forbes,* June 2, 2017, https:// www.forbes.com/sites/jpmorganchase/2017/06/02/americas-comeback-city -the-rebirth-of-detroit/#2ec012bb37a5/. For more detail on the JPMorgan Chase Detroit initiative, see "A Model of Recovery for America's Cities" (originally published in *Politico,* May 18, 2017), JPMorgan Chase, https:// www.jpmorganchase.com/corporate/news/stories/model-recovery-cities.htm/.

114 "America's comeback city": See JPMorgan Chase, "America's Comeback City: The Rebirth of Detroit."

114 "inclusive collaboration and public-private partnership": See JPMorgan Chase, "A Model of Recovery for America's Cities."

115 Despite global criticism and a rebuke from the United Nations: After

visiting Detroit, Catarina de Albuquerque, special rapporteur on the human right to water and sanitation, stated: "It is contrary to human rights to disconnect water from people who simply do not have the means to pay their bills. I heard testimonies from poor, African American residents of Detroit who were forced to make impossible choices, to pay the water bill or to pay their rent." As reported by World Bank/Allison Kwesell, "In Detroit, City-Backed Water Shut-Offs 'Contrary to Human Rights,' Say UN Experts," UN News, October 20, 2014, https://news.un.org/en/story/2014/10/481542-detroit-city-backed-water-shut-offs-contrary-human-rights-say-un-experts/. See also Amber Ainsworth, "Detroit Sees Drastic Drop in Number of Water Shutoffs This Year," Click On Detroit, April 17, 2019, https://www.clickondetroit.com/news/detroit-sees-drastic-drop-in-number-of-water-shutoffs-this-year/. And there are consequences beyond the immediate misery to targeted residents. When shutoffs are concentrated in particular communities, which they tend to be, pipes serving those communities lose their biofilm, destroying the buffer between the water flowing through them and the lead in the pipes. As a result, in neighborhoods with lots of shutoffs, lead content is dangerously high, forcing, for example, schools to shut down their water systems. Simon Albaugh, "Shutoffs Continue as the People of Detroit Fight for Water as a Human Right," Nation of Change, January 14, 2019, https://www.nationofchange.org/2019/01/14/shutoffs-continue-as-the-people-of-detroit-fight-for-water-as-a-human-right/.

115 **lack of water and sanitation services:** See Mary Schuermann Kuhlman, "Detroit Water Activists Urge Gov. Whitmer to Provide Free Water Stations During the Coronavirus Pandemic," *Detroit Metro Times*, March 23, 2020, https://www.metrotimes.com/news-hits/archives/2020/03/23/detroit-water-activists-urge-gov-whitmer-to-provide-free-water-stations-during-the-coronavirus-pandemic. See also Khushbu Shah, "How Racism and Poverty Made Detroit a New Coronavirus Hotspot," Vox, April 10, 2020, https://www.vox.com/identities/2020/4/10/21211920/detroit-coronavirus-racism-poverty-hot-spot.

117 **Since 2000, multinational utilities and engineering firms:** Sharmila Murthy of Suffolk University Law School explains that this change was driven partly by the belief that expertise provided by the private sector could surpass that available in government. These ideas were supported by examples of public utilities failures throughout the world. Sharmila L. Murthy, "The Human Right(s) to Water and Sanitation: History, Meaning and the Controversy over Privatization," *Berkeley Journal of International Law* 31, no. 1 (2013): 123–24. See also Leila M. Harris, Jacqueline A. Goldin, and Christopher Sneddon, eds., *Contemporary Water Governance in the Global South: Scarcity, Marketization and Participation* (New York: Routledge, 2013), 124–25.

117 **"solve environmental challenges":** Veolia online, https://www.veolianorthamerica.com/who-we-serve/. Veolia also says: "Ensuring access to basic services, fair distribution of resources and conserving them for future generations are crucial challenges for our communities. Veolia works toward these goals on a daily basis by consistently monitoring our CSR and ambitions add to our appeal with all our stakeholders, which most importantly

include our customers, our employees, and our investors." Veolia online, https://www.veolia.com/africa/en/propos/veolia-en-afrique/corporate-social -responsibility/.

117 **"solve the world's most complex challenges"**: "Solving Our Customers' Toughest Waters and Process Challenges Wherever They Occur," Suez Water Technologies & Solutions, https://www.suezwatertechnologies.com/LP -Brand?gclid=Cj0KCQjwtMvlBRDmARIsAEoQ8zRFKPZzkUXmCBg OWOwVsQUkCb1o-f8CYYAU6SQn5kWfevFybr-fGrwaAkqGEALw _wcB/.

118 **"make a positive contribution to our customers, communities"**: Steve Robertson, CEO, "Our Corporate Responsibility Policy," Thames Water, August 2018, https://www.thameswater.co.uk/-/media/Site-Content /Corporate-Responsibility/CRS-2017-18/Policies-and-other-pdfs/Corporate -Responsibility-Policy-2018.pdf.

118 **"we should value water more"**: The United Nations agrees. In 2010, the UN General Assembly and Human Rights Council declared a human right to safe drinking water, affirming, as one commentator describes it, "the fundamental importance of water for human dignity."

120 **They exclude communities:** See Murthy, "The Human Right(s) to Water and Sanitation: History, Meaning and the Controversy over Privatization."

120 **And because the contracts between water corporations and public authorities:** Ibid., 139.

120 **when corporations take over water systems:** As Sharmila Murthy states, "Incentives to be efficient—and generate a profit—do not necessarily result in providing good services to *all,* which is critical from a human rights perspective." Ibid., 136.

123 **Emmett Carson:** As quoted in Natasha Singer, "The Silicon Valley Billion-aires Remaking America's Schools," *New York Times,* June 6, 2017, https:// www.nytimes.com/2017/06/06/technology/tech-billionaires-education -zuckerberg-facebook-hastings.html/.

124 **Cyber-charters are notorious for cheating scandals:** See Kristen Taketa, Morgan Cook, and Jaclyn Cosgrove, "Online Charter Schools in L.A. and San Diego Counties to Close After Indictments," *Los Angeles Times,* May 28, 2019, https://www.latimes.com/local/lanow/la-me-ln-edu-charter-school -indictments-20190528-story.html/.

124 *Liberating Learning*: See Terry M. Moe and John E. Chubb, *Liberating Learning: Technology, Politics, and the Future of American Education* (San Fran-cisco: John Wiley & Sons, 2012).

125 **The stay-at-home schooling:** See Katherine Mangu-Ward, "Regulatory Barriers to Online Tools Will Fall," and Sonia Shah, "More Restraints on Mass Consumption," in "Coronavirus Will Change the World Permanently. Here's How," *Politico,* March 19, 2020, https://www.politico.com/news /magazine/2020/03/19/coronavirus-effect-economy-life-society-analysis -covid-135579; see also Caroline Alphonso, "'The Education World Has Been Turned Upside Down': Online Learning May Reshape the Classroom," *Globe and Mail,* March 25, 2020. https://www.theglobeandmail.com/canada /article-as-online-learning-rolls-out-education-may-change-forever/.

128 **JPMorgan Chase egregiously flouted financial laws and regulations:**

See press release, "Justice Department, Federal and State Partners Secure Record $13 Billion Global Settlement with JPMorgan for Misleading Investors About Securities Containing Toxic Mortgages," U.S. Department of Justice, November 19, 2013, https://www.justice.gov/opa/pr/justice-department-federal-and-state-partners-secure-record-13-billion-global-settlement/. For more on how JPMorgan Chase helped cause the financial crash, see Jessica Silver-Greenberg and Ben Protess, "JPMorgan Chase Faces Full-Court Press of Federal Investigations," *New York Times,* March 26, 2013, https://dealbook.nytimes.com/2013/03/26/jpmorgan-chase-faces-full-court-press-of-federal-investigations/. Since the 2013 settlement, JPMorgan Chase has continued to be on the wrong side of the law, cited for, among other things, risky investment practices, improper increases in monthly minimum payments for credit card customers, foreclosure abuses, altering results of outside analyses of securitized mortgages that turned out to be toxic, lying to regulators, using manipulative schemes to transform money-losing power plants into powerful profit centers, fraudulent and unlawful debt-collection practices, manipulating electricity markets, bribery, forcing homeowners to buy overpriced property insurance, violating securities laws, manipulative conduct in trading credit default swaps, failing to alert authorities about its client Bernie Madoff's suspicious transactions, deficiencies in money-laundering controls, manipulating the foreign exchange market, and charging African American and Hispanic mortgage borrowers higher rates than similarly situated white customers. See Philip Mattera, "JPMorgan Chase: Corporate Rap Sheet," Corporate Research Project, last updated February 3, 2017, https://www.corp-research.org/jpmorganchase/.

130 **For want of a 75-cent face mask:** Farhad Manjoo, "How the World's Richest Country Ran Out of a 75-Cent Face Mask," *New York Times*, March 25, 2020, https://www.nytimes.com/2020/03/25/opinion/coronavirus-face-mask.html.

131 **"Crimson Contagion":** See David E. Sanger, Eric Lipton, Eileen Sullivan, and Michael Crowley, "Before Virus Outbreak, a Cascade of Warnings Went Unheeded," *New York Times*, March 19, 2020, https://www.nytimes.com/2020/03/19/us/politics/trump-coronavirus-outbreak.html.

132 **Predict:** Jim Robbins, "The Ecology of Disease," *New York Times*, July 14, 2012, https://www.nytimes.com/2012/07/15/sunday-review/the-ecology-of-disease.html.

133 **poor and low-income people would be:** See Jennifer Valentino-DeVries, Denise Lu, and Gabriel J. X. Dance, "Location Data Says It All: Staying at Home During Coronavirus Is a Luxury," *New York Times,* April 3, 2020, https://www.nytimes.com/interactive/2020/04/03/us/coronavirus-stay-home-rich-poor.html?referringSource=articleShare.

134 **The coronavirus pandemic is the perfect example:** See "In Conversation with Anand Giridharadas: Can the Oligarchy Survive Coronavirus?" April 21, 2020, https://www.youtube.com/watch?v=_56cofRjsI4.

134 **One undeniable result:** Statistics compiled from https://inequality.org/facts/.

141 **Supreme Court Justice Louis Brandeis is reputed to have said:** Peter

Scott Campbell writes: "After spending years on this project [searching for the source of the quote], I have been able to come up with an answer: He definitely did not say it. Or maybe he did." Campbell provides statements from Brandeis that closely resemble the one quoted and suggests the latter may be a conflation of these or possibly words spoken in conversation by Brandeis. See Peter Scott Campbell, "Democracy v. Concentrated Wealth: In Search of a Louis D. Brandeis Quote," 16 *Green Bag* 2D 251 (Spring 2013), University of Louisville School of Law Legal Studies Research Paper Series No. 2014-11, http://www.greenbag.org/v16n3/v16n3_articles _campbell.pdf.

6. Democracy Unbound

146 **There was a sense, even early in the pandemic, that big changes were afoot:** See Lilliana Mason, "Government Service Regains Its Cachet," and Eric Klinenberg, "Less Individualism," in "Coronavirus Will Change the World Permanently. Here's How," *Politico*, March 19, 2020, https://www .politico.com/news/magazine/2020/03/19/coronavirus-effect-economy-life -society-analysis-covid-135579; Interview transcript, "Nobel Laureate Economist Joe Stiglitz: Combat the Coronavirus Pandemic with Progressive Capitalism," *Democracy Now!*, March 19, 2020, https://www.democracy now.org/2020/3/19/joseph_stiglitz_says_trump_s_response.

148 **"We hold these truths to be self-evident":** The original speech was made by Martin Luther King, Jr., on August 28, 1963. The story is retold in the "I have a Dream" speech at History.com, January 15, 2020, https://www .history.com/topics/civil-rights-movement/i-have-a-dream-speech/.

149 **Chokwe Lumumba:** Quotations are from Bhaskar Sunkara, "Free the Land: An Interview with Chokwe Lumumba," Jackson Rising Pressbooks, https://jacksonrising.pressbooks.com/chapter/free-the-land-an-interview -with-chokwe-lumumba/.

152 **Cooperation Jackson:** See https://cooperationjackson.org/.

153 **Chokwe Antar Lumumba:** Quotations from Jamiles Lartey, "A Revolutionary, Not a Liberal: Can a Radical Black Mayor Bring Change to Mississippi?," *The Guardian,* September 11, 2017, https://www.theguardian .com/us-news/2017/sep/11/revolutionary-not-a-liberal-radical-black -mayor-mississippi-chokwe-lumumba/.

153 **"an example of what government for the people can be":** This quote is from Mayor Lumumba's chief of staff, Safiya Omari. As quoted in D. D. Guttenplan, "Is This the Most Radical Mayor in America?," *The Nation,* November 17, 2017, https://www.thenation.com/article/is-this-the-most -radical-mayor-in-america/.

154 **"talk with her about the cooperative businesses they'd developed":** Ibid.

155 **together known as the Arab Spring:** The Arab Spring began in Tunisia on December 17, 2010, when pro-democracy protesters took to the streets, occupied the squares, and overthrew the government. It quickly spread to other Arab nations—Egypt (January 25, 2011), Syria (January 26), Yemen

(January 27), and Bahrain (February 14). The movement's slogan, "The people want to bring down the regime," was realized in part with regimes toppled in some countries, like Tunisia, Egypt, and Libya, but by mid-2012 it had become abundantly clear that movement goals of greater democracy and economic equality would not be realized.

156 **They began by crafting a "tactical briefing":** See the full text at https://www.micahmwhite.com/occupywallstreet/.

161 **two hundred progressive luminaries from around the world:** The letter can be found at https://medium.com/@BComuGlobal/open-letter-to -the-people-of-barcelona-66a72e938c22/.

162 **With her signature issue, the $15 minimum wage:** See Ben Gilbert, "Amazon Tried to Remove a Seattle City Councilmember and Lost," *Business Insider,* November 20, 2019, https://www.businessinsider.com/amazon -seattle-kshama-sawant-interview-on-election-2019-11/.

163 **"it's only a collective organized effort":** Sawant has had other victories beyond the $15 minimum wage—boosting rights for renters, revealing cozy relationships between big business and the city council, and publicizing Amazon's tax-avoidance strategies—but, again like Lumumba and Colau, she's also realistic about the problems in her city, and the world, and the limits of her position in government. "We are talking about massive dysfunctions," she says, "a system that is absolutely not working for the vast majority of human beings." Climate change demands quickly moving away from fossil fuels to renewable energy, and inequality and extreme poverty must be attacked, she says. These are not things you can do from a perch on a city council. But "you've got to start somewhere," she says.

167 **He championed privatization and market solutions:** See Farhad Manjoo, "Barack Obama's Biggest Mistake," *New York Times,* September 18, 2019, https://www.nytimes.com/2019/09/18/opinion/obama-2008 -financial-crisis.html?smid=nytcore-ios-share/.

168 **Noam Chomsky describes it:** See Democracy Now!, "Noam Chomsky on Trump's Disastrous Coronavirus Response, Bernie Sanders & What Gives Him Hope," April 10, 2020, https://www.youtube.com /watch?v=zRvqkUoiKJo.

173 **It's telling that just over half of American millennials say:** The figure is taken from a Harvard University study and reported by Max Ehrenfreund, "A Majority of Millennials Now Reject Capitalism, Poll Shows," *Washington Post,* April 26, 2016, https://www.washingtonpost.com/news/wonk/wp /2016/04/26/a-majority-of-millennials-now-reject-capitalism-poll-shows/.

173 **61 percent report responding positively:** See Stef W. Kight, "Exclusive Poll: Young Americans Are Embracing Socialism," Axios, March 10, 2019, https://www.axios.com/exclusive-poll-young-americans -embracing-socialism-b051907a-87a8-4f61-9e6e-0db75f7edc4a.html/.

173 **43 percent of Americans agree:** See Mohamed Younis, "Four in 10 Americans Embrace Some Form of Socialism," Gallup News, May 10, 2019, https:// news.gallup.com/poll/257639/four-americans-embrace-form-socialism.aspx/.

173 **"siren song of socialism":** Vice President Mike Pence, as reported by Lauren Gambino, " 'We're Here to Win': US Democratic Socialists Move to

Center Stage," *The Guardian,* August 6, 2019, https://www.theguardian
.com/politics/2019/aug/06/democratic-socialists-us-alexandria-ocasio
-cortez-bernie-sanders/.

173 **socialism "would be a disaster for our country":** Jamie Dimon, in his
annual letter to shareholders, as reported by Dominic Rushe, "Billionaire
JP Morgan Chief Attacks Socialism as 'a Disaster,'" *The Guardian,* April 4,
2019, https://www.theguardian.com/business/2019/apr/04/jamie-dimon
-socialism-jp-morgan-banker-disaster/.

173 **more than one hundred democratic socialists currently holding office:**
Among them are Khalid Kamau, a city councillor in South Fulton, Georgia,
and a Black Lives Matter organizer; Ruth Buffalo, an indigenous state representative in North Dakota; Mik Pappas, a district judge in Pennsylvania;
six democratic socialists recently elected to Chicago's city council (along
with progressive mayor Lori Lightfoot); and Gabriel Acevero, elected as a
representative to the Maryland House of Delegates. See Gambino, "'We're
Here to Win': US Democratic Socialists Move to Center Stage."

Afterword

184 **as Angela Davis notes:** Interview transcript, "Uprising & Abolition:
Angela Davis on Movement Building, 'Defund the Police' & Where We Go
from Here," *Democracy Now!*, June 12, 2020, https://www.democracynow
.org/2020/6/12/angela_davis_historic_moment.

185 **Most "new" corporations have joined in:** See, for example, Tarpley
Hitt, "The Companies with the Most Hypocritical Black Lives Matter
Messaging," *Daily Beast,* June 5, 2020, https://www.thedailybeast.com
/the-companies-with-the-most-hypocritical-black-lives-matter-messaging
-from-fox-to-facebook; Terry Nguyen, "Consumers Don't Care About
Corporate Solidarity. They Want Donations," Vox, June 3, 2020, https://
www.vox.com/the-goods/2020/6/3/21279292/blackouttuesday-brands
-solidarity-donations; Tejal Rao, "Food Brands Tweet #BlackLivesMatter,
but What's Behind the Words?" *New York Times,* June 6, 2020, https://www
.nytimes.com/2020/06/11/dining/food-brands-black-lives-matter-social
-media.html?auth=login-email&login=email; Rachel Lerman, "From Wake
Word to Woke Word: Siri and Alexa Tell You Black Lives Matter, but Tech
Still Has a Diversity Problem, *Washington Post,* June 10, 2020, https://www
.washingtonpost.com/technology/2020/06/10/big-tech-black-lives-matter/.

186 **Dr. Keeanga-Yamahtta Taylor:** Interview transcript, "Defund Police:
Keeanga-Yamahtta Taylor Says Budgets Wrongly Prioritize Cops Over
Schools, Hospitals," *Democracy Now!*, June 1, 2020, https://www.democracy
now.org/2020/6/1/keeanga_yamahtta_taylor_defund_us_police.

186 **Dr. Cornel West describes it:** Interview transcript, "'America's Moment
of Reckoning': Cornel West Says Nationwide Uprising Is Sign of 'Empire
Imploding,'" *Democracy Now!*, June 1, 2020, https://www.democracynow
.org/2020/6/1/cornel_west_us_moment_of_reckoning.

INDEX

Amazon, 15, 20, 27, 41, 56, 163
  Flex, 102
  as monopoly, 74, 92, 94
  worker welfare at, 98–100
American Petroleum Institute, 65, 75
Appadurai, Anjali, 76
Apple, 20, 56, 94, 124
Arab Spring, 155–7
artificial intelligence (AI), 100,
    104–5, 123

bailouts, 4, 134, 143–4, 146, 156–7,
    170
Baker, James E., 65
Bakule, Justin, 21–2, 29
Bannon, Stephen, 62
Barcelona en Comú party, 160–2
Barlow, John Perry, 92
Barrett, Chris, 166–70
Barro Blanco dam, Panama, 84
B corps (benefit corporations), 32,
    79–81
Bechtel, 120
Beech, Hannah, 132
Ben & Jerry's, 17, 19
Berle, Adolf, 31
Berman, Tzeporah, 21

Bezos, Jeff, 27
Biden, Joe, 144, 168
Big-Box Swindle (Mitchell), 42
B Lab, 79–80
Black Act of 1723 (UK), 59–60
Black Lives Matter, 16, 174, 185
BlackRock, 21, 46–7
Blair, Tony, 7–8, 113
Boeing, 69–70
Boost (nutraceutical), 51–2
Boot, Max, 111
Brandeis, Louis, 141
Bridge International Academies,
    122–3, 125–6
British American Tobacco, 41
(BP) British Petroleum, 18, 47
  Deepwater Horizon disaster of,
    37–40, 56, 72
British South Sea Company, 59–60
Browne, Lord John, 18–9, 33, 36–40,
    44, 45
Brown, Gordon, 64
Brown, Wendy, 109–11, 130, 133,
    139–40
Buffett, Warren, 53
Buiter, Willem, 72–3
Business Roundtable, 3, 66, 114

carbon emissions, 17, 19–20, 43–4, 53–7, 75, 174
    offset programs for, 81–5, 167
    regulation of, 63–7, 73, 161, 185
Carson, Emmett, 123
certification regimes, 76–81
charter schools, 115, 121–7
Chavez, Cesar, 150
CheatNeutral.com, 82–3
Chemical Safety and Hazard Investigation Board, 38
Children's Food and Beverage Advertising Initiative, 73
Chomsky, Noam, 161, 168
Chubb, John, 124
Citizens United v. Federal Election Commission, 89
Civil Rights Act, 148–9
climate change, 11, 13, 148, 172, 184. *See also* carbon emissions
    carbon emissions tied to, 17, 19–20, 43–4, 53–7, 63–7, 73, 75, 81–5, 161, 167, 174, 185
    corporate obfuscation on, 43–7
    disease tied to, 4, 48–9, 132, 182–3
    Paris accord on, 15, 43–5
Coalition for Inclusive Capitalism, 19
coal production, 41, 47, 63, 66–7, 84–5, 177
Coca-Cola, 11, 15, 17, 26, 30, 42, 66, 116
    nutraceutical drinks by, 49, 51–2
    water offset program by, 85–8
Cochabamba, Bolivia, 120
Colau, Ada, 153–5, 159–62, 164–5, 168–70, 180–1
colonialism, 60, 126, 184–6
Consumers International, 42
Cooperation Jackson, 152–3
coronavirus/pandemics, 3, 5, 13, 21, 41, 99, 115, 125
    bailouts stemming from, 4, 134, 143–4, 146, 170
    climate change's tie to, 4, 48–9, 132, 182–3

deregulation's impact on, 63–6
economic *vs.* human loss in, 111–2
readiness/preparation for, 130–3
social state's depletion and, 4, 26–7, 130–1, 133–4, 143–4, 145–8, 170, 178, 182–3
Trump's response to, 20, 26–7, 64–5, 111–2, 130–2, 143, 178
corporate social responsibility (CSR)
    evolution of, 16–9
    legal limitations on, 31–4
    as money-making tool, 28–30, 32–3, 41–2
    obfuscation involving, 44–7, 49–52, 74–8, 86–8
    self-interest as limitation in, 12, 15, 18–9, 24–34, 37–58, 66–73, 77–81, 87, 90, 106, 127–30, 143–4, 178–9, 185
    tax avoidance and, 24–8
corporations, 3, 11, 16. *See also* privatization; regulation
    automation/AI and, 100, 104–5
    bailouts of, 4, 134, 143–4, 146, 156–7, 170
    certification regimes of, 76–8
    data collection by, 94–6
    debt carried by, 65–6
    democracy's decline under, 4–5, 9–10, 61–3, 74–5, 89–90, 91–5, 105–6, 110, 115, 128–30, 135–41
    direct relationships between consumers and, 95–7
    economization of personal value by, 107–12
    governance as goal of, 113–8
    law as founding element of, 31–5, 57, 60, 81, 89, 182
    lawbreaking by, 53–8
    "personhood" of, 31, 89
    political activism to curtail, 145–75, 180–7
    privatization as goal of, 112–43

profit/self-interest as driving
purpose of, 12, 15, 18–9,
24–34, 37–58, 66–73, 77–81,
87–8, 90, 106, 127–30, 143–4,
178–9, 185
right-wing's synergy with, 125,
139–43, 186
tax cuts for, 5, 24–8, 126, 128–30,
133–4, 139, 143, 147, 163,
170, 173, 185
worker welfare and, 4, 36–41,
97–103, 124–5, 128, 130, 141,
150, 174, 180–1, 185
The Corporation (Bakan), 4, 14, 166,
169
Cowlar (smart collar), 98–9
Coyne, John, 13, 19, 29
creative capitalism, 11, 121, 126
Crimson Contagion, 131
CSR. *See* corporate social
responsibility

Daszak, Peter, 132
Dauvergne, Peter, 17, 41–2, 45,
76, 78
Davis, Angela, 184
Davos, Switzerland, 7–14, 22–8, 91,
104, 112–3
*Decision Making in Environmental
Law*, 73
Deepwater Horizon disaster, 37–40,
56, 72
Defense Production Act (DPA), 64–5
democracy
corporate-based decline of, 4–5,
9–10, 61–3, 74–5, 89–90,
91–5, 105–6, 110, 115,
128–30, 135–41
political protests' role in, 145–51,
154–9, 164–5, 174–5, 181,
186–7
political service as step to, 151–4,
159–69, 172–5, 181
social state as necessity for, 145–8,
167–75, 183–7
democratic socialism, 146
de Swardt, Cobus, 53

Detroit, Michigan, 113–5,
127–8
Dimon, Jamie, 3, 7–9, 25–6,
173
deregulation push by, 66–7
privatization push by, 112–6,
127–8
Dodd, Merrick, 31

Edelman, Richard, 12–3, 19, 116,
127–8
education, 174, 183, 186
cyber-based, 124
funding cuts, 24, 129, 143, 185
privatization of, 115, 120–7, 137,
167
teacherless, 123–6
Elmore, Bartow, 88
environment. *See also* climate change
Deepwater Horizon disaster and,
37–40, 56, 72
deregulation's impact on, 63–7,
68, 72–3, 94, 174–5, 185
Green New Deal and, 174
as "new corporation" focus, 3–5,
9–13, 17, 19–22, 24–30, 41–9
obfuscation by corporations on,
44–7, 54–8
pandemics tied to, 4, 48–9, 132,
182–3
Paris accord's impact on, 43–5
Environmental Defense Fund, 78
Ernst & Young, 12, 18
Ethiopian Airlines, 69–70
ExxonMobil, 15, 45, 47, 75

FAA Reauthorization Act, 68
Facebook, 92, 94, 124
Fair Labor Standards Act, 97
Federal Aviation Administration
(FAA), 68–70
FedEx, 20, 41, 78
15-M. *See* Los Indignados
financial crisis of 2008, 16, 68, 72,
128, 146, 154, 159
bailouts for, 144, 156–7
Fink, Larry, 21, 46–7

First USA, 166
Floyd, George, 16, 41, 183–6
Ford, 21
Francis, Pope, 81–3, 88, 180
Friedman, Milton, 12, 92
Friedman, Patri, 92

Ganz, Marshall, 149–51, 158, 181
Gates, Bill, 11, 29
    privatization push by, 120–1,
        123–4, 126–7
Geffner, Dana, 77
Giridharadas, Anand, 94, 127–9,
        133, 138
GlaxoSmithKline, 51–2, 56, 78
GM, 20, 65
González, Juan, 163–4
Google, 15, 26, 41, 56, 124
    anti-union efforts of, 97–8
    monopolistic aspects of, 92, 94
Gore, Al, 7
Green New Deal (GND), 146, 174
Grenfell Tower, London, 71–2
Gresta, Bibop, 7–10, 91, 104,
        112–3
Guendelsberger, Emily, 99
Gupta, Arun, 51
Gutelius, Beth, 99–100

H1N1 flu pandemic, 131
Hanauer, Nick, 134, 139
Hardt, Michael, 141, 148, 157–8,
        180–1
Harvard Law Review, 31
Hastings, Reed, 123
health care, 136–7, 146, 163, 170,
        173–4, 185
    Affordable Care Act for, 167
    employment-based, 134
    funding cuts to, 4, 24, 26–7
Hedges, Chris, 145
Hoffmann-La Roche, 56
Honeywell, 20, 29–30, 41
Hong, Sun-ha, 105
Horlicks (nutraceutical), 51–2
Hubbard, Ben, 132
Hyperloop Transportation
        Technologies, 7–9, 91, 113

immigration, 11, 15–6, 20, 48–9,
        114, 138–9
indigenous people, 47, 174–5,
        179–80, 183–5
Los Indignados (15-M), 155–60
Institute for New Economic
        Thinking, 22
International Anti-Corruption
        Day, 53
International Monetary Fund, 102
Internet of Things (IOT), 95–6
IRI Consultants, 97–8
Isdell, E. Neville, 85

Jackson, Mahalia, 168
Jackson People's Assembly, 152
Jain, Sanjay, 112–3
Johnson, Boris, 111–2
Johnson & Johnson, 55–6, 66
Johnson, Robert, 22–3
Joint Authorities (aviation), 69–70
JPMorgan Chase, 3, 7–9, 25–6,
        29, 66
    financial crisis of 2008 and, 128
    privatization push by, 112–6,
        127–8

Kelleher, Dennis, 63
Keller, Valerie, 12–3, 18–9, 29
Kenan, W. R., Jr., 50
Kimmelman, Jay, 122–3, 126–7
King, Martin Luther, Jr., 148–9
King, Ronnie, 71
Klinenberg, Eric, 146
Kobori, Michael, 30
Koch Industries, 12, 41

labor unions, 4, 97–8, 100, 124–5,
        128, 130, 141, 150, 174, 180–1
Lac-Mégantic, Quebec, 72
Lasn, Kalle, 156
Leveson, Nancy, 39
Lewis, Brandon, 71
LGBTQ rights, 11, 92
Liao, Carol, 80
Liberating Learning (Chubb/Moe),
        124
Lion Air, 69–70

Lumumba, Chokwe (Edwin Finley Taliaferro), 149–53
Lumumba, Chokwe Antar, 153–4, 161, 164, 168–70
Luna, Fausto, 101
Lustgarten, Abrahm, 37–8, 40

Macron, Emmanuel, 23
Madoff, Ray, 172
Mangu-Ward, Katherine, 125
Manjoo, Farhad, 131, 167
Mason, Lilliana, 146
Matten, Dirk, 15
May, Elizabeth, 172
May, Shannon, 122, 126–7
May, Theresa, 23
McCabe, Luke, 166
McGhee, Heather, 180
Merkel, Angela, 23
Merrill, Mike, 107–10
Microsoft, 11, 56, 116, 120, 124
Mission Racer (game), 99–100
Mississippi Freedom Democratic Party, 149
Mississippi Summer Project, 149
Mitchell, Stacy, 42, 73–6, 99, 129
Modi, Narendra, 23
Moe, Terry, 124
Moldbug, Mencius, 92
Monbiot, George, 61, 147
Monsters, Inc. (film), 14–7
Motrin, 55
Musk, Elon, 8

NASA, 69
National Labor Relations Act, 97
National Rifle Association, 151
Nature Conservancy, 77, 87
Navidi, Sandra, 8–10, 25, 113
Nestlé, 49–50, 119, 121
New Deal, 60–1, 144, 167, 172–4
Ngäbe people, 84
NGOs (nongovernmental organizations), 7, 20
  corporate alignments with, 50, 52, 77–8, 81, 87–8
Nike, 11, 116, 166
nutraceutical products, 49–52

Obama, Barack, 162, 166–7
Ocasio-Cortez, Alexandria, 173–4
Occupational Safety and Health Administration (OSHA), 39
Occupy Seattle, 162, 168
Occupy Wall Street, 16, 155–9, 168
offsetting programs
  for carbon emissions, 81–5, 167
  for water, 85–8
Olivera, Oscar, 120
Orr, Kevyn, 115

Paris Agreement on Climate Change (Paris accord), 15
  effectiveness of, 43–5
Pence, Mike, 173
Petro-Canada, 75
Phillip, Stewart, 47–8, 175, 179–80
political citizenship, 128, 136
  democracy's protection via, 145–75, 180–1, 186–7
  grassroots organizing as, 149–51, 161, 164–5, 174–5, 180–1
  protesting as, 150–1, 154–9, 164–5, 174–5, 181, 186–7
  running for office as, 151–4, 159–69, 172–5, 181
Polman, Paul, 12, 19, 29
Popkin, Barry, 50
Porro, Álvaro, 155
Porter, Michael, 13, 19, 29, 43, 116
Prahalad, C. K., 121
Predict program, 132
privatization, 112–4
  democracy's decline due to, 110, 115, 128–30, 135–42
  of education, 115, 120–7, 137, 167
  under Obama, 167
  right-wing's synergy with, 125, 139–43, 186
  social state's destruction for, 127–43
  as tenet of "new" corporations, 116–8, 127–43, 147
  wage inequality tied to, 134–9
  of water services, 115, 117–20, 127, 137, 175
Procter & Gamble, 17, 20, 42, 66

public services. *See also* education;
    privatization
    funding cuts to, 4, 24, 129, 143,
      185
    privatization of, 4–5, 114–44, 167,
      175

racism, 11, 25, 60, 114, 133, 148,
      163, 174, 183
    corporations' impact on, 139–43,
      170
    poverty's connection to, 184–6
Ravitch, Diane, 117–8, 123–6, 137
Raza, Nayeema, 75
Reagan, Ronald, 62, 93, 140, 146
recycling, 17, 20, 75
regulation, 10, 24, 59
    AI use to avoid, 100, 104–5
    via antitrust laws, 93
    via B corps, 79–81
    Citizens United's impact on, 89
    by consumer actions, 74–7, 81, 88
    democracy's protection via, 61–3,
      74–5, 89–90, 93–5, 106
    and deregulation push, 62–73,
      89–90, 91–106, 129–30,
      139–41, 143, 146–7, 163, 171,
      174–5, 179, 185
    direct-to-consumer campaigns
      skirting, 95–7
    financial crisis of 2008 tied to, 16,
      68, 72, 128, 156–7
    independent contractor use to
      avoid, 101–3
    by NGOs, 77–8, 81
    offsetting of damage *vs.*, 81–8
    purpose of, 60–2, 68, 83, 88–90
    and self-regulation as conflict of
      interest, 5, 71–3, 77–8, 81, 87,
      90, 106
    worker protections via, 97–101
Reich, Robert, 27, 129, 134, 143
Reid, Sue, 21
Republic of New Afrika (RNA),
      149–50
Responsible Care, 73
Resurrection (Tolstoy), 177

Riese, Martin, 118–9
Rockefeller, John D., 93
Roosevelt, Franklin D., 60–1, 97,
      144, 167, 172–4
Run to Failure (Lustgarten), 37–8, 40
Rushkoff, Douglas, 111

Sandel, Michael, 86, 135–8
Sanders, Bernie, 168–70, 173
Save the Children, 77–8
Sawant, Kshama, 138, 162–3, 164–6,
      168–70
Schiffrin, Anya, 22–3
Schlossberg, Tala, 75
Schneider, Mark, 50
Schwab, Klaus, 10–3, 23–9, 89–90,
      103, 116, 127
Seasteading society, 92
sexism, 11, 60, 98, 114, 133, 148,
      163, 180, 183
Sharma, Ruchir, 66
Sherman Antitrust Act of 1890, 93
Skarlicki, Daniel, 18, 30
socialism, 134, 146, 173
social state
    corporate destruction of, 127–44,
      182–6
    democracy's connection to, 4–5,
      9–10, 105–6, 128–30, 135–9,
      145–8, 167–175, 183–7
    funding cuts to, 4, 24, 26–7,
      128–31, 133–5, 143, 185
    pandemic response and, 4, 26–7,
      130–1, 133–4, 143–4, 145–8,
      170, 178, 182–3
Sossion, Wilson, 125–6
Spence, Michael, 22
Srinivasan, Balaji, 92
stakeholder capitalism, 10–4, 32–4,
      116
*Standard Oil Co. of New Jersey v. United
      States,* 93
Stiglitz, Joseph, 22, 24–5, 68, 70–1,
      146
Stout, Lynn, 31–2
Superhubs (Navidi), 8
Super Bowl LI, 15

Tasini, Jonathan, 98, 172

taxation, 5, 24–8, 126, 128–30, 133–4, 139, 143, 147, 163, 170, 173, 185

Taylor, Keeanga-Yamahtta, 186

Texas City, Texas disaster, 37–9

Thatcher, Margaret, 62, 136, 141

Thiel, Peter, 92

Thompson, E. P., 59–60

Thunberg, Greta, 46

Thunder Horse oil rig, 39

Tobin, Dennis, 80

Toffel, Michael, 15–6

Tolstoy, Leo, 177

Tooze, Adam, 112

Triangle Shirtwaist Factory fire, 97, 103

Trudeau, Justin, 7, 23

Trump, Donald, 10, 12, 15, 140, 170–1
    coronavirus response by, 20, 26–7, 64–5, 111–2, 130–2, 143, 178
    deregulation as focus of, 62–73
    tax reform under, 24–8, 134
    WEF speech by, 22–4, 67

Tylenol, 55

Uber, 21, 101–3

Unilever, 13, 15, 19, 29, 121
    nutritional products by, 49, 51–2

Union of Concerned Scientists, 65

United Farm Workers, 150

United Kingdom (UK), 59–60, 71

United Nations, 50, 77, 115
    Clean Development Mechanism, 83–4
    Intergovernmental Panel on Climate Change, 44, 46

U.S. Chamber of Commerce, 64–5

van Beurden, Ben, 43

Vitingo (nutraceutical), 51–2

Volkswagen scandal, 53–7

Waber, Ben, 100

wage inequality, 4, 11, 13, 16–7, 59–60, 134–9

Walmart, 17, 20–1, 29, 41, 74–5

Warren, Elizabeth, 80

water offset programs, 85–8

water services, 174
    privatization of, 115, 117–20, 127, 137, 175

WEF. *See* World Economic Forum

Weissman, Robert, 44, 57, 90

West, Cornel, 186–7

White, Micah, 155–9, 165, 178, 180–1

white supremacy, 140–1, 184

Wilkins, Matt, 75

Winners Take All (Giridharadas), 94

Wise, Jeff, 63

worker welfare, 41, 185
    independent contracting's impact on, 101–3
    via labor unions, 4, 97–8, 100, 124–5, 128, 130, 141, 150, 174, 180–1
    monitoring devices and, 98–100
    occupational *vs.* process-based measures for, 36–40

World Bank, 122, 126

World Economic Forum (WEF), 7–14, 22–8, 116–7, 122
    Trump speech at, 22–4, 67

World Forum for Ethics in Business, 54

World Health Organization, 52, 119

World Wildlife Fund (WWF), 77–8, 87

xenophobia, 4, 12, 23, 139, 170

Zuboff, Shoshana, 95–6

Zuckerberg, Mark, 123–4, 126